An Anthropology of Absence

Mikkel Bille · Frida Hastrup
Tim Flohr Sørensen
Editors

An Anthropology
of Absence

Materializations of Transcendence and Loss

 Springer

Editors
Mikkel Bille
University of Copenhagen
Copenhagen
Denmark
mbille@hum.ku.dk

Frida Hastrup
University of Copenhagen
Copenhagen
Denmark
frida.hastrup@anthro.ku.dk

Tim Flohr Sørensen
University of Aarhus
Hoejbjerg
Denmark
farktfs@hum.au.dk

ISBN 978-1-4419-5528-9   e-ISBN 978-1-4419-5529-6
DOI 10.1007/978-1-4419-5529-6
Springer New York Dordrecht Heidelberg London

Library of Congress Control Number: 2010923406

Printed on acid-free paper

Springer is part of Springer Science+Business Media (www.springer.com)

Acknowledgements

The editors would like to thank the Danish Research School of Cultural Heritage, the Graduate School of Regional Studies, and the Department of Cross-Cultural and Regional Studies at the University of Copenhagen for funding the seminar *The Presence of Absence: Materiality and Beyond* in April 2008, from where most of the chapters of this book originate. We are grateful to all the participants in the seminar, including those whose papers are not presented in this volume.

Chapter 9 'Absent Powers: magic and loss in post-socialist Mongolia' by Lars Højer has been published in *Journal of the Royal Anthropological Institute* 15(3), 575–591. We are grateful to the original publisher for permitting us to reprint the work here.

Copenhagen, Denmark

Mikkel Bille
Frida Hastrup
Tim Flohr Sørensen

Contents

Contributors

Mikkel Bille is an assistant professor at University of Copenhagen. He holds a PhD in anthropology from University College London and has a background in near eastern archaeology. His research has focused on the material and social negotiation of heritage, ranging from UNESCO heritage proclamations to quotidian practices among the Bedouin in southern Jordan. Bille's current interest centres on the material orchestration and social conceptualizations of atmospheres, particularly how light is used as a social and material phenomenon.

Lotte Buch is a PhD Student at the Department of Anthropology, University of Copenhagen, working on a project about social suffering and violence in the Occupied Palestinian Territories. Buch is also affiliated with the Research- and Rehabilitation Centre for Torture Victims (RCT) in Denmark. She holds an MA in anthropology from University of Aarhus, Denmark, and an MA in social anthropology from Goldsmiths College, University of London.

Victor Buchli is Reader in Material Culture at University College London. He received his PhD in Archaeology and Anthropology from University of Cambridge and was later Junior Research Fellow at Sidney Sussex College, Cambridge. His previous books include An Archaeology of Socialism (Berg 1999) – an ethno-historical study of a constructivist housing block in Moscow, Archaeologies of the Contemporary Past (Routledge 2001) with Gavin Lucas – an examination of the critical issues which arise when the archaeological method is applied to the study of contemporary material culture, and Interpreting Archaeology (Routledge 1995) co-edited with Ian Hodder et al. He has also edited The Material Culture Reader (Berg 2002), the five volume Material Culture: Critical Concepts in the Social Sciences for the Major Works Series, Routledge Publishers (2004) and with C. Alexander and C. Humphrey, Urban life in Post Soviet Asia (Routledge 2007). Buchli has been managing editor of the Journal of Material Culture, and is founding and managing editor of Home Cultures with Berg Publishers – an interdisciplinary journal for the critical study of the domestic sphere.

Severin Fowles is an assistant professor at Barnard College and Columbia University. His research interests include the archaeology of religion, iconography, and the evolution of societies in opposition to the state. Fowles specializes in the ancestral Pueblo archaeology of the American Southwest and is the author of "The Magician's Progress: A Critique of True Religion", forthcoming from the School of Anthropological Research Press.

Frida Hastrup is a postdoctoral fellow at the Department of Anthropology, University of Copenhagen. She holds a PhD in anthropology from the University of Copenhagen, and her doctoral research focused on notions and practices of recovery after the Asian tsunami in 2004 based on fieldwork in a fishing village in Tamil Nadu, India. Hastrup's current research addresses local responses to climatic changes in the Bay of Bengal area with a specific focus on flooding, cyclones and coastal erosion.

Lars Højer is associate professor at the Department of Cross-Cultural and Regional Studies, University of Copenhagen. Højer holds a PhD in anthropology from University of Cambridge and has done extensive fieldwork in Mongolia, focusing on social, economic, and religious transition processes. His current research concentrates on minority issues related to Western China.

Anja Marie Bornø Jensen is a PhD student at the Department of Anthropology, University of Copenhagen. She has worked extensively with anthropological perspectives on organ donation and conducted several field studies among donor families and healthcare staff in The United States and in Denmark. Jensen holds an MA in anthropology from University of Copenhagen.

Lynn Meskell is Professor at the Department of Anthropology, Stanford University. Meskell's research and teaching interests include a broad range of fields, including Egyptian archaeology, ethnography in South African, identity and sociopolitics, gender and feminism, and ethics. Her current research examines the constructs of natural and cultural heritage and the related discourses of empowerment around the Kruger National Park, ten years after democracy in South Africa. Another project is focused on the social constitution of the figurine worlds at Çatalhöyük, Turkey. Meskell is founding editor of the Journal of Social Archaeology, and has published several books, including *Object Worlds in Ancient Egypt: Material Biographies Past and Present* (Berg 2004).

Fiona R. Parrott is a research fellow at the London School of Hygiene and Tropical Medicine. Her interests include the material and visual culture of loss, remembrance and separation in Britain and Africa. Parrott holds a PhD in anthropology from University College London, and her doctoral research focused on death, memory and the home in London. Parrott's current work in Northern Malawi focuses on perceptions of death and fertility among people living with HIV in the context of freely available antiretroviral therapy. She also works with psychiatric patients in the UK on a project exploring the impact of secure psychiatric care on patients' relationships to their children.

Layla Renshaw lectures in forensic archaeology and anthropology at the School of Life Sciences, Kingston University, London, and is course director of the BSc in Forensic Science there. Renshaw holds a PhD in Anthropology from University College London, and her thesis focused on the relationship between memory, materiality and the contested representations of the past elicited by the exhumation of Republican mass graves from the Spanish Civil War. In addition to forensic investigations, she has participated in civil war exhumations throughout Spain, and her ongoing research interests include the materiality of bodies and objects, the politics of exhumation, and the role of memory and material evidence in forensic investigations into the traumatic past.

Tim Flohr Sørensen has recently submitted his PhD thesis in archaeology at the University of Aarhus. He has a background in landscape archaeology (University of Wales Lampeter) and Near Eastern archaeology (University of Copenhagen), and now he works mainly with material culture, movement and emotion in prehistoric as well as contemporary Danish contexts. Sørensen's PhD research focuses on the choreography of movement and emotion in cemeteries, and the interaction between materiality, affectivity and the senses. Other research interests include lighting, landscape, architecture, design and methodology.

Part I
Toward an Anthropology of Absence

Chapter 1
Introduction: An Anthropology of Absence

Mikkel Bille, Frida Hastrup, and Tim Flohr Sørensen

The Corporeality of Absence

After losing his arm in the battle of Santa Cruz de Tenerife in 1797, Lord Nelson took the pain he felt in his missing limb to be a "direct proof of the existence of the soul" (Ramachandran and Hirstein 1998: 1604). What Lord Nelson had experienced was a phenomenon first identified by the physician Silas Weir Mitchell in the late nineteenth century as "phantom pains". During the American Civil War, Mitchell treated and studied soldiers with nerve injuries and post-traumatic disorders, who described to him the experience of sensing their amputated limbs (Wade 2003: 518). Since then, phantom pains have been medically defined as the painful sensation of missing limbs, i.e. a sensuous experience of something which is materially absent. However, even before Mitchell's studies and coining of the term, pain felt in missing limbs and the sense that an amputated limb is still attached to the body had been elements in philosophical treatises. René Descartes, for instance, argued that sensations in amputated limbs testify to the unreliability of the senses (Wade 2003: 518–520).

In the social realm, too, people experience "phantom pains" in the form of sensing the presence of people, places and things that have been obliterated, lost, missing or missed, or that have not yet materialized. Such absences can be spurred by an array of conditions, ranging from the quotidian or personal, such as homesickness, involuntary childlessness, melancholia or nostalgia, to the dramatic, such as bereavement after catastrophes, war or crime, or the destruction of people, monuments and buildings as epitomised by the bombing of Hiroshima, the destruction of the Bamiyan Buddhas in Afghanistan or the attack on the World Trade Center in New York. In all of these cases, the absent elements are sensuously, emotionally and ideationally present to people, and are articulated or materialized

M. Bille (✉) and F. Hastrup
University of Copenhagen, Copenhagen, Denmark
e-mails: mbille@hum.ku.dk; frida.hastrup@anthro.ku.dk

T.F. Sørensen
University of Aarhus, Højbjerg, Denmark
e-mail: farktfs@hum.au.dk

M. Bille et al. (eds.), *An Anthropology of Absence: Materializations of Transcendence and Loss*, 3
DOI 10.1007/978-1-4419-5529-6_1, © Springer Science+Business Media, LLC 2010

in various ways through narratives, commemorations, enactments of past experiences or visualisations of future scenarios.

Taking phantom pains as our point of departure, this volume essentially suggests, through a wide range of case studies, that what may be materially absent still influences people's experience of the material world. We argue for a need to see the relationship between the present and the absent as more complex than simply consisting of two antonymic categories. Rather, as an ambiguous interrelation between what is there and what is not, absences are cultural, physical and social phenomena that powerfully influence people's conceptualizations of themselves and the world they engage with. The objective of this book – captured in the notion of *an anthropology of absence* – is therefore to probe into the specific ways absences have or take power, and thereby have important bearing on people's social, emotional and material lives.

The various contributions argue that a paradox exists in the properties of presence and absence showing that they inherently depend on one another for their significance to be fully realised and even conceptualised, and that the processes through which the properties gain significance are local, complex and not necessarily consistent. The power of absence, such as an amputated arm, longing for parenthood, revolution, the coming of Messiah, or the negative imprint of a Buddha statue or the memorial "Reflecting Absence" at the site of the World Trade Center, consists in the ability of such absences to imply and direct attention towards presence. Thus, phenomena may have a powerful presence in people's lives precisely *because* of their absence; a paradox that we refer to as "the presence of absence". In investigating this paradox as a cultural phenomenon, we want to point to the mutual interdependence in people's lives of the materially present and the materially absent, and bring to the fore central questions concerning cultural conceptualizations of ontological and material categories.

Philosophies of Absence

The insight that absence has presence is not new, but has been vividly discussed, particularly in existential and post-structural philosophy. In Søren Kierkegaard's writings, the absent is what triggers the aesthete to pursue the thought of seducing whatever he finds intriguing. Kierkegaard's character, Johannes the Seducer, is stimulated not so much by the act of seduction and the actual conquering of the desired object, as by longing for what he does not possess, that which is still tedious but could become interesting (1988 [1843]). Longing becomes the symptom of absence as a fundamental driving force behind human action, suggesting that once the person or thing that was longed for has been obtained, and the longing thus has vanished, not only will the motivation for action disappear, but the action itself will cease to exist. The action spurred by longing is thus annihilated by its fulfilment. In turn, this leads to longing for something or someone else and for new actions. To Kierkegaard, longing is not only defined by the spatial absence of a person or thing, but more importantly by the perceived emotional immediacy of what is absent and the way that this absence is constitutive of social relations and actions.

In a similar vein, Arthur Schopenhauer saw this longing or desire – or "will" in his terminology – as intertwined with a most fundamental human condition of suffering: "All *willing* springs from lack, from deficiency, and thus from suffering" (1966 [1818]: 196). At the same time, Schopenhauer argued that this suffering could be resolved through ascetic behaviour and a basic denial of the will (Janaway 1998: 25), celebrating abstention and absence as the redeemers of pain – which was in itself a result of the lack of what was desired for. No matter how many desires we fulfil, there will always be new desires and aspirations – hence new suffering – and thus in Schopenhauer's pessimistic view, it would be better to avoid desires entirely and exist, instead, in pure ascetic abstention.

The consequence of Schopenhauer's line of reasoning is a self-effacing form of existence, bordering on total non-existence. This may lead us to consider for a moment a philosophical line of reasoning that suggests the existence of an absolute form of absence. Philosopher Patrick Fuery (1995), for example, argues that absence may be divided into two registers, "primary absence" and "secondary absence". Primary absence is defined as "absence-in-itself", as existing outside of any relation to presence; it is "just absence" (1995: 2). While philosophically intriguing, the concept of primary absence does not easily apply to studies of the social world. On the other hand, secondary absence, in Fuery's terms, is derived from, and defined by, its relational connection to presence. This means that absence and presence become inherently intertwined. As Fuery explains, "Something is absent because it is not present, but the significant detail is that the absent something is figured as potentially present" (1995: 1). To Fuery, like Kierkegaard, the *feeling* of absence is a source of desire; desire towards the person, thing or place that is absent.

Absence, similarly, constitutes a key component in Jean-Paul Sartre's exploration of negation (2005 [1943]), famously exemplified by a meeting with "Pierre" in a café. Coming to a café expecting to meet Pierre, but discovering that Pierre is not there, Sartre argues that not only is Pierre missing from the café, but his attention towards Pierre's absence means that the café and its tables, chairs, mirrors, lights and people disappear: "In fact Pierre is absent from the *whole* café; his absence fixes the café in its evanescence" (2005 [1943]: 34). In other words, directing the attention to something absent makes present things and people disappear, and in Sartre's example, the absence of Pierre dissolves the attention to the café and thus makes it disappear phenomenologically. This means that the presence or the absence of phenomena – be it persons, things, events or places – does not necessarily depend either on absolute, positive occurrences or the absolute lack of such, but may just as well reside in the way the experience of phenomena differs from expectations and preconceptions. Along the same lines, philosopher Drew Leder argues that our bodies may disappear (meaning *not appearing*) when we engage with the world outside the body, whereby focus is turned away from the body itself and it disappears from consciousness (1990: 26–27); "I forget my feet until the moment I stumble" (1990: 85). In addition, the body of the other may even become more phenomenologically manifest than the disappearing body of oneself, because of the attention drawn to the otherness of the other's body.

The process of directing one's attention to the other took a different turn with Jacques Derrida (1973). Derrida argued that significance resides not in the specific contents of phenomena. Instead, significance is created through heterogeneity, because the meaning of a phenomenon must be described by way of other phenomena and the ways in which it is different from (or similar to) these. Hence, according to Derrida, the meaning of a phenomenon is always derived from describing other signifiers, and the actual meaning instead rests in the difference of signifiers. Thereby meaning is not in the phenomenon itself, but in what it is not.

These philosophical thoughts were given a concrete expression in 1985, when philosopher Jean-François Lyotard curated an exhibition in Paris called *Les Immatériaux*, or "The Immaterials" (Lyotard and Chaput 1985; see also Wunderlich 2008). The exhibition explored new technologies and media, in particular digitalisation, which were seen as a means of transforming the material form of human reality, pushing it towards an immaterial form. As machines have taken over most of the industrial production, humans are instead responsible for the processing of data. This point was made at Lyotard's exhibition by dematerializing the art object, which was turned into a system of communication in order to reveal the values and power by which the art objects were circumscribed. The boundaries of art objects were vague and intangible, and it was difficult to grasp where one object stopped and the next began, suggestive of an immaterial infinity. It has been argued (Crowther 1992: 194) that even though many of the forms explored in the exhibition had been long-existing, the postmodern condition brought them to the forefront of our consciousness, offering an awareness of an infinite and largely immaterial web of analysability and transformation.

The novelty of this awareness may be somewhat overstated in the light of the artistic and technological explorations that were made in the early twentieth century within the field of art photography. Leading artists like László Moholy-Nagy and Medardo Rosso experimented with photography in the first decades of the century and considered the technology a means of immaterializing objects. Taking photographs of sculptures was seen as a way of transforming the sculpture's solid and concrete matter into "an almost immaterial substance" in Moholy-Nagy's words (cited in Johnson 2004: 72) by staging strong and contrasting lighting effects on the sculpture in the studio and developing the photograph with a pronounced emphasis on shadows and abstract forms. In this way, the traditional figurative sculpture could be dissolved and transformed into light and shadow. Rosso bluntly stated that the consequence of the technological transformation of the sculpture by way of photography was that the "material does not exist (…). Nothing is material in space" (cited in Moure 1997: 171). Conversely, photography was also appreciated as a means of materializing the impalpable and of giving "tangible shape to light" (Moholy-Nagy cited in Johnson 2004: 77), thereby positioning photography as a paradoxical technology: suspending the solid on the one hand and materializing the intangible on the other.

Moholy-Nagy's declaration that photographs turned sculpture into "an almost immaterial substance" calls for attention to this paradox, and the "almost" becomes revealing (discussed by Buchli, this volume). Lyotard's attempt to present the notion of the immaterial in artistic form in the postmodern era reveals some of the same paradoxes relating to the material-immaterial intersection. Even though Lyotard considered data absorbed into a digitalized matrix to be immaterial, its communication still rested on tangible forms; forms that could be touched, heard and seen. Even digitalisation must thus also make do with turning the material into an "almost" immaterial form.

Presence and Absence in Everyday Life

Although we may draw on such philosophical insights, our aim here, however, is somewhat different. We wish to situate absences in everyday practice, by investigating how absences are important social, political and cultural phenomena that impinge on people's lives. The common denominator for the chapters is thus, that they offer concrete studies of that which, in one sense or another, is not there, but yet has a bearing on everyday life, thereby focusing head-on on the intersections of presence and absence. Obviously, dramatic absences in the wake of war, terror, famine or catastrophes receive vast media attention, yet at the heart of this volume are also those micro-processes that unfold in everyday life with local meanings and effects. More particularly, by focusing on situations where notions of loss, absent things, people, ideas or phenomena are at stake, the chapters take their point of departure in particular engagements with material worlds to show how people define, negotiate and understand themselves through things or their absence.

The volume resonates with the expanding literature on material culture, materiality and objectification within the past three decades (Brown 2003; Hodder 1982; Hodder and Hutson 2003; Ingold 2000; Latour and Weibel 2005; Meskell 2004; Miller 1987; Miller 2005a; Shanks and Tilley 1987). Research on material culture has convincingly shown how cultural, spiritual and individual lives are inherently dependent upon and constituted by their interconnections with organic and inorganic things. In other words, these discussions have often demonstrated how social relations are played out within material registers. Most contributors here also employ a distinct material culture perspective in their research by focussing on that which is not materially there, conceptualised as immaterial, or on the material processes by which absence is understood and commemorated.

With his seminal work on *The Gift* from 1924, Marcel Mauss was one of the first scholars to clearly demonstrate the power and agency of things in people's social lives. In his classic discussion of gift giving, Mauss found that a gift by far exceeded being an object of pure generosity. Rather, gift giving should be seen as part of a total social system forming structures of reciprocal exchange between different social actors. In his effort to explain the fact that an obligation to reciprocate gifts is a universal rule of all societies, Mauss pointed to the idea that a gift is not an inactive object, but one which is animated; in the case of the Maōri, by the spirit (*hau*) of the thing. Thus, even when transmitted or re-circulated, Mauss argued, the gift still possesses something of the giver and contains a form of identity (2002 [1954]: 15). Consequently, the givers' accumulated imprints are present in the spirit of the object, even if the object has been removed from the giver.

Even though Mauss implicitly demonstrated the power of things, and even of abandoned things, in so doing, he maintained that the gift embodied social implications and obligations. In the 1980s, archaeologists and anthropologists interested in material culture centred in Cambridge began focussing more directly on the significance of material culture as constitutive of social interaction, supplementing previous linguistic, interpretative, symbolic turns in the social sciences and humanities. The focus on the material not only prescribes attention to the physical infrastructure of social life, but also suggests that materiality and material culture are formative of the social. By now, artifacts can be recognised as potentially having social effects through their very "thingliness" (Gell 1998; Ingold 2000; Miller 2005a; Tilley et al. 2006).

Nevertheless, there has been a profound interest in the *meaning* of things, often at the expense of interest in the way they present themselves sensuously; a theme particularly prevalent in the phenomenological turn in the early 1990s (Csordas 1994; Gosden 1994; Jackson 1996; Tilley 1994). Further attempts at theorising presence have also recently been influential, particularly in relation to explorations of means of interacting with transcendent or immaterial phenomena whether in the shape of religious authorities, globalized digital networks, experiencing ghosts or other fluid and ephemeral phenomena (e.g. Degen and Hetherington 2001; Gordon 1997; Kapstein 2004; Lacoste 2007; Sassen 2002). A lesson learnt from these studies is that it appears that the more people attempt to approach and conceptualize the immaterial, the more specific are the ways such conceptualisations are materialized (Miller 2005b: 28).

The focus on presence rather than meaning – as two simultaneous and complementary elements of an engagement with the material world – is hence by no means new, as particularly attested to in semiotic discussions on representation and presentation (Armstrong 1971, 1981; Gumbrecht 2004; Keane 1997, 2007; Pitkin 1967). Anthropologist Robert Armstrong proposed this point in 1971 in his seminal study of the agency of Yoruba art. Here he demonstrated the inadequacy of approaching Yoruba art as invested with symbolic content by the artist, whereby meaning is seen as located outside the very artifact. Such an approach, Armstrong argued, overlooks and denies the artifacts' selfhood and their *affecting presence*. In Armstrong's words: "it is the artist who brings about the work, but it is the work that presents" (1971: 25). Upon being created, the work of art personifies or realizes the idea behind its creation, whereby its prototype loses its significance for the artifact's existence; after its creation, the piece of art embodies the prototype. Thus, to Armstrong, "the work stands in the relationship of immediacy, not of mediation" (1971: 25–26; see also Meskell 2004).

This relationship is also apparent in debates about fetishism. In these discussions the question is to what extent things, aside from their material being, have inherent meanings that produce *presence* and effect, or whether things are simply a surface of a deeper essence that needs interpretation (Ellen 1988; Gumbrecht

2004; Maniura and Shepherd 2006; Masuzawa 2000; Pels 1998; Pietz 1985, 1987, 1988; Spyer 1998; Taussig, 1980, 1993). In a similar line, anthropologists Henare et al. (2007) have recently proposed "an ontological break-through" within anthropology and stressed the need to think through things, arguing that in a world of multiple ontologies, things are not only *representing* but can be *identical* with their meaning. Such versatile ontologies, we argue, shed light on the lived experience of the simultaneity of presence and absence.

Another understanding of presence that informs several of the contributions here is that of historian Eelco Runia, who understands presence as "'being in touch' – either literally or figuratively – with people, things, events, and feelings that made you into the person you are" (Runia 2006a: 5). For example Runia (2006a, b) argues that in commemorative practices, a focus on "meaning" falls short of explaining the performed and actual engagement with the material world. Runia thereby advocates that in terms of memory, presence as being in touch is complementary to the attention towards meaning and at least as important (see also Ankersmit 2006; Bentley 2006; Domanska 2006; Gumbrecht 2004, 2006; Peters 2006). Professor of Judaic Studies, James E. Young demonstrates this role of presences and absences in the case of Holocaust memorials. He argues that the displayed debris of Holocaust victims' personal belongings rise "in a macabre dance of memorial ghosts. Armless sleeves, eyeless lenses, headless caps, footless shoes: victims are known only by their absence, by the moment of their destruction. In great loose piles, these remnants remind us not of the lives that once animated them, so much as of the brokenness of lives" (Young 1993: 132–133). In this sense, the memorial invokes a simultaneous distance and proximity of the Holocaust, whereby the internalisation of presence, as being-in-touch, unfolds as more than mere spatial proximity and equally as more than a cognitive capacity to construct meaning and recollection.

Anthropologist Matthew Engelke (2004, 2005, 2007) has most recently addressed the complex intersection of presence and the immaterial as pertaining to Christian worship of God. In a study of the Masowe Church, a Charismatic Christian community in Zimbabwe that rejects reading the Bible, Engelke, drawing on Hegel, argues for a dualistic view of presence divided between material presence ("sensible presence of Christ") and immaterial presence ("the presence of God in the Spirit"). According to Engelke, the sacred immaterial presence of God comprises a paradox in its necessity to transcend or rather to reject the object-character of religious devotion. The physicality of the Bible as a book and even the church as a material institution are repudiated, and the community thereby takes the perceived superiority of the immateriality of the word to an extreme. This leads Engelke to conclude that: "the problem of presence is a problem of representation – of how words, objects, and actions get defined as such and, in the process, become significant" (2007: 252). The central question for Engelke is what role material objects – and we may add physical places – play for people trying to achieve nearness to God (cf. Coleman 1996; Holloway 2006; Ong 1967).

Even though these approaches are influential and foundational to most chapters in this volume, they still rely on the identifiable *presence* of an object, i.e. that the given active object is, in fact, a materially manifest thing. While existing material culture studies have undoubtedly offered many new perspectives on human engagement with the material world, with this volume we suggest that the ideas of the agency and efficacy of present things can benefit from developing perspectives on the absent things. This will expose how absence – even if absence is only perceived absence – may have just as much effect as material presence. As a way of turning the concept of phantom pains on its head, one could argue that an insensible or numb limb, even though materially there, may importantly affect people's life, exactly because of its sensuous absence. We thus take absence to be as much of an occurrence in real life as presence, and we attempt to explicate the need to acknowledge the intersections between what is considered to be there and what is not.

Paradoxically, then, what characterises many of the contributions in one way or the other is that the absence of one thing attracts attention to or even provokes the production of another thing, mediating the absent thing as a stand-in, a surrogate or a proxy. This relates to what Bille in his chapter calls the "paradox of immateriality", drawing on Miller's proclamation that "the very clarity within this mission toward immateriality brings out the inherent contradiction that follows from the impossibility of ever transcending the process of objectification itself" (Miller 2005b: 22). Through such objectifications, some of the objects people surround themselves with "serve as mediation with the present, others as mediation with the past, the value of the latter being that they address a lack" (Baudrillard 1996: 83). Transgressing the temporal separation of past and present, this point becomes particularly apparent in studies of death, memory and bereavement, as Jensen, Parrott and Sørensen, show in this volume, where specific things may bind the living and the dead across temporal distance and "preserve a material presence in the face of embodied absence" (Hallam and Hockey 2001: 18). While that may be the case in some of the contributions, it is also apparent that there are cases where it is precisely the lack of objectification of an absence that forms the conceptualizations of the world, for example through an image prohibition or political taboo (Fowles 2008, this volume, Renshaw, this volume).

Absences, however, are not exclusively an aspect of material culture; absences are everywhere, ranging from the largely irrelevant to those crucial to understand: Absence of certainty, absence of loved ones, absence of recognition and so on. It may seem superficial to focus on cases where objects mediate absences, or cases where absent things shape human lives, rather than on other absences such as, say, political concealment of acts or the muting of minorities or dissident voices. However, this is not to be seen as a mere neglect on our part, but rather as an attempt to underscore the point, also made elsewhere, that the material world is by no means innocent or passive, but may in fact testify to previous injustice, or serve as a vehicle of producing intended political lacunae.

Throughout the chapters, it becomes clear that absence is not a mere spatial term meaning "being away from", just as presence is not only to be understood as spatial proximity in the sense of "being in front of" or "being near". What might appear as a binary opposition between presence and absence is in fact often conceptualized within a continuous and ambiguous spectrum as discussed above. From this perspective, it is clear that there is a need for an anthropology of absence, directing our attention towards questions like: How are objects, people and phenomena "there" from an experiential perspective, even though they are "not there" from a positivist perspective? How are losses presented in the everyday lives of the bereaved? How are religious ideals of transcendence materialized? How are past events, histories or future expectations materially manifested in the present? Running as an additional undercurrent in many of the chapters is the methodological issue of how to study something which is gone, metaphysical in nature, deliberately or accidentally destroyed, or not yet materialized.

Perspectives on the Agency of Absence

As intimated above, important perspectives on absence emerge from various scholarly disciplines. Archaeology, which forms an academic background of many of the contributors, is frequently understood as the study of the remote past and not of contemporary or recent society (pace Buchli and Lucas 2001; Gould and Schiffer 1981). Yet, the core of archaeology is basically the study of material things. The archaeological perspective means that material culture is exploited as a source of social and cultural knowledge in its own right, complementing or replacing textual or verbal information. But archaeology is also increasingly entering contemporary politics by revealing political prosecution, destruction of heritage and silencing of alternative voices. As the presence of absence may be ontologically, epistemologically and existentially difficult to cope with, or even communicate as outlined previously, the archaeological perspective may reveal how it may be constructive to explore not only what people say or write about their experience of absence (about ontological problems, loss and transcendence), but also what they *do* in the presence of absence; how they go about the paradox that something can be there even though it is not there, and how bodily practices and material culture may add insights to people's perceptions of the absent. Within recent archaeology, important steps have been taken concerning the issue of absence. Archaeologist Severin Fowles is one of the prime proponents of the turn towards a "negative archaeology". He has explored the possibilities of "an archaeology of taboo" by addressing the issue of what to infer from an absence of an object or category of objects from the archaeological records. Fowles raises the important issue of "whether the *absence* of pig bones at certain sites can itself point to the presence of a formal religious taboo" (2008: 19). Such an approach to things as intentionally constructed absences points to the possibility that an absence can contain social importance and not just be a result of a lack of access to solid evidence (see also Bailey 2007). On a methodological note, Fowles' analysis can also be seen more generally to raise the question of how to make inferences from an absent objectification to the existence of societal values or phenomena. In Fowles' case, the taboo on pigs hence re-addresses the famous archaeological dictum that the absence of evidence is not evidence of absence.

Sociologist Kevin Hetherington (2004) similarly addresses the potency of the absent through the notion of an "agency of absence" with regard to consumption and ensuing disposal practices. He argues that disposal is not a matter of merely getting rid once and for all of objects considered to be waste. Instead, disposing of objects is an ongoing process that hinges on an inherent mobilisation of absence. As Hetherington notes: "The absent can have just as much of an effect upon relations as recognisable forms of presence can have. Social relations are performed not only around what is there but sometimes also around the *presence* of what is not" (2004: 159). Anthropologist Debbora Battaglia also observes how certain places in Maho village on Sabarl Island, Papua New Guinea, are entirely unmarked yet still delineated with a sense of invisible "no trespassing signs". These define where deceased people have danced, and the places are to be avoided out of respect for the deceased. At the same time, this avoidance is not carved permanently in stone and disappears with the dissolution of the memory of the people who once danced there: "The significance of this space, its capacity to affect behaviour, and the space as such vanish along with those who project it; they reemerge in the same place or elsewhere under the gaze of different persons with different memories. Social behaviour, temporal orders, the social landscape itself are redefined by the invisible agency of an 'active absence': the experience of non-activity special to active constituents of a human history" (Battaglia 1990: 198).

Another aspect of absence is its close link to political processes, as suggested in the scholarly literature dealing with the politics, meanings and narratives of commemoration at Ground Zero in New York and the Bamiyan Buddhas. Marita Sturken (2004) has taken us through the physicality of dust, piles of rubble and architecture to show how the absence of the Twin Towers "has spoken more loudly, and with more resonance, than their presence ever could have" (2004: 319). In cases such as the planned memorial of 9/11 named "Reflecting Absence", it becomes clear that absences, emptiness and voids are the primary aesthetic forms of memorial design (cf. Huyssen 2003: 49–71). This points to the importance of studying lived experience that must also include a study of the elements of human life that are affected by or even hinge on absence, as will be shown by the chapters in this volume.

Similarly, one of the points that may be drawn from geographer Tim Edensor's exploration of ruins and the ruined is that our sensation of the world within the margins of order often shrouds the sensible qualities of the things we engage with. Ruins, in this light, draw attention to the provenance and tactility of buildings and objects, emphasising texture and gravity in sensuous as well as affective terms, which are otherwise largely absent from the smoothness of everyday consumer objects and spaces (Edensor 2005b: 324). The duality of absence and presence is contained within the confrontation with the incomplete; that which shows absence not as an entire existential emptiness, but as a defective continuity, something that is in need of completion or from which parts are missing. Such incompleteness may be encountered in Edensor's exploration of ruins (2001, 2005a, b), where the traces of past activities are articulated as absent through clothes and tools left behind, and their wear and tear. These are the identifiers of "that which appeared not to be there, 'a host of ghostly signs and traces'" (2005a: 158). Not only do these traces evoke the bodies of the people that are now absent, but the wear and tear of abandoned clothes and objects furthermore stir an empathetic flow between the body in the present and the body that is absent (2005b: 329; see also Sørensen 2008).

Absence, furthermore, has potent, traumatic, and devastating consequences in light of political prosecution. Whether in the case of missing men in Argentina (Crossland 2000, 2002), the disappearance of men and women in Cyprus (Cassia 2005), oppression of Human Rights in Morocco (Slyomovics 2005), forensic archaeology and DNA technology merging with juridical practices and personal stories in Srebrenica (Wagner 2008) or the deportation of non-citizens in Montréal (Burman 2006), absence appears as an emotionally, politically, even juridically delicate matter, where uncertainty, social propriety, history, longing and a cause to fight for shape the lives and identities of millions of people across the globe (e.g. Sider and Smith 1997; Trouillot 1997). Because of the potent power of absence, the question of presenting what others regard as pivotal to keep hidden has continuously caused social upheaval. In cases ranging from the 1977 Oscar nominated movie "The Message", starring Anthony Quinn, where Prophet Muhammad is never revealed, to museums choosing to display Brazilian Candomblé saint stones, intended to remain hidden (Sansi-Roca 2005), or to cover up the bodies of Egyptian Mummies in the Manchester Museum, closure on and concealment of the past, of people and their objects, remain a potent and contested question. In this volume, this political potency is the particular focus in the study of exhumation of disappeared victims of the Spanish Civil War (Renshaw, this volume), and in the study of the lives of the women in occupied Palestinian territory who are married to imprisoned men (Buch, this volume).

Absence is therefore not just a theoretical concept implied as the default logical antonym to presence; it is also a corporeal, emotional and sensuous phenomenon articulated in distinctly concrete, political and cultural registers. The agency of the absent – whether in terms of disposal, religious transcendence, planned obliteration, suppression of past events and histories or accidental bereavement – is never finite, but entangled in the dynamics of potential reverberation, reappearance, transformation and return. Thus, absence as well as presence can be approached through a study of the multitude of complex sensuous engagements with the world, as these are practiced through paradoxical intersections of what is there and what is not. As Fowles (this volume) challengingly argues: "absences are special kinds of things". The question of why some things matter to people can hence be paralleled by the question of why some absent things matter.

Towards an Anthropology of Absence

On our path towards an anthropology of absence, we may consider how the present and the absent intersect or may in fact be mutually constitutive within Christian theology. In his chapter on absent things, forming the second part of the introductory section, Severin Fowles (Chap. 2) points out that with Mary Magdalene's discovery of the lost body of Jesus in the tomb, absence may not only be a powerful sensuous experience, such as standing on an empty high-street, but may indeed be quintessential in understanding the religious, ethical, or political world around us (cf. Cort 2006). This resonates with philosopher Jean-Luc Nancy (2008), who argues that the Christian present rests on the hope of the future return of a person who lived in the past, i.e. the hope of the Second Coming of Christ (or, *parousia* from Greek "presence"); "*Parousia* is – to be set apart from the very thing that approaches, to be a gap with and in itself. *Parousia* – or presence close to – differs and is deferred: in this way it is there, imminent, like death in life" (Nancy 2008: 59).

Taking up Hans Christian Andersen's story of the Emperor's new clothes, Fowles further shows how absence of clothes has been received radically different in terms of nudity in contrast to nakedness: "The nude was presented to the nineteenth century consumer of art as a whole specimen that lacked nothing – indeed, it served as the very image of human perfection [...] The nakedness of the native, on the other hand, was fundamentally a thing of deprivation". By tying together anthropological writings from Morgan to Latour, Fowles shows how definitions of absence become central points not only of understanding oneself, but also of understanding and constructing the "Other".

Succeeding Fowles' essay, the significance of various forms of absence in everyday life is investigated through four interrelated headings, namely "Embodying Absence", "Temporalities of Absence", "Materializing Remembrance" and "Ambiguous Materialities". The first register of absence, explored in part II, concerns the way the relationship between the missing person, body and skeleton is perceived and entangled in the moral and political scene of reconciliation, recuperation and grief. Absence, here, is centered on the role of the deceased body – or parts of it – in the lives of those left behind. The second register of absence, investigated in part III, is characterised both by its futurity and by different stances towards the past. This form of absence implies that what is missing is something that has yet to be given a fixed position in history or that has yet to materialize and manifest itself, as in the cases where people experience a loss that has yet to be clearly defined. The third register of absence, explored in part IV, concerns ways of presenting someone or something that has passed away or disappeared. This implies practices of commemoration, enactments of memory and the recollection of history. In this register of absence, social propriety is often at stake, when commemorating people in ways that may not correspond to everyone else's commemorative practices. Hence, not only is the honour of the deceased at play, so too, is the propriety of the bereaved. As to the fourth register of absence, the focus of part V, the conceptualization of absence may not correspond to any materialistic conception of what is there, but resides rather in the realm of the cultural and historical ideas about transcendent powers, asceticism and immateriality. Such forms of absence entail a desire to transcend material form by denying it, such as in cases of religious worship of non-material entities.

In part II of this book on embodying absence, Layla Renshaw (Chap. 3) raises the problem of how personal stories and memories of civilians killed by Francoist militias in Spain during the Civil War can be represented, when much of their biographies and the events surrounding their deaths have been politically suppressed. Renshaw explores how excavating and identifying the material remains of the dead become part of shifting and unpredictable courses of events in relation to presences and absences of memories and imaginaries of the dead, and of lacking representations of the dead while they were missing. As one example of the role of absence in everyday life, she highlights how cemeteries, where the deceased are re-buried, may not be the primary sites of commemoration for bereaved individuals, who choose instead to visit the sites where their relatives are no longer buried, but where they have so far spent most of their death.

While Renshaw positions the body on an infected political scene revolving around truth, reconciliation and nationalism, Anja Marie Bornø Jensen (Chap. 4) on the other hand, takes a more intimate view on the body as it is conceptualized in the emotional and commemorative practices of people engaged in organ donation. Her chapter focuses on the perceptions of absence and presence among relatives of organ donors in the USA, by analyzing how the deceased are seen as present in the lives of their relatives, because parts of their bodies live on in other (anonymous) people. Because of the literal embodiment of the donor in the life of someone else, the bereaved relatives, aided by organizations lobbying for organ donation, construct narratives that render the donor immortal. In that sense, the absence of a relative is not complete, because the deceased donor is thought to live on as a "hero" in other people, in a sense in line with Mauss' description of the *hau*.

In part III of the volume, the issue of time is addressed as crucial to ways of understanding absence in the wake of social emergencies. The chapters on temporalities of absence highlight the ways in which missing people or things bring about a tension between progression and suspension of expected life courses, as also discussed in Renshaw's chapter. In these cases, closure is not an option, either because absence is indefinite, or because reclaiming the ability to plan ahead seems more important than coming to terms with a past event.

Lotte Buch's contribution (Chap. 5) demonstrates how the wives of Palestinian men who have been imprisoned during the political conflict live in a state of liminality or suspended subjectivity because they are defined more or less exclusively by the temporal absence of their husbands. Buch refers to this as "derivative presence", indicating that the social status of the wife of a captive is a function of the imprisonment of her husband, which is seen as a temporal situation, regardless of the actual duration of the prison sentence. Buch shows that in a hierarchy of suffering, the wives of captives occupy an entirely different position than do the wives of martyrs, who in the national mythology have made a heroic and ultimate sacrifice for the sake of the nation. While both groups of wives suffer the absence of their husbands, the wives of the captives live with an ambiguous and temporally blurred kind of absence, which precludes them from laying claim to any privileged social position and ultimately suspends their personal agency.

The relation between subjectivity and temporality is also explored by Frida Hastrup (Chap. 6) in her study of how the Asian tsunami, striking the village of Tharangambadi on the coast of Tamil Nadu, robbed people not only of their loved ones, home and property, but of "a present room to manoeuvre within a recognisable horizon of expectation". Drawing on Veena Das' (2007) notion of subjectivity as conditioned by duration, Hastrup focuses on the gradual recovery process in the village by concentrating on the role of lost objects, ruined houses, water-damaged domestic utensils and on local efforts at appropriating the relief materials donated by humanitarian organizations. Hastrup thereby demonstrates how recovery is played out in a curious material register and is aimed at restoring a durable present and a sense of a future plot for everyday life. This resembles what Yael Navaro-Yashin (2009) has termed "ruination", which she defines as "the material remains or artifacts of destruction and violation, but also the subjectivities and residual effects that linger like a hangover, in the aftermath of war and violence" (2009: 5).

Part IV explores how absence plays a powerful part in commemorative practices. Susanne Küchler (1997) has convincingly shown this in her studies of the Malangan statues, which are left to rot or given to Western collectors after their ritual use. Her studies show that remembering is an engagement with absence, where particular kinds of objects "are capable of serving as vehicles that both hold at bay as well cement a road to the realm of the invisible" (Küchler 1997: 54). Taking up this clue, Tim Flohr Sørensen (Chap. 7) investigates the practices of inscription on gravestones in Danish cemeteries, addressing the issue of the voids that are often seen on the stones. The empty spaces left for future inscription of a name of a person not yet deceased equally illustrates the temporal confusion of presence and absence, in that the uncompleted gravestones come to work as memorials over deaths that have not yet occurred, yet tell stories of social values of gender, economy and propriety of caring. In addition, the lacunae at the cemeteries breach distinctions between the material and the emotional through acts of anticipation as well as the active preparation of affective continuity.

The emotional presence that charges these forms of absence is further pursued in Fiona R. Parrott's (Chap. 8) study of displays of photographs and other items picturing deceased individuals in South London households. Parrott shows how the photographs are engulfed in potent negotiations of remembrance, household dynamics and the durability of relations between the living and the dead. The chapter demonstrates that the absence of a loved one is often presented through mundane consumer objects that have no apparent relation to the dead, but which are invested with the presence of the missing person in the lives of the bereaved.

Inherent in the discussion of absence and presence, is also the question of an opposition between the material and the immaterial. Just as we propose to view presence and absence as completely entangled, it may be equally untenable to produce a clear oppositional separation between the material and the immaterial. To consider one extreme position, we may return to the notion of the fetish. Masuzawa argues that "the fetish is materiality at its crudest and lowest; it points to no transcendent meaning beyond itself [...] It is this special tie to materiality, or rather, this ineradicable essence of the fetish *as* materiality, and the alleged absence of any symbolic (or supra-material) dimension that distinguishes fetishism from idolatry" (2000: 248). Such an approach suggests a separation between material and immaterial, but as part V of the volume shows, it seems at times more productive to operate with a notion of ambiguous materialities where objects must be seen within a spectrum of material-ness and sensuous encounters, rather than in terms of material versus immaterial (as also suggested by Fowles, this volume, and Rowlands 2005). This resonates with the work of Webb Keane (2003, 2005) who has suggested that the concept of "bundling" may describe the coexistence of various material qualities in the same object (see also Limbert 2008; Meneley 2008). The chapters in the section revolve around the multiple ontologies of the material and immaterial. Here, the importance of the presence of absence relies on transcending, defying or repudiating the categories of material and immaterial. What emerges from this is also the necessity to explore the transcendence, even reversal, of categorizations of material and immaterial, the present and absent.

Lars Højer (Chap. 9) argues that the socialist years in Mongolia deprived people of traditional comprehension of spirit powers, resulting in an irretrievable loss of knowledge. However, via Marilyn Strathern (2004), Højer argues that the loss of a certain kind of knowledge has the effect of directing people's ways of attending to the world towards a "compelling unknown". He thus shows that concealment works as a potent presence that through charms and imaginaries draws focus to "what is important by virtue of not being there, by virtue of being a powerful centre of gravity where only nothing – or rather no *thing – is* yet".

In a similar way, Mikkel Bille (Chap. 10) addresses the ambiguous material registers that Bedouin in Jordan make use of to protect themselves against evil eyes and spirits. Some of the material objects previously used to ward off misfortunes are increasingly seen as idolatrous within a literal understanding of Islam that favours a particular kind of asceticism. To reconcile this tension, the specific materiality of the objects employed for protection paradoxically becomes all the more important, verging on a dematerialization of material objects inscribed with the Word of God. But, not only is absence here seen within the realm of spiritually contested means of protection, importantly, the contested protective objects are simultaneously part of nostalgic narratives, where objects, along with the lack of tents in the landscape testify to how people's Bedouin roots have disappeared. Nostalgia is one of those everyday phenomena where it is evident how the presence of absence impinges on people's life. Yet as Susan Stewart warns, "the past it seeks has never existed except as narrative, and hence, always absent, that past continually threatens to reproduce itself as a felt lack" (1993: 23). From cultural heritage proclamations to narratives of the good-old-days, rapid social upheavals direct the attention to an absence that may be utopian, yet "the sentiment itself, the mourning of displacement and temporal irreversibility, is at the very core of the modern condition" (Boym 2001: xvi). We thereby return to Kierkegaard's, Schopenhauer's and Fuery's notions of desire and longing; in this case a desire for a different "pre-modern" time.

Further exploring the notion of ambiguous materialities in line with the discussion about early twentieth century art photography, Lyotard's *Les Immatériaux* and the post-structural critique, Victor Buchli's (Chap. 11) contribution takes up the techno-scientific paradoxes at the intersection of the material and the immaterial by highlighting prototype technologies. Buchli suggests that recent manufacturing technologies (Rapid Manufacturing) have the capacity to deconstruct the presentic bias in traditional industrial production that emphasizes a concrete and immediate relationship between prototype, materials, producer and product. These intimate connections are broken with new means of transferring prototypes across the globe via electronic media. However, Buchli also suggests that this relationship may be revolutionizing in terms of industrial production, but not necessarily as an idea, building the argument on the early Christian separation of idol and icon, where the icon becomes a material proxy for an immaterial notion of the divine. As a consequence of these relationships, Buchli argues that we may better approach the present and the absent through the notion of "propinquity", denoting that that which is near may yet not necessarily be "present", and that artifacts may thus contain aspects of both the material and the immaterial.

In the commentary Lynn Meskell (Chap. 12) summarizes the perspectives offered by the contributors, particularly relating to the archaeological perspective on the material world, and suggests how the various avenues explored in the chapters may offer new ways of understanding the significance of human and material engagements, in the past and present.

The overall suggestion put forward in this book is that people's engagement with the world does not simply consist in deducing the meaning of people, places and things or what they represent, but also in *presencing* that which is absent in one way or another. In proposing an anthropology of absence, we therefore want to highlight how missing, lost or immaterial phenomena are emotionally and experientially significant. With this volume, we hope to challenge material culture studies to move beyond its presentist bias and beyond a focus on the boundaries between the material and the immaterial, and instead point to the complex intersections, repudiations and tensions between what is considered present and absent in people's everyday lives. As many of the chapters show, *the presence of absence* does indeed go beyond the material, beyond representation and meaning, and relate to the sensuous and ontological understanding of the lived world constituted by both positive, negative and absent material imprints.

References

Ankersmit, F. R., 2006. "Presence" and Myth. *History and Theory*, 45(3), 328–336.

Armstrong, R. P., 1971. *The Affecting Presence. An Essay in Humanistic Anthropology*, Chicago: University of Illinois Press.

Armstrong, R. P., 1981. *The Powers of Presence: Consciousness, Myth, and Affecting Presence*, Philadelphia: University of Pennsylvania Press.

Bailey, D., 2007. The Anti-rhetorical power of representational absence: incomplete figurines from the Balkan Neolithic, in *Material Beginnings: a Global Prehistory of Figurative Representation*, eds. C. Renfrew and I. Morley, Cambridge: McDonald Institute, 117–126

Battaglia, D., 1990. *On the Bones of the Serpent: Person, Memory and Mortality in Sabarl Island Society*, Chicago: Chicago University Press.

Baudrillard, J., 1996. *The System of Objects*, London: Verso.

Bentley, M., 2006. Past and "Presence": revisiting historical ontology. *History and Theory*, 45(3), 349–361.

Boym, S., 2001. *The Future of Nostalgia*, New York: Basic Books.

Brown, B., 2003. *A Sense of Things: The Object Matter of American Literature*, Chicago: University of Chicago Press.

Buchli, V. and G. Lucas (eds.), (2001). *Archaeologies of the Contemporary Past*, London: Routledge.

Burman, J., 2006. Absence, "Removal," and Everyday Life in the Diasporic City: Antidetention/ Antideportation Activism in Montréal. *Space and Culture*, 9(3), 279–293.

Cassia, P. S., 2005. *Bodies of Evidence. Burial, Memory, and the Recovery of Missing Persons in Cypros*, New York, Oxford: Berghan Books.

Coleman, S., 1996. Words as things: language, aesthetics and the objectification of protestant evangelicalism. *Journal of Material Culture*, 1(1), 107–128.

Cort, J. E., 2006. Installing absence? The consecration of a Jina image, in *Presence: The Inherence of the Prototype within Images and Other Objects*, eds. R. Maniura and R. Shepherd, Aldershot; Burlington, VT: Ashgate.

Crossland, Z., 2000. Buried lives: forensic archaeology and Argentina's disappeared. *Archaeological Dialogues*, 7(2), 146–159.

Crossland, Z., 2002. Violent spaces: conflict over the reappearance of Argentina's disappeared, in *The Archaeology of 20th Century Conflict*, eds. J. Schofield, C. Beck and W. G. Johnson, London: Routledge, 115–131.

Crowther, P., 1992. *Les Immatériaux* and the Postmodern Sublime, in *Judging Lyotard*, ed. A. Benjamin, London: Routledge, 192–205.

Csordas, T. J. (ed.), (1994). *Embodiment and Experience: The Existential Ground of Culture and Self*, Cambridge: Cambridge University Press.

Das, V., 2007. *Life and Words. Violence and the Descent into the Ordinary*, Berkeley, Los Angeles & London: University of California Press.

Degen, M. and K. Hetherington, 2001. Guest editorial: hauntings. *Space and Culture*, 5(11/12), 1–6.

Derrida, J., 1973. Differance, in *Speech and Phenomena, and Other Essays on Husserl's Theory of Signs*. Evanston: Northwestern University Press, 129–160.

Domanska, E., 2006. The material presence of the past. *History and Theory*, 45(October), 337–348.

Edensor, T., 2001. Haunting in the ruins: matter and immateriality. *Space and Culture*, 5(11/12), 42–51.

Edensor, T., 2005a. *Industrial Ruins: Space, Aesthetics and Materiality*, Oxford: Berg.

Edensor, T., 2005b. Waste matter – the debris of industrial ruins and the disordering of the material world. *Journal of Material Culture*, 10(3), 311–332.

Ellen, R., 1988. Fetishism. *Man, New Series*, 23(2), 213–235.

Engelke, M., 2004. Text and performance in an African church: the book, "live and direct". *American Ethnologist*, 31(1), 76–91.

Engelke, M., 2005. Sticky subjects and sticky objects. The substance of African Christian Healing, in *Materiality*, ed. D. Miller, Durham: Duke University Press, 118–139.

Engelke, M., 2007. *A Problem with Presence. Beyond Scripture in an African Church*, Berkeley: University of California Press.

Fowles, S., 2008. Steps toward an archaeology of taboo, in *religion, archaeology, and the material world*, ed. L. Fogelin, Southern Illinois University: Center for Archaeological Investigations, 15–37.

Fuery, P., 1995. *The Theory of Absence: Subjectivity, Signification and Desire*, Westport: Greenwood Press.

Gell, A., 1998. *Art and Agency: An Anthropological Theory*, Oxford: Oxford University Press.

Gordon, A., 1997. *Ghostly Matters: Haunting and the Sociological Imagination*, Minneapolis: University of Minnesota Press.

Gosden, C., 1994. *Social Being and Time*, Oxford: Blackwell.

Gould, R. A. and M. B. Schiffer (eds.), (1981). *Modern Material Culture: The Archaeology of Us*, New York: Academic Press.

Gumbrecht, H. U., 2004. *Production of Presence: What Meaning Cannot Convey*, California: Stanford University Press.

Gumbrecht, H. U., 2006. Presence achieved in language (with special attention given to the presence of the past). *History and Theory,* 45(October), 317–327.

Hallam, E. and J. Hockey, 2001. *Death, Memory and Material Culture,* New York: Berg.

Henare, A., M. Holbraad and S. Wastell (eds.), (2007). *Thinking Through Things: Theorising Artifacts Ethnographically,* London: Routledge.

Hetherington, K., 2004. Secondhandedness: consumption, disposal, and absent presence. *Environment and Planning D: Society and Space,* 22(1), 157–173.

Hodder, I., 1982. *Symbols in Action: Ethnoarchaeological Studies of Material Culture,* Cambridge: Cambridge University Press.

Hodder, I. and S. Hutson, 2003. *Reading the Past: Current Approaches to Interpretation in Archaeology,* Cambridge: Cambridge University Press.

Holloway, J., 2006. Enchanted spaces: the séance, affect, and geographies of religion. *Annals of the Association of American Geographers,* 96(1), 182–187.

Huyssen, A., 2003. *Present Pasts: Urban Palimpsests and the Politics of Memory,* Stanford, CA: Stanford University Press.

Ingold, T., 2000. *The Perception of the Environment: Essays in Livelihood, Dwelling and Skill,* London: Routledge.

Jackson, M. (ed.) (1996). *Things As They Are: New Directions in Phenomenological Anthropology,* Bloomington: Indiana University Press.

Janaway, C., 1998. Schopenhauer as Nietzsche's Educator, in *Willing and Nothingness: Schopenhauer as Nietzsche's Educator,* ed. C. Janaway, Oxford: Clarendon Press, 13–36.

Johnson, G. A., 2004. 'An almost immaterial substance': photography and the dematerialization of sculpture, in *Immaterial: Brancusi, Gabo, Moholy-Nagy.* Cambridge: Kettle's Yard, 71–88.

Kapstein, M. T. (ed.), (2004). *The Presence of Light: Divine Radiance and Religious Experience,* Chicago: The University of Chicago Press.

Keane, W., 1997. *Signs of Recognition: Powers and Hazards of Representation in an Indonesian Society,* Berkeley: University of California Press.

Keane, W., 2003. Semiotics and the social analysis of material things. *Language & Communication,* 23(4), 409–425.

Keane, W., 2005. Signs are not the garb of meaning: on the social analysis of material things, in *Materiality,* ed. D. Miller, London: Duke, 182–205.

Keane, W., 2007. *Christian moderns: Freedom and fetish in the mission encounter,* Berkeley: University of California Press.

Kierkegaard, S., 1988 [1843]. *Enten-Eller,* Copenhagen: Gyldendal.

Küchler, S., 1997. Sacrificial economy and its objects: rethinking colonial collecting in Oceania. *Journal of Material Culture,* 2(1), 39–60.

Lacoste, J.-Y., 2007. Perception, transcendence and the experience of God, in *Transcendence and Phenomenology,* eds. C. Cunningham and P. M. Candler, London: SCM Press, 1–20.

Latour, B. and P. Weibel (eds.), (2005). *Making Things Public: Atmospheres of Democracy,* Cambridge, MA: MIT Press.

Leder, D., 1990. *The Absent Body,* Chicago: Chicago University Press.

Limbert, M., 2008. The sacred date: gifts of God in an Omani Town. *Ethnos,* 73(3), 361–376.

Lyotard, J.-F. and T. Chaput, 1985. *Les Immatériaux,* Paris: Centre National d'Art et de Culture Georges Pompidou.

Maniura, R. and R. Shepherd, 2006. *Presence: The Inherence of the Prototype within Images and Other Objects,* Aldershot, Burlington, VT: Ashgate.

Masuzawa, T., 2000. Troubles with materiality: the ghost of fetishism in the nineteenth century. *Comparative Studies in Society and History,* 42(2), 242–267.

Mauss, M., 2002 [1954]. *The Gift: The Form and Reason for Exchange in Archaic Societies,* London: Routledge.

Meneley, A., 2008. Oleo-signs and quali-signs: the qualities of olive oil. *Ethnos,* 73(3), 303–326.

Meskell, L., 2004. *Object Worlds in Ancient Egypt: Material Biographies Past and Present,* London: Berg.

Miller, D., 1987. *Material Culture and Mass Consumption,* Oxford: Blackwell.

Miller, D. (ed.) (2005a). *Materiality,* Durham, NC: Duke University Press.

Miller, D., 2005b. Materiality: an introduction, in *Materiality,* ed. D. Miller, Durham: Duke University Press, 1–50.

Moure, G., 1997. *Medardo Rosso,* Centro Galego de Arte Contemporánea: Santiago de Compostela.

Nancy, J.-L., 2008. *Dis-Enclosure: The Deconstruction of Christianity,* New York: Fordham University Press.

Navaro-Yashin, Y., 2009. Affective spaces, melancholic objects: ruination and the production of anthropological knowledge. *Journal of the Royal Anthropological Institute,* 15(1), 1–18.

Ong, W., 1967. *The Presence of the Word: Some Prolegomena for Cultural and Religious History,* New Haven: Yale University Press.

Pels, P., 1998. The spirit of matter. On fetish, rarity, fact, and fancy, in *Border Fetish: Material Objects in Unstable Spaces,* ed. P. Spyer, London: Routledge, 91–121.

Peters, R., 2006. Actes de présence: presence in fascist political culture. *History and Theory,* 45(3), 362–374.

Pietz, W., 1985. The problem of the fetish I. *RES: Journal of Anthropology and Aesthetics,* 9, 5–17.

Pietz, W., 1987. The Problem of the Fetish II: The Origin of the Fetish. *RES: Journal of Anthropology and Aesthetics,* 13, 23-45.

Pietz, W., 1988. The problem of the fetish IIIa: Bosman's guinea and the enlightenment theory of fetishism. *RES: Journal of Anthropology and Aesthetics,* 16, 105–123.

Pitkin, H. F., 1967. *The Concept of Representation,* Berkeley: University of California Press.

Ramachandran, V. S. and W. Hirstein, 1998. The perception of phantom limbs: The D. O. Hebb lecture. *Brain,* 121, 1603–1630.

Rowlands, M., 2005. A materialist approach to materiality, in *Materiality,* ed. D. Miller, Durham: Duke, 72–87.

Runia, E., 2006a. Presence. *History and Theory,* 45(February), 1–29.

Runia, E., 2006b. Spots of time. *History and Theory,* 45(October), 305–316.

Sansi-Roca, R., 2005. The hidden life of stones: historicity, materiality and the value of candomblé objects in Bahia. *Journal of Material Culture,* 10(2), 139–156.

Sartre, J.-P., 2005 [1943]. *Being and Nothingness: An Essay on Phenomenological Ontology,* London: Routledge.

Sassen, S. (ed.), (2002). *Global Networks: Linked Cities,* London: Routledge.

Schopenhauer, A., 1966 [1818]. *The World as Will and Representation,* New York: Dover Publications.

Shanks, M. and C. Tilley, 1987. *Social Theory and Archaeology,* Cambridge: Cambridge University Press.

Sider, G. and G. Smith (eds.), (1997). *Between History and Histories: The Making of Silences and Commemorations,* Toronto: University of Toronto Press.

Slyomovics, S., 2005. *The Performance of Human Rights in Morocco,* Philadelphia: University of Pennsylvania Press.

Spyer, P. (ed.), (1998). *Border Fetishisms: Material Objects in Unstable Spaces,* London: Routledge.

Stewart, S., 1993. *On Longing: Narratives of the Miniature, the Gigantic, the Souvenir, the Collection,* Durham: Duke University Press.

Strathern, M., 2004. *Partial connections,* Walnut Creek, CA: AltaMira Press.

Sturken, M., 2004. The aesthetics of absence: rebuilding ground zero. *American Ethnologist,* 31(3), 311–325.

Sørensen, T. F., 2008. Urban exploration as archaeological engagement: a review of http://infiltration. org/ – 'the zine about places you're not supposed to go'. *European Journal of Archaeology,* 10(1), 89–91.

Taussig, M., 1993. *Mimesis and Alterity: A Particular History of the Senses,* London: Routledge.

Taussig, M. T., 1980. *Devil and Commodity Fetishism in South America,* Chapel Hill: North Carolina University Press.

Tilley, C., 1994. *A Phenomenology of Landscape: Places, Paths and Monuments,* Oxford: Berg.

Tilley, C., W. Keane, S. Küchler, M. Rowlands and P. Spyer (eds.), (2006). *Handbook of Material Culture,* London: Sage.

Trouillot, M.-R., 1997. *Silencing the Past: Power and the Production of History,* Boston: Beacon Press.

Wade, N. J., 2003. The legacy of phantom limbs. *Perception,* 32, 517–524.

Wagner, S. E., 2008. *To Know Where He Lies: DNA Technology and the Search for Srebrenica's Missing,* Berkeley: University of California Press.

Wunderlich, A., 2008. *Der Philosoph im Museum: die Ausstellung "Les Immatériaux" von Jean François Lyotard,* Bielefeld: Transcript Verlag.

Young, J. E., 1993. *The Texture of Memory: Holocaust Memorials and Meaning,* Bloomington: Indiana University Press.

Chapter 2
People Without Things

Severin Fowles

> "... well then, let's have less of that. Let's have radically,
> radically less of that."
>
> – John Zerzan *(in Versluis 2008:160)*

Introduction

It is easy to understand the puzzlement of colleagues who are unsure what to make
of the increasing number of anthropologists who bemoan anthropocentrism. We
can forgive their sideways glances when they hear that social scientists are "now
look[ing] to gain maturity by burying the corpse of our imperial majesty: society"
(Miller 2005: 37). Or when they learn that posthumanism is a growing project in
the humanities (Wolfe 2003). Or that the latest iteration of phenomenology has little
to do with people and is instead concerned with how objects perceive one another
(Harman 2005).

What is going on? Why are so many scholars in the humanities and social sciences eager to write about everything *except* actual people? "These days," observes
Bill Brown (2004: 2), "you can read books on the pencil, the zipper, the toilet, the
banana, the chair, the potato, the bowler hat..." – not, mind you, books written by
pencil manufacturers or by agri scientists detailing the best ways to grow bananas
and potatoes. Rather, these are books written within disciplines that not so long
ago only had eyes for other eyes (that is, for other humans) but now find they have
much more to say about zippers and telephone poles.

The "turn toward things" in late twentieth and early twenty-first century social
theory could be variously interpreted, but most regard it as a critical response to
the textual turn of the 1970s and 1980s, which, in its excessive variants, reduced
the world to a series of texts authored and read by culturally situated human

S. Fowles (✉)
Barnard College, Columbia University, New York, NY, USA
e-mail: sf2220@columbia.edu

M. Bille et al. (eds.), *An Anthropology of Absence: Materializations of Transcendence and Loss*,   23
DOI 10.1007/978-1-4419-5529-6_2, © Springer Science+Business Media, LLC 2010

subjects. "The culture of a people," wrote Geertz (1973: 452), "is an ensemble of texts, themselves ensembles, which the anthropologist strains to read over the shoulders of those to whom they properly belong." Importantly, the "culture of a people" within this body of theory included not only structured practices such as cockfights, but also structured matter itself (i.e., material culture), all of which was of analytical interest only insofar as it transmitted encoded human meanings.

It is now generally acknowledged that the textual turn's privileging of the human interpreter and its reduction of the material world to mere semantic placeholders went too far. We are all, suggests John Frow, working in "the *aftermath* of a theoretical paradigm which sought to imagine the world rigorously in terms of a play of representations" (Frow, 2004: 347, emphasis added). The recent focus on materiality, in this sense, can be understood as a response to a world reduced to discourse, filled with unstable meanings that have been cut free from anything solid or unproblematically "out there". It can be understood, in other words, as a corrective to certain strands of late twentieth century social theory in which the real seemed to be lost in the hyperreal and in which the world was left feeling a bit like shadows and fog.

The result has been a remarkable interdisciplinary effort to raise the status of *things*, to tip our hats to their agentive presence in the world, to explore their hidden materiality, and to expose the powers they command. Old understandings of the social as an exclusively human phenomenon are being reassembled and recast as a vast brier patch of relations in which multitudes of nonhumans get caught up – an imbricated collective of people and things. In this bold new vision of the social, objects take center stage: the humble air pump becomes the co-author of modernity (Latour 1993), and Marx's actual felt coat co-authors the discursive coat that emerges in *Capital* as an exemplar of the commodity form (Stallybrass 1998).

To a certain extent, the argument being advanced in this work is that by attending to things in themselves, we stand in a much better position to understand people in themselves, due to the inescapable conclusion that people and things are mutually constitutive. There is, however, a more radical extension of this argument that draws upon overtly postcolonial language to make the claim that the traditionally heavy focus on the human in the humanities is not only analytically limiting but downright immoral. We are told that "the imperialist social and humanist discourses" (Olsen 2003) have debased the world of nonhuman objects by treating them as "subalterns" (Olsen 2003) who have been "colonized" (Pinney 2005) by human "tyrants" (Miller 2005).[1] Things, concludes Latour (1999: 214), "deserve better. They deserve to be housed in our intellectual culture as full-fledged social

---

[1] It was remarked by the editors that to interweave the essays by Olsen (2003), Pinney (2005) and Miller (2005) in this way does a disservice to their individual arguments, insofar as each essay has its own broader agenda. This is a fair critique; however, all explicitly draw inspiration from Latour who is largely the originator of the postcolonial thing-rhetoric in which Olsen, Pinney, and Miller all indulge. And it is this common rhetoric that I find noteworthy, particularly so, because it seems to be deployed toward numerous ends.

actors." Needless to say, this is strong language that needs to be unpacked in a more extensive treatment than I am able to offer here. Nevertheless, its mere invocation provides a sense of the broader agenda and passion underlying the recent theorization of things, materiality, and nonhuman agency. Things, rather than people, have become our subjects as part of a strange project of decolonization in the humanities, designed to establish a new form of democracy extended to both humans and nonhumans. This is the liberatory politics of what Latour (1993) refers to as symmetry, a concept I will return to shortly.

The turn toward things has much to recommend it, but let us not fool ourselves into thinking that it has finally offered a comprehensive view of the world and its doings. Every car has its blind spots, and my primary argument in this chapter is that thing theory's[2] major blind spot is, quite literally, that which is unseen – or, rather, that which is absent but nevertheless experienced as a presence precisely because its absence is marked or emphatic. Indeed, my worry is that in the rush to take things seriously, we have over-privileged a crude notion of presence linked to physicality and tangibility, as if the only meaningful relations were those between entities that can be seen, smelt or felt. My worry is that this new materialism tends to blind us to that more complicated world of relations in which, packed between the multitudes of self-evident things, are crowds of non-things, negative spaces, lost or forsaken objects, voids or gaps – absences, in other words, that also stand before us as entity-like presences with which we must contend.

The reason for this blind spot, it seems to me, is closely linked to the particular brand of "posthuman postcolonialism" just noted. If much of the motivation behind the turn toward things has been to empower the position of nonhuman objects by demonstrating that they are truly self-standing presences in the world – presences that follow their own agendas and are not, therefore, reducible to human discourse about them – then absent objects emerge as an especially awkward category. One might say, for instance, that a set of keys jangling about in one's pocket has its own autonomous steely quality that permits it to have an effect upon the actions of key-users. But consider the keys that have been misplaced and so are present only as an absence. These absent keys also impinge upon us in a strongly sensuous fashion: one registers the absence of keys with distress, gropes about the emptiness in one's pocket, and, defeated, is left standing in the cold outside one's apartment. Both the keys and the absence of the keys have material effects on the world. And yet, while we are able to write about the present key as a viable actor (e.g., Latour 2000), it is more difficult to write about the absent key in similar terms, for the latter only appears to exist when acknowledged by a human subject. The absent thing, in other words, seems to rely upon at least a mild anthropocentrism, and it is precisely this anthropocentrism that we are increasingly encouraged to reject on both philosophical and ethical grounds.

---

[2] Or its variants: materiality studies (Miller 2005), material engagement theory (Renfrew 2004), symmetrical archaeology (Shanks 2007; Witmore 2007), and the like.

The remainder of the essay is divided into two parts. The first part expands upon the core paradox just noted: that absence seems to be both derivative and strangely autonomous vis-à-vis the perceiving human subject. In the process, I revisit a classic example of symmetrical analysis within Latour's writing to underscore the challenges presented by this paradox to contemporary studies of the relations between people and things generally. The second part moves beyond critique to consider what is to be gained by following Bille, Hastrup, and Sørensen's (this volume) lead in granting absence its presence. As an archeologist of "pre-modernity," I have special interests in what is to be gained vis-à-vis our understanding of those indigenous societies that, in the older literature, were defined precisely by what they lacked – the so-called stateless societies. As I suggest below, it is here that the flickering relationship between absence and presence casts a particularly intense light on the politics of attending to what is missing and why.

The Carnality of Absence

Let me begin, then, by briefly returning to the celebrated turn toward things. As much as it marks an entrée into a new domain of inquiry, it is also, quite clearly, a reactionary move designed to counter the excesses of certain variants of social constructivism in which one cannot talk about the world except as something that is talked about. In contrast, the response in recent years has been to emphasize the resistance of things to what we may say or think about them, to focus upon the alterity and autonomy of nonhumans, even if that alterity can only be vaguely sensed rather than rigidly defined. Standing in opposition to ideas or meanings, things are "what's encountered as opposed to what's thought," writes Bill Brown (2004: 5). They are defined by their carnality, by their ability to sensuously intrude upon our lives. There is a "suddenness with which things seem to assert their presence and power: you cut your finger on a sheet of paper, you trip over some toy, you get bopped on the head by a falling nut" (Brown 2004:4).

If we imagine a fundamental division between things and ideas about things, between what is encountered and what is thought, then the absences of the world might be viewed as somewhat closer to ideas. We can imagine scenarios in which a spouse is gone on an extended journey, leaving the one at home to feel the acute pain of the spouse's absence. More grandly, we can follow Marx in thinking about history weighing like a nightmare on the mind of the living. At either scale, that which is gone or has passed – that which is absent – certainly has a powerful presence, but one might explain away these present absences by saying that it is really the *idea* of the loved one, or the *idea* of the past that weighs upon us. And this would be to argue, therefore, that we are not in the province of materiality, not in the world of things.

Still, there are other species of absence that are encountered more suddenly as object-like entities that stand over against us and demand response. The absence of people on the city street at midday can make you stop and hurriedly wonder, "Where did all the people go? What's going on?" Or you may reach for your wallet only to find it missing – stolen – pulling the rug from beneath whatever your plans for the day had been. These sorts of absences have greater impact. Like Brown's falling nut, they intrude on your life and bop you on the head.

When absences become object-like, when they seem to exist not merely as an afterthought of perception but rather as self-standing presences out there in the world, they begin to acquire powers and potentialities similar to things. Object-like absences (or what Fuery (1995: 2) refers to as quasi-presences), in this sense, become full participants in the social characterized by their own particular politics and, at times, their own particular emotional and semiotic charge.

Zoe Crossland (2002) writes of precisely this sort of phenomenon in her work on the disappeared of Argentina, those thousands of individuals abducted and killed during the period of military rule in the late 1970s and early 1980s. Crossland attends to the problem of absence as it evolved in the aftermath of this extremely violent and unstable time in the country when clandestine commando units took individuals from their homes with neither warning nor trial nor official acknowledgment. Thousands of gaping physical and emotional holes were suddenly carved out of the families of the disappeared, and Crossland reveals the manner in which these absences shifted from negative to positive as they became critical political objects around which communities rallied in protest.

It is telling, in this regard, that some vocal Argentinean families vigorously opposed the efforts of the forensic archeologists brought in as part of the formal judicial inquiries to exhume and identify the individuals anonymously interred in the military's mass graves – not, of course, because they opposed the effort to publicly acknowledge the violence, but rather because the presence of the disappeared's remains threatened to bring about a premature closure to the political struggle for accountability. Like Barthes's (1981) photograph – which offers us a presence (the photograph) that is immediately overwhelmed by a deathly absence (the photographed scene, now passed) – the identification and return of corpses paradoxically consummated the disappearance of the disappeared, pushing them into the category of the "that-has-been". Absence, in this case, was actively maintained and protected, for it was there that surviving families found the power of protest.

This is to say that absences perform labor, frequently intensifying our emotional or cognitive engagement with that which is manifestly not present. Lately, this point has even come to be made by archaeologists struggling to understand societies deep in antiquity (Fowles 2008). Douglass Bailey (2007), for instance, has recently revisited the curious case of the faceless figurine, a common archaeological object of the Neolithic and earlier periods in Europe. How, asked generations of archaeologists, are we to understand a figurine with detailed genitalia and body decoration but with a face that is either entirely absent or reduced to an indistinct nubbin? Unsurprisingly, most commentary has concluded that presence and value must be positively correlated (so great is the bias toward presence). Hence, large breasts and genitalia are regularly taken to indicate a concern with the female body and its fertility, while the absent face supposedly reveals a disinterest in what was going on above the neck. Bailey, however, offers an entirely different reading, drawing upon work in cognitive psychology to suggest that we take the absence of the face as evidence of the face's *enhanced* significance. "One is forced to ask: Where is the detail of human expression, the face, the head?" (Bailey 2007: 118). And one is also forced to fill the gap, to project a face or subjectivity or emotional state onto the void. The missing face, then, is not a text to be read so much as it is an inscrutable thing that demands the construction of a text.

This is to say, again, that absences cannot be reduced to ideas. Regardless of the meanings that we, as semiotic animals, may nail to their doors, absences – no less than presences – also inhabit the material world on the far side of signification. They come both before and after human perception, and in this way gain a kind of independence from the perceiving human subject. Absences push back and resist. They prompt us into action. And like present things, absences also have their distinctive affordances and material consequences that are not only prior to meaning but can, of their own accord, direct the process of signification itself.

This is perhaps most evident in the way so many religious traditions have relied upon voids both to signify and, more importantly, to provoke novel reflection upon the divine. The empty throne icon in early Buddhist art directed the viewer's attention toward the transcendence of the Buddha (Tanaka 1998), and in the ancient Nabatean tradition the deity was made present by a niche within a niche, a void within a void (Patrich 1990: 51). We are most familiar with such negative signification as it has figured in the Abrahamic religions where the paradox of God's simultaneous presence and absence in the world is an obvious theme. Mary Magdalene did not go to Christ's tomb, find it empty, and say, "Ah well, there's nothing here; we can all go home now and worry ourselves with other matters." The emptiness, of course, was *constitutive* of Christ's divinity, a basic theological stance that has also underwritten a long history of Judeo-Christian and Islamic iconoclasm in which the faithful periodically reinstated the supposed purity of iconographic absence (see also Engelke 2007).

For Daniel Miller (2005), the religious examples just cited are properly viewed as components of a much more basic tension between the material and the immaterial. "Humanity," he writes in the introduction to a recent volume entitled *Materiality*, "constantly returns to vast projects devoted to *immateriality*, whether as religion, as philosophy, or... as the practice of finance" (Miller 2005: 28, emphasis added). As should be clear from this comment, Miller treats "immateriality" as an umbrella term to describe not only the spiritual realm, but also everything from academic theories to exchange value. What unifies them all, he contends, is that each rests "on the same paradox: that immateriality can only be expressed through materiality" (2005: 28). This is an important point, and there is a sense in which the tension between immateriality and materiality highlighted by Miller parallels the tension at the heart of the present volume, insofar as one might equally say that absence can only be expressed, paradoxically, through presence. However, the comparison can only be taken so far. Miller's immaterial stands on the side of

Brown's world of ideas as that which is thought rather than encountered,[3] and the goal, as I see it, must rather be to draw the immaterial into the field of encounter and expose the ability of non-things no less than things, immateriality no less than materiality, and absence no less than presence to intrude upon human lives and stand, object-like, before perceiving subjects.

I want to expand upon this observation with a brief example drawn from the work of one of the great champions of material things, Bruno Latour. The example I have in mind is Latour's (1999: 176–180) analysis of the ontological status of guns in the debate between the National Rifle Association and anti-gun lobbyists. It is an example that has the advantage of being widely regarded as an exemplar of posthumanist or symmetrical analysis and, as such, has been rehearsed in the related literature with remarkable frequency (e.g., Dant 2005: 81–2; Ihde 1990: 26–7; Knappett 2008; Robb 2004; Smith 2003). A large part of its appeal lies in the simplicity of the example: in one corner, anti-gun activists brusquely claim that "guns kill people", and so they would like to see gun sales restricted; in the other corner, the NRA counters by claiming that "guns don't kill people; *people* kill people." Hence, they argue we should crack down on criminals and not the guns themselves, the latter of which they present as neutral objects, mere tools that can be used properly or improperly.

Latour steps into this debate by posing a rhetorical question designed to expose the underlying biases of both sides: "Which of them," he asks, "the gun or the citizen, is the actor in this situation?" His answer, of course, is that, strictly speaking, neither citizens nor their guns are culpable when viewed as discrete agents. Rather, responsibility must lie on the shoulders of *someone else*, on some new hybrid agent, on the "citizen-gun" or the "gun-citizen":

> You are different with a gun in your hand; the gun is different with you holding it. You are another subject because you hold the gun; the gun is another object because it has entered into

---

[3] This read of Miller's recent work was contested by the editors; however, I stand behind it. For Miller, the "world confronts us as material culture" (2005: 8), whereas "humanity reaches toward the *conceptualization* of the immaterial" (2005: 28, emphasis added). True, Miller lays great emphasis upon the supposedly dialectical manner in which people and things bring each other into being. This he refers to as the process of objectification: "In objectification all we have is a process in time by which the very act of creating form creates consciousness or capacity such as skill and thereby transforms both form and the self-consciousness of that which has consciousness, or the capacity of that which now has skill" (2005: 9; see also Miller 1987). Or as he puts it more simply: "we need to show how the things people make, make people" (2005:38). This is all well and good, but it is an odd dialectic indeed that begins with an opposition between consciousness and form *and also ends* with an opposition between consciousness and form, or both begins and ends with people and things, or subjects and objects, or what have you. More to the point, however, by stressing the opposition between materiality and immateriality, Miller moves away from an understanding of materiality as a culturally specific understanding of the material world, to one in which materiality is concrete rather than abstract and sensuously encountered rather than imagined. This is how he is able to claim that "immateriality can only be expressed through materiality."

a relationship with you. The gun is no longer the gun-in-the-armory or the gun-in-the-drawer
or the gun-in-the-pocket, but the gun-in-your-hand, aimed at someone who is screaming.
(Latour 1999: 179–180).

Latour, then, offers a characteristically simple and elegant twist on an old debate, a
move toward analytical symmetry that places the presence of things and people on
a level playing field.

But has he really done justice to the debate and the various positions involved?
Without question, a turn toward things is achieved, and we begin to appreciate the
world as a network of actors, some human and some nonhuman, whose encounters
and alliances transform the state of affairs and collectively lead to violence or non-
violence. Nevertheless, as the relations between hard material things become illumi-
nated, a shadow is simultaneously cast upon the many absent things that have their
own part to play in the action.

This becomes clearer when we suspend the project of symmetry for a moment and
consider more carefully the situated positions of the humans involved, particularly the
members of the NRA. What would they have to say about Latour's seemingly
straightforward contention that "Citizen + Gun = CitizenGun"? To be sure, they might
argue that the gun is neutral and so should not really enter into the equation at all. But
the core of their argument has consistently been that an American citizen is not a
full citizen without a gun or, rather, without the possibility of owning a gun. Hence,
their endless references to the Second Amendment, the alleged insurance that citizens
as citizens have the right to bear arms. For the NRA, in other words, there is no
CitizenGun, precisely because citizenship has already been defined in hybrid terms
as the union of a person and a gun (or potential gun). Take away the guns, and what
one is left with is not a society of peace-loving citizens, but a society with no citizens at all. One is left with a society of individuals stripped of true citizenship,
individuals who carry with them the stigma of absent rights as much as absent guns.
In other words, if...

person + gun (or potential gun) = citizen
... then following the NRA's mathematics...
citizen – gun = less-than-a-citizen + ~~gun~~.

What the NRA is centrally concerned with is *the spectre of the crossed-out gun*. The
person-plus-gun-minus-gun, in their analysis, cannot walk away a citizen precisely
because this new hybrid carries in its hand a politicized absence rather than a gun. It
carries a denial of a right that, if not exactly god-given, then was at least given by a
semi-mythical group of founding ancestors. And this is the funny thing about
humans: one cannot add and subtract relations without leaving residues. "You are a
different person with the gun in your hand," notes Latour (1999: 179). But you are
also a different person having formerly had a gun in your hand. That is, you are a
different person when gripping a crossed-out gun. On the battlefield you may be a
prisoner-of-war; in American politics you are – so claims the NRA – another-disen-
franchised-victim-of-liberal-big-government.

Naked Society

It makes sense that the dedicated participants in the turn toward things would have little to say about *absent* things.[4] Despite their material impact and the relative autonomy they achieve, absent things fall into the blind spot of thing theory due to the stigma of their unseemly origins – their illegitimate birth in human perception. If one roundly rejects phenomenology in favor of a posthuman relational philosophy (as does Latour), then one is far more inclined to write essays about hard, metal guns as opposed to absent or banned guns. And if one rejects idealism in favor of a new materialism (as do an increasing number of anthropologists and archaeologists), then one is far more inclined to write essays about the physicality of the decaying corpse as opposed to the strange and ghostly presence of the absent family member.

And yet, if we turn to consider earlier periods in the history of anthropology, the situation does not look much better. The problem of absence has always been a peripheral concern at best, which is surprising insofar as the discipline's dominant subject matter, until relatively recently, was comprised of non-Western societies defined precisely by what they lacked. Stateless society, pre-capitalist economies, tribes without rulers, people without history – these were the curiosities of the colonial frontier that animated most early theory-building in anthropology. "Acephalous" was another term sometimes used to describe such societies, and here we might draw a comparison between the archaeologist holding his faceless Paleolithic figurine and the ethnographer struggling to grasp the logic of the apparently headless (leaderless) tribe. If, for Bailey (2007), the absent face of the figurine implicitly prompts us to fill in the gap and project a missing subjectivity, then the missing head of the tribal society in Africa, Australia, or the Americas surely served as its own prompt for the early twentieth century ethnographer. How was social order maintained in the absence of true government and strong leaders? What filled this curious gap? Generations of scholars steeped in functionalist theory advanced their own answers, building models in which religion, kinship or some other phenomenon stood in for the missing political system.

I do not intend to revisit these dusty anthropological arguments in any length. But I do want to emphasize the degree to which a vast swath of humanity has become tangled up in the problem of absence, albeit implicitly. Take, for instance, one of anthropology's founding texts, Lewis Henry Morgan's *Ancient Society*, and the manner in which absence served as a key concept in both the method of cross-cultural comparison as well as Morgan's resultant theory of social evolution.

---

[4] In discussing what he refers to as "delegation," Latour (1999: 189) does observe that by using and engaging with crafted artifacts "we hourly encounter hundreds, even thousands of absent makers who are remote in time and space, yet simultaneously active and present." But this is a separate issue. Indeed, there is a certain irony here as well insofar as we only "encounter" Latour's absent makers from the situated perspective of the (human) analyst standing outside the action and tracing out indexical relations – the very sort of anthropocentrism Latour typically opposes. Be that as it may, the absent things discussed above always seem to fall outside a Latourian analysis.

Significantly, Morgan approached the question of stateless society by working backward from the present; the task of the ethnologist, he suggested, was to begin with the modern nation-state and, through a process of elimination, to successively remove evolutionary benchmarks, working one's way through the ethnographic diversity of the world down to the most primitive of tribes. Morgan put it this way:

> ... [by following] along the several lines of human progress toward the primitive ages of man's existence, and removing one by one his principal institutions, inventions, and discoveries, in the order in which they have appeared, the advance made in each period will be realized. (1974: 29).

"The principle contributions of modern civilization," he continued, "are the electric telegraph; coal gas; the spinning-jenny;" etc., and so the ethnologist must begin by stripping society of these and the many other technologies introduced during the Industrial Age. Then "should be removed the modern sciences; religious freedom and the common schools; representative democracy;" etc. (1974: 30). Remove coinage, civil law, and cavalry. Then poetry, the potter's wheel, the popular assembly. On and on, down through domesticated plants and dug-out canoes, until, "when this work of elimination has been done," when humanity has been stripped of all its things, "we shall have approached quite near the infantile period of man's existence" (1974: 36) – which in the anthropology of the day was essentially equivalent to aboriginal Australia or Tierra del Fuego.

Morgan's model was not merely teleological. Certainly, his founding principle was that the modern European or Euro-American state marked an endpoint toward which all non-modern societies have naturally aspired as part of the grand "plan of the Supreme Intelligence" (1974: 563). What I find more interesting, however, is the analytical method he employed to draw non-Western societies into the evolutionary metanarrative. Morgan stripped away things and institutions as a means of revealing and situating primitivity, an act of methodological disrobing that cannot be divorced from the deep-seated Victorian preoccupation with the nakedness of native peoples. During the nineteenth century "nakedness symbolized readability and legibility" writes Philippa Levine (2008: 198–199). "To unclothe was to uncover the truth about the native." Thus were indigenous bodies on the colonial frontier systematically disrobed and photographed as a form of scientific documentation and anthropometric study. Such photographs, mailed back to Europe, became iconic evidence of the native's lack of civilization and their generally abject state of humanity left unfulfilled. "The scantily-clad native," observes Levine (2008: 196), "was doubly marginalized – by clothing, or its lack, as well as by culture, or its lack. Lacking history, lacking shame, lacking clothes, the native epitomized the absence of civilization..." (see also Stevens 2003).

Nineteenth century prudishness undoubtedly imbued the colonized subject's lack of clothes with a special charge, but there was more at work here than the mere sight of skin. In this respect, we might contrast the documentary photograph of the "naked" native taken by the colonial traveler, with its alter-ego, the painted "nude" of Victorian high art, which also exhibited the disrobed body according to very particular conventions. The key difference between the two is that, unlike the image of the naked native, the aestheticized "nude" of the artist was not truly "lacking clothes," if by this we mean that it was somehow considered less than complete. The nude painting was presented to the nineteenth century consumer of art as a whole specimen that lacked nothing – indeed, it served as the very image of human perfection (Clark 1956). The nakedness of the native, on the other hand, was fundamentally a thing of deprivation. The Victorian blushed before the naked native as a way of acknowledging that something morally required was missing (clothing, but perhaps also an appropriate sense of shame), while he could gaze upon the painting of a nude in a gallery with impunity, for the nude was as she was meant to be.

To be naked is also to stand in a very particular relation to desire, and in the case of the scantily-clad native, she (the gendering here is necessary) was frequently represented as the object of a voyeuristic colonial gaze. Louis Montrose (1993: 179–81) comments upon Jan van der Straet's late sixteenth century illustration of Vespucci's "discovery" of America (Fig. 2.1) to make this point:

> Here a naked woman, crowned with feathers, upraises herself from her hammock to meet the gaze of the armored and robed man who has just come ashore; she extends her right arm toward him, apparently a gesture of wonder – or, perhaps, of apprehension. Standing with his feet firmly planted upon the ground, Vespucci observes the personified and feminized space that will bear his name. This recumbent figure, now discovered and roused from her torpor, is about to be hailed, claimed, and possessed as *America*. (Montrose 1993: 179–180)

The native – and the virgin resources of the landmass she represents – are clearly what the European explorer has longed for during his months of sea travel. But more importantly, the discourse of desire within the image seems to go in both

Fig. 2.1 "Vespucci Discovers America," by Jan van der Straet (ca. 1580)

directions, for van der Straet has presented the native as both desired and desiring. With her arm extended, she reaches as if to touch not only an excessively clothed man, but also a man laden with wondrous material *things*. Ships at his back, a sword at his hip, a cruciform staff in his right hand, and an astrolabe held forward in his left hand, dangling before the native like a hypnotist's watch, Vespucci's presence on the shore reveals to the native, in an instance, that she is impoverished, that she is a creature of absence.

As typically understood, absence is equated with incompleteness and so becomes a source of longing. This assumption was made particularly explicit by Freud in his infamous contention that the woman's missing penis led both men and women to accommodate the physiological absence in deep, psychological ways: women were driven to envy, men to fetishistic substitution. But it also underwrote the European colonial project. Below, I will suggest that we should be suspicious whenever we encounter a theory that takes the link between absence and longing for granted. Returning to *Ancient Society*, however, one could say that the primitives of this and many other early anthropological texts were naked rather than nude because, while they may not have been cognizant of their lack of coinage, the potter's wheel, writing, history, religion, government, etc., they were nevertheless tragically incomplete. The Victorian's primitive was like Freud's woman: driven by an unconscious desire, as it were, to fill a void. The very notion of evolutionary progress relied upon a hidden teleological compulsion for society to acquire more and more of its missing things, gradually filling out a checklist of civilization's predetermined accomplishments. Progress was driven by the phantom pains of the acephalous society as it subconsciously sensed its own headlessness. Whether they knew it or not, the naked native *desired* to be modern – this, at least, was the conceit of the time.

Of course, the nineteenth century ended long ago, and it is reasonable to ask what any of this has to do with twenty-first century anthropology, particularly insofar as most contemporary ethnographers seem so preoccupied by postcoloniality that they cannot be bothered to think about the precolonial world. But to ignore the precolonial or premodern is to do merely that; indeed, without a viable alternative to the myth of progress, the old evolutionary metanarratives tend to linger in the shadows. (Are not premodern societies still being defined by what they lack, that lack simply now having become "modernity" itself?) This point is not lost on Latour who has, with characteristic daring, offered his own revised history of the world or, as he puts it, his own "servant narrative" to counter the master narrative of the West (Latour 1993, 1999: 198–215).[5] This is not the place to discuss Latour's broader claims, his careful dissection of the genealogy of "purification" and his critique of the modernist

---

[5] Very much in the style of Rousseau's (1992) *Discourse on Inequality*, Latour is explicit in denying the factuality of his counternarrative; it is, he suggests, purely a rhetorical strategy to assist us in imagining alternatives to the myth of progress (Latour 1999: 201). And yet, Latour's counternarrative, like Rousseau's, is only compelling because he seems to convince himself of its empirical validity in the course of its presentation.

separation of nature and culture. I do, however, want to briefly draw attention to certain features of Latour's narrative that, ironically enough, are shared with Morgan's and are likewise bound up with the problem of primitive absence we have been considering.

The most obvious similarity is that both Latour and Morgan imagine a world history in the singular, proceeding along a unidirectional trajectory from an early society with few things to a modern society with many. Of the two, Morgan is more explicit and includes long lists of technological devices, instruments, property types, and institutions acquired over the course of evolutionary time. However, Latour is writing in a similar vein when he stresses the growing "scale of collectives and the [increasing] number of nonhumans enlisted in their midst" (Latour 1999: 195). Indeed, both seem to regard time's arrow as if it were affixed to a giant historical scale designed to measure the world's mounting and increasingly unwieldy mass. Morgan writes that,

> Since the advent of civilization, the outgrowth of property has been so immense, its forms so diversified, its uses so expanding and its management so intelligent in the interests of its owners, that it has become, on the part of the people, an unmanageable power. The human mind stands bewildered in the presence of its own creation. (Morgan 1974: 561)

Latour is similarly struck by the degree to which "modernity" has come to be overwhelmed by the swarms of objects that act more like subjects and vie with us for control over events. Following Michel Serres (2007: 224–34), he refers to these nonhuman actors – guns and astrolabes, for example – as "quasi-objects," subject-like things that constantly mediate our experience and transform our goals. Today's world is thick with such quasi-objects, while the premodern world, Latour contends, was less burdened.[6] Be that as it may, the more general conclusion that humans have come to inhabit increasingly heavy and entangled material worlds over the past 40,000 or so years is taken by many to be inescapable.[7] Ever more things, it would seem.

---

[6] Ever slippery, Latour both supports and denies this trajectory in his writings. Here, I am concerned with his discussion in *Pandora's Hope* where Latour's story is one "in which the further we go the more articulated are the collectives we live in" (1999: 212), in which "time enmeshes, at an ever greater level of intimacy and on an ever greater scale, humans and nonhumans with each other" (1999: 200).

[7] The notion that the world has somehow become thicker with things over time is implicit in many disciplines, but it tends to be archeologists who truly make this explicit. Ian Hodder (2006), for instance, has recently discussed the Neolithic Revolution as a process of intensified entanglement with nonhumans that has propelled us down the road toward our current material heaviness. The problem is that the "material heaviness" of society is typically measured by the quantity of *artifacts* (see also Dant 2006) – in other words, by the quantity of human-constructed objects that have come to occupy a world formerly filled with "natural" materials. Which is to say that the notion is premised upon a division between the things of nature and the things of culture, only the latter of which are assumed to mediate human lives and contribute to the overall material burden of society. And this division is precisely what Latour (1993) refers to as the untenable practice of analytical purification. Below, I will also suggest that the seemingly simple assumption that modernity is characterized by an ever greater material burden falls apart further once we accept absent things as viable participants in human entanglements.

Significantly, both Latour and Morgan also assume that history involves the *accretion* of certain sorts of material objects, those of subsequent ages adding to, rather than replacing, those of prior ages. Morgan may have written in terms of the growth of property while Latour stresses the accumulation of human entanglements with nonhumans, but each founds their argument on an additive principle. And this is why Latour, like Morgan, also finds it useful to recount his history of world by working *backwards*, stripping away successive relations between people and things from the present down through the ages:

> To tell my tale, I will open Pandora's box backward; that is, starting with the most recent types of folding [i.e., the most recent exchange of properties between people and things], I will try to map the labyrinth until we find the earliest (mythical[8]) folding. As we will see… no dangerous regression is involved here, since all the earlier steps are still with us today. (Latour 1999: 201–202)

At the end of the story, we are left standing in Latour's own basement, his prima-tological "Level 1." Morgan went a step further, digging all the way to what he referred to as "the zero of human society," but in both accounts the result is the same: an act of disrobing, a work of elimination designed to reveal our naked beginnings.

Needless to say, the comparison I have just drawn is hardly fair to Latour's project, which he undertakes precisely to oppose the modernist myth of progress as exem-plified in the writings of Morgan. But while one might write off the similarities as superficial, I have highlighted them to make a somewhat deeper point. Much con-temporary scholarship, even when it explicitly critiques modernist narratives, remains wedded to an understanding of premodern societies as "societies without." Absence, in other words, continues to be central to the conceptualization of pre-modernity, and we find that we have not moved far beyond the old image of the impoverished forager roaming the landscape with his absent modernity silently in tow. Modern is to primitive as presence is to absence – this is what it means to be naked, to be stateless, to be without a head.

Should we aim, then, for understandings of nonmodern and non-Western societies that solely attend to that which is present? Should we find ways to discuss gift economies that are not "precapitalist," or stone tool technologies that are not "pre-Industrial," or kin-based societies that are without the underlying stigma of state-lessness? This would seem the reasonable solution.

There is, however, a second option that promises, I think, to take us further. What if, rather than ignoring the absences that seem to cling to anthropological models of non-modern societies, we took these absences seriously, wiped them clean of their stigma, granted them their presence, and explored their material effects? What if we approached the missing things of society – and here we should speak of all societies, be they primitive or modern – as possessions precisely because they are missing or not present.

---

[8] See footnote 5.

The challenge presented by this second option is not just to overcome the materialist impulses of contemporary social theory in which our only meaningful encounters are with the hard, present things that press against us. We must overcome the insidious affiliation of absence with *longing* and *desire* as well. That is, we must do away the assumption that every absence in the world is a void in need of being filled. As noted above, this assumption has, in part, a Freudian heritage, but its sources can also be traced in the deeper progressivist discourse of colonialism. Europeans clearly took it for granted that native people on the colonial frontier, once they were made aware of their nakedness, would naturally desire to clothe themselves. (The missionary's retelling of the Biblical story of Adam and Eve was, after all, meant to transform nudity into a nakedness in search of clothing.) But they also extended this logic from clothing to things like domesticated plants and animals, all the way up to political institutions. Once made aware of their lack of agriculture, foragers would, naturally, want to correct this absence and become civilized farmers. Once they realized their acephalousness, the natives would obviously long for a head of state.

The alternative to this sort of conceit is to acknowledge that absence need not be a source of longing at all. Quite to the contrary, absence can be aggressive; it can be cultivated; it can mark the *overt rejection* of that which is not present. Consider the gun debate discussed in the previous section. If we indulge in imagining a future in which handguns in the U.S. have been banned, there is no question that members of the NRA would regard their crossed-out guns as painful absences, as a palpable lack in need of remedy and renewed lobbying. But for those lobbyists who fought for the ban, the crossed-out gun would be experienced as a kind of fulfillment and a completion of true citizenship as they envision it. Now consider a much more radical example: the increasing number of people in far left circles who advocate doing away with, not just guns, but *all* mass-produced things, indeed who advocate doing away with "civilization" itself. Often referred to as primitivists or neo-Luddites, this community is certainly engaged in their own work of elimination, but instead of an act of disrobing that results in an image of deficiency, here one encounters elimination as a constructive act aimed at building greater levels of individual autonomy and ecological sustainability (see Shepard, 1998; Zerzan 1994a). Doing without, in this context, is a way of embracing absence and making it perform political work.

Transfer this vision to the ethnographies of the colonial frontier, and we no longer find ourselves confronted by a congeries of unevolved societies lacking government. Rather, we are in a very different terrain of deliberate or object-like absences, a terrain famously referred to by Pierre Clastres as the "society against the state."

> Even in societies in which the political institution is absent, where for example chiefs do not exist, *even there* the political is present, even there the question of power is posed: not in the misleading sense of wanting to account for an impossible absence, but in the contrary sense whereby, perhaps mysteriously, *something exists within the absence*. (Clastres 1987: 22–23)

For Clastres, that something was a paradoxical "powerless power" in which certain individuals were granted empty positions of leadership precisely so that would-be dominators could be kept in check by the community at large.

Two assumptions underlie Clastres's argument. First, it is taken as axiomatic that "the State" was not a novel institutional apparatus cut from whole cloth in the Near East some six millennia ago, but is better understood as a frightening image of systematic domination that has always haunted human societies. David Graeber (Graeber, 2004; see also Fowles 2010) has recently extended Clastres's argument, observing that ethnographers have, in fact, encountered this very image of domination in the relationships egalitarian societies frequently have with a violent and despotic world of spirits. In such societies, observes Graeber, the effort to thwart would-be despots in day-to-day human interactions "appears to spark a kind of equally elaborate reaction formation, a spectral nightworld inhabited by monsters, witches or other creatures of horror. And it's the most peaceful societies which are also the most haunted" (Graeber 2004: 25). There is much more to this argument, of course, but the central claim is that it was precisely because they were able to imagine what they were missing that non-state societies were able to be "non-state" for as long as they were.

The second assumption follows from the first: insofar as the State has always been with us as a dangerous possibility, it is never merely absent. The stateless society, for Clastres, is always a society against the state, which is to say it is a society with a ~~state~~ led by leaders with extreme ~~power~~... similar to the way the NRA is worried about becoming a society filled with ~~guns~~, or the way neo-primitivists aim for a world with ~~cell phones, SUVs~~, and ~~computers~~. None of these absent things come naturally. Like a dugout canoe, all require a great deal of excavation to construct. And neither the society clothed by the state nor the society clothed by the ~~state~~ is any more naked than the other.

Conclusion

I began this essay by commenting on the recent turn toward things in social theory, and so there is a certain irony in ending with references to neo-primitivists and "societies against the state" who have turned away from things – or, at least, who have turned away from a wide array of things they find offensive. The move was intentional, however, for it is in those moments when something has been actively rejected and aggressively avoided that we become especially aware of the flickering nature of absence and presence. "Well then, let's have less of that. Let's have radically, radically less of that," proposes John Zerzan (Versluis 2008: 160) in classic Luddite fashion. Less technology, fewer possessions, no political representatives, no agriculture even. Certainly, this sort of project presents a challenge to the materialism of contemporary society, but my argument has been that it also presents a challenge to the materialism of contemporary social theory. The world sought by Zerzan is one in which absences (of planes, of stockyards, of the state) are embraced and regarded as their own sort of highly evolved artifacts, wonderful possessions that the neo-primitive explorer boldly carries with her as she confronts a slumbering and complacent modernity that lacks such absences.

Thus, we arrive at a final question: once we accept the presence of absence (already a significant move away from the plenism of much recent writing on materiality, actor networks, and the like), are we then left to think through the absence of presence? Perhaps so. Indeed, how else are we to understand the neo-primitivist's characterization of the material heaviness and clutter of consumer culture as a *"landscape of absence* wherein real life is steadily being drained out by debased work, the *hollow* cycle of consumerism and the *mediated emptiness* of high-tech dependency" (Zerzan 1994b: 144, emphasis added)? Presence and absence seem to collapse in upon themselves when we realize that, for the neo-primitivist, what is absent from modern consumerism is absence itself, now encountered as freedom from the chains of high-tech things. To lack an absence, in other words, is to be burdened by a present thing that makes one incomplete.

In sum, absences are a special category of things. I have suggested that they must be regarded as part of the material world, part of the world of encounter that stands over against us. And yet, they are also foreign to that world, insofar as an absence always marks one or a limited number of nonpresent things drawn out of the infinite number of things that are, in fact, not present in a given context. This makes the absent thing an odd expatriate of the world of ideas that has taken up residence in the world of encounter. Once we have come to terms with this fact, we will be in a position to see both the naked native and the naked emperor in a somewhat different light. And from amidst the crowds in attendance, we will be able to exclaim, with ironic sincerity: "Look at the Emperor's new clothes. They're beautiful!"[9]

References

Bailey, D. 2007. The anti-rhetorical power of representational absence: incomplete figurines from the Balkan Neolithic. In: *Material Beginnings: A Global Prehistory of Figurative Representation*, eds. C. Renfrew and I. Morley, 117–26. Cambridge: McDonald Institute.
Barthes, R. 1981. *Camera Lucida – Reflections on Photography*. New York: Hill and Wang.
Brown, B. 2004. Thing theory. In: *Things*, ed. B. Brown, 1–16. Chicago: University of Chicago Press.
Clark, K. 1956. *The Nude: A Study in Ideal Form*. Princeton: Princeton University Press.
Clastres, P. 1987 [1974]. *Society Against the State*. New York: Zone Books.
Crossland, Z. 2002. Violent spaces: conflict over the reappearance of Argentina's disappeared. In: *Matérial Culture: The Archaeology of Twentieth-Century Conflict*, eds. J. Schofield, W. Johnson and C. Beck, 115–131. New York: Routledge.
Dant, T. 2005. *Materiality and Society*. New York: Open University Press.

---

[9] Cf. Miller's (2005: 32) use of the tale of the emperor's new clothes in which this classic fictional meditation on absence serves as a prompt for a discussion, not of clotheslessness, but rather of material clothes themselves and the manner in which they transform us into a "clothing/person." Miller's argument follows in step with Latour's analysis of the citizen-gun and is born, I suggest, of the same sidestepping of the presence of absence as a matter of theoretical inquiry.

———. 2006. Material civilization: things and society. *The British Journal of Sociology* 57(2):289–308.

Engelke, M. 2007. *A Problem of Presence: Beyond Scripture in an African Church.* Berkeley: University of California Press.

Fowles, S. 2008. Steps toward an archaeology of taboo. In: *Religion, Archaeology, and the Material World*, ed. L. Fogelin. Carbondale: Center for Archaeological Investigations, Occasional Paper No. 36.

———. (2010) A people's history of the American Southwest. In: *Considering Complexity*, ed. S. Alt. Denver: University of Colorado Press.

Frow, J. 2004. A pebble, a camera, a man who turns into a telegraph pole. In *Things*, ed. B. Brown, 346–361. Chicago: University of Chicago Press.

Fuery, P. 1995. *The Theory of Absence: Subjectivity, Signification, and Desire.* Westport: Greenwood Press.

Geertz, C. 1973. Deep play: notes on the Balinese cockfight. In *The Interpretation of Cultures*, pp. 412–54. New York: Basic Books.

Graeber, D. 2004. *Fragments of an Anarchist Anthropology.* Chicago: Prickly Paradigm Press.

Harman, G. 2005. *Guerrilla Metaphsics: Phenomenology and the Carpentry of Things.* Chicago: Open Court.

Hodder, I. 2006. *The Leopard's Tale: Revealing the Mysteries of Catalhoyuk.* London: Thames and Hudson.

Ihde, D. 1990. *Technology in the Lifeworld.* Bloomington: Indiana University Press.

Knappett, C. 2008. The neglected networks of material agency: artefacts, pictures and texts. In *Material Agency: Towards a Non-Anthropocentric Approach*, ed. C. Knappett and L. Malafouris, 139–156. New York: Springer.

Latour, B. 1993. *We Have Never Been Modern.* Cambridge, MA: Harvard University Press.

Latour, B. 1999. *Pandora's Hope: Essays on the Reality of Science Studies.* Cambridge, MA: Harvard University Press.

Latour, B. 2000. The Berlin key or how to do words with things. In *Matter, Materiality and Modern Culture*, ed. P. Graves-Brown, 10–21. New York: Routledge.

Levine, P. 2008. States of undress: nakedness and the colonial imagination. *Victorian Studies* 50(2):189–219.

Miller, D. 1987. *Material Culture and Mass Consumption.* New York: Blackwell.

Miller, D. 2005. Materiality: an introduction. In *Materiality*, ed. D. Miller, 1–50. Durham: Duke University Press.

Montrose, L. 1993. The work of gender in the discourse of discovery, In *New World Encounters*, ed. S. Greenblatt, 177–216. Berkeley: University of California Press.

Morgan, L.H. 1974 [1877]. *Ancient Society, or Researches in the Lines of Human Progress from Savagery through Barbarism to Civilization.* Gloucester, MA: Peter Smith.

Olsen, B. 2003. Material culture after text: re-membering things. *Norwegian Archaeological Review* 36(3):87–104.

Patrich, J. 1990. *The Formation of Nabatean Art: Prohibition of a Graven Image Among the Nabateans.* The Magnes Press, Jerusalem: The Hebrew University and Leiden: E.J. Brill.

Pinney, C. 2005. Things happen: or, from which moment does that object come? In *Materiality*, ed. D. Miller, 256–272. Durham: Duke University Press.

Renfrew, C. 2004. Towards a theory of material engagement. In *Rethinking Materiality: The Engagement of Mind with the Material World*, eds. E. DeMarrais, C. Gosden, and C. Renfrew, 23–31. Cambridge: McDonald Institute for Archaeological Research.

Robb, J. 2004. The extended artefact and the monumental economy: a methodology for material agency. In *Rethinking Materiality: The Engagement of Mind with the Material World*, eds. E. DeMarrais, C. Gosden and C. Renfrew, 131–139. Cambridge: McDonald Institute Monographs.

Rousseau, J.-J. 1992 [1754]. Discourse on the Origin and Foundations of Inequality. In *The Collected Writings of Rousseau, Vol. 3*, eds. R.D. Masters and C. Kelly, 17–67. Hanover: University Press of New England.

Serres, M. 2007 [1980]. *The Parasite*, translated by L. R. Schehr. Minneapolis: University of Minnesota Press.

Shanks, M. 2007. Symmetrical archaeology. *World Archaeology* 39(4).

Shepard, P. 1998 [1992]. A post-historic primitivism. In *Limited Wants, Unlimited Means*, eds. J.M. Gowdy, 281–325. Washington, DC: Island Press.

Smith, A. 2003. Do you believe in ethics? Latour and Ihde in the trenches of the science wars (or: Watch out, Latour, Ihde's got a gun). In *Chasing Technoscience: Matrix for Materiality*, eds. D. Ihde and E. Selinger, 182–194. Bloomington: Indiana University Press.

Stallybrass, P. 1998. Marx's coat. In *Border Fetishisms: Material Objects in Unstable Spaces*, ed. P. Spyer, 183–207. New York: Routledge.

Stevens, S.M.. 2003. New World Contacts and the Trope of the 'Naked Savage.' In *Sensible Flesh: On Touch in Early Modern Culture*, ed. E.D. Harvey, 124–140. Philadelphia: University of Pennsylvania Press.

Tanaka, K. 1998. *Absence of the Buddha Image in Early Buddhist Art*. New Delhi: D.K. Printworld.

Versluis, A.. 2008. Interview with John Zerzan. *Journal for the Study of Radicalism* 2(1):155–168.

Witmore, C.L. 2007. Symmetrical archaeology: excerpts of a manifesto. *World Archaeology* 39(4).

Wolfe, C. 2003. *Animal Rites: American Culture, the Discourse of Species, and Posthumanist Theory*. Chicago: University of Chicago Press.

Zerzan, J. 1994a. Future primitive. In *Future Primitive and Other Essays*, pp. 15–46. New York: Autonomedia.

Zerzan, J. 1994b. Feral. In *Future Primitive and Other Essays*, pp. 144–146. New York: Autonomedia.

Part II
Embodying Absence

Chapter 3
Missing Bodies Near-at-Hand: The Dissonant Memory and Dormant Graves of the Spanish Civil War

Layla Renshaw

Introduction

This contribution will look at the case of Spain's mass graves containing the remains of tens of thousands of civilians killed by the Francoist regime during the Spanish Civil War (1936–1939) and its aftermath. These graves are located in both urban and rural communities of all sizes, throughout Spain. Since 2000, these graves and the remains within them have become the focal point for intense investigative and commemorative activity, primarily structured by a campaign to exhume and formally rebury these remains. This campaign has achieved a rupture in the long-held "pact of silence", which has hitherto surrounded the Civil War. This contribution is based on ethnographic interviews and participant observation in two small rural communities in Castile Leon, while, over three years from 2003, they experienced the extended process of exhumation, identification and reburial of bodies of Republicans buried in unmarked graves on the edge of their communities.

Interviews and collection of life histories were undertaken with a cross-section of the different constituencies involved in the Spanish Republican exhumations: the relatives of the dead, the archaeologists and forensic practitioners conducting exhumations, and Republican memory campaigners who co-ordinate the exhumations and lobby to draw government and media attention to the graves. Focusing on the Spanish case, and considering this material alongside ethnographies of exhumation in other contexts, namely Cyprus and Argentina, this chapter seeks to highlight the complexities inherent in conceptualizing the status of missing people, missing bodies, and concealed bodies, and the way these three may become conflated in encounters with the traumatic past, particularly those encounters which take the form of exhumation and reburial.

The Spanish Civil War started through a military coup headed by General Francisco Franco against Spain's elected government, a Leftist coalition which came to be known as the Republican side. The war was fought over a spectrum of

L. Renshaw (✉)
School of Life Sciences, Kingston University, London, UK
l.renshaw@kingston.ac.uk

M. Bille et al. (eds.), *An Anthropology of Absence: Materializations of Transcendence and Loss,* 45
DOI 10.1007/978-1-4419-5529-6_3, © Springer Science+Business Media, LLC 2010

class and ideological oppositions, which varied across the diverse regions of Spain, but was characterized in many parts of the country by the extreme levels of violence experienced by civilian populations, far away from the battle lines (Preston 1989; Thomas 1990). In the field sites discussed in this chapter, the violence was enacted by locally-organized militias who selected their victims through personal knowledge of their ideology and political affiliation, taking them on forced round-ups and abductions, known euphemistically as *paseos*, or "taking a stroll" followed by mass executions and burials.

Events in two of these communities in Castile Leon in Northwestern Spain illustrate the range of repressive measures experienced by civilians in the Spanish Civil War and serve to contextualize the exhumations, which took place there. In my first field site, 22 men were shot within a few days in the summer of 1936, including the serving Mayor and most of the elected councilors. In my second field site, civilians were rounded up from several villages further afield, with a reported 47 individuals killed and buried in a clearing on the edge of the village. In the aftermath of the killings, informant accounts describe the extreme gendered violence and physical humiliation which the female relatives of the dead were subjected to. Male relatives of the dead experienced bouts of incarceration, forced labour and torture. There was an absolute prohibition on mourning the dead, or making any public representation of these deaths. The actual names of these two communities and their residents are not used here because of the enduring sensitivity surrounding discussions of these experiences.

These conditions were highly effective in producing a state of atomization in the relatives of the dead, resulting in the breakdown of the transmission of memory between generations, even within the confines of the family home. My older generation of informants in their seventies and eighties describe an atmosphere of fear and intimidation throughout the dictatorship, and into the early years of democracy. The children of this generation describe a pervading silence and sense of rupture in personal and family biographies which accord closely with the findings of many historians and anthropologists now working on Spanish Civil War memory (Graham 2004; Richards 2002). The breakdown in the transmission of memory in the private realm was reinforced by the total occupation of the public realm by an extreme Francoist memory politics (Aguilar and Humlebæk 2002), which in the aftermath of the war saw the initiation of new commemorative holidays, monumental architecture, street names and text books, all representing a Francoist version of the past. Following the death of Franco in 1975, the delicate transition to democracy was achieved through a "pacted" or conditional understanding amongst a broad spectrum of politicians to draw a line over the past. This understanding was described as "the pact of amnesia" or "the pact of silence." In this climate, a direct confrontation with the traumatic past, and with the question of the thousands of unmarked Republican graves, was viewed by a wide cross-section of Spanish society as destabilising and threatening to the new democracy (Desfor Edles 1998).

In 2000, a Madrid-based journalist named Emilio Silva returned to his family's ancestral village of Priaranza del Bierzo in Leon. Visiting the graves of other deceased family members in the village cemetery caused Silva to reflect on the absence of his paternal grandfather's grave. His grandfather, also called Emilio Silva, was known to have been killed by Francoist forces in one of the thousands of extrajudicial political killings of civilians that characterized the Spanish Civil War (Silva and Macías 2003). Silva's journalistic response was to prove pivotal to the foundation of a Republican memory campaign, as seen in this extract from one of the extended interviews I undertook with him. In this, he describes the article he wrote about his grandfather, which compared the Spanish Republican dead to the *Desaparecido*, or the disappeared of Argentina:

> "In September of 2000, I published an article in the newspaper 'Leon Chronicle' that was entitled: "My Grandfather, too, was a *Desaparecido*", and in this I complained that Spain has applauded the detention of Pinochet and Garzón has initiated trials in Argentina, and Chile, others in Guatemala and here we have *Desaparecido* but that don't exist. I wrote this without knowing the dimension of the problem or anything. I wrote this article very angrily and I put my phone number at the bottom". (Emilio Silva, Co-founder of the Association for the Recuperation of Historical Memory, Madrid)

An exhumation in Priaranza del Bierzo was successfully undertaken in October 2000. In December of that year, Emilio Silva and Santiago Macias co-founded the Association for the Recuperation of Historical Memory (ARMH). Other exhumations followed. By the end of 2005, more than 500 corpses had been recovered in over 60 exhumations (Ferrándiz 2006: 8). Fernandez de Mata (2004) has characterised the radical rupture in the prevailing Spanish memory politics as the "mass grave phenomenon", highlighting the centrality of exhumation as a catalyst to a new public discourse on the past. The impact for Spanish society and possible directions of this new form of public archaeology is explored by Gonzalez-Ruibal (2007). A detailed account of the movement's development is given by the co-founders in the book they authored together (Silva and Macías 2003).

As clearly shown by the comparisons drawn by Emilio Silva in the interview excerpt above, and the comparison explicit in his article "My Grandfather, too, was a *Desaparecido*", the exhumation, scientific identification and reburial of the victims of Civil War violence have, in part, followed the model of action of the tribunals and truth commissions around the world, particularly in Latin America. Despite following the precedents furnished by international cases, there are clear points of divergence between the Spanish exhumations, and those occurring in other historical and political contexts. These points of divergence centre upon the ways in which different categories of the dead have been and are conceptualized, and highlight the complex status of three different categories of victims of conflict or violence: the buried body; the missing body; and the disappeared person, all of which may be positioned differently on the axis of presence and absence.

The disappeared in the Argentine context were carried off by a state apparatus that could be faceless and remote to the families of the victims, and had layers of bureaucracy, status and chains of command to hide behind. In Cyprus, survivors from civil war were displaced and thus separated from the physical locales where the missing victims were last seen, and where the dead might be buried, whereby physical separation compounded the separation from the dead (Kovras 2008). In these cases, there is an absence of knowledge surrounding the physical whereabouts of victims of violence and the circumstances of their death. This absence of certainty surrounding the victims' status can in fact make them more potently present, as the possibility of life remains, and they continue a kind of existence in the space created by the uncertainty of their families and communities, and within public discourse and imagination (Robben 2005).

There were many different forms of violence and disappearance experienced during the Spanish Civil War and its aftermath, but the killings in my field sites during the very early stages of the war can be characterized as locally-organized, intimate, and according to local narratives, as fratricidal. The habits, ideology, domestic arrangements, and material property of victims might be intimately known to perpetrators. Victimization occurred through existing networks of social relationships, in which people variously denounced and defended neighbours and relatives. Although the Spanish Civil War and the subsequent dictatorship saw significant levels of displacement, exile and the depopulation of rural areas, I encountered many incidents in my field sites where the families of victims and perpetrators continued to inhabit the same small communities and traverse the same spaces in which the killings and burials occurred. In my field sites, the barriers between the living and the dead were not those created by anonymity or physical displacement as in Argentina or Cyprus, but were created by the repressive dictatorship, fragile transition to democracy, and the near 70-year time lag between the killings and the onset of exhumation.

These categories of the dead from conflict and political violence contain within them an inherent potentiality to be located, uncovered and returned in various forms to their relatives and communities. The inherent instability of a missing or clandestinely buried body lies in the potential for the living to effect some change upon the status of the dead through the physical intervention of exhumation. Along with the enduring physical properties of the skeleton, this means that the absent dead are a site of unresolved emotion and ongoing political tension, even "outliving" generations of mourners. This potentiality and tension may be activated even after decades of apparent dormancy, as seen in the exhumation of Republican graves in Spain since 2000, or the exhumations of Serbian dead from World War II, in a post-socialist climate of resurgent nationalisms (Verdery 1999).

This contribution will also look in detail at how the absence of the Republican dead in Spain is experienced, and the paradoxical or dissonant ways of knowing about the dead, which have emerged in these communities. Such absence and the different conceptualizations of the missing people enable knowledge of the dead to be both taboo and matter-of-fact, and the bodies themselves to be simultaneously remote and near-at-hand. An understanding of how the dead may be conceptualized in Spain shows that the Spanish war dead may also constitute an enduring site of political and emotional instability, and potentiality, albeit in a way that has been necessarily less visible than the tensions surrounding the missing in Argentina and Cyprus.

A consideration of some of the experiences of exhumation in Argentina and Cyprus reveal the potential for a painful ambiguity or confusion between the missing person and the missing body contained within the act of exhumation. In these cases, exhumation may succeed in bringing forms of resolution, but may also fail to fully activate or fulfill that potentiality inherent in the instability of the missing body. For this reason, exhumations may also provoke ambivalent, even hostile, reactions, from the bereaved. In the light of these experiences in Argentina and Cyprus, the degree to which exhumation activates or fulfills the perceived potentiality of the Spanish war dead can be questioned by looking at some of the experiences in my field sites.

"Bring Them Back Alive": The Absent Dead as A Site of Active Political Tension

The status of bodies of victims of conflict and political violence as absent is integral to their categorisation, and to the calls of the bereaved for recognition of the fact and circumstances of the deaths. The unresolved location and status of the human remains become a structuring activity in campaigns that may, in fact, have a much broader scope, calling for acknowledgment or adjudication over whole historical periods and regimes, such as Argentina's junta, or the Turkish military action in Cyprus. As human remains may structure these far-reaching engagements with a traumatic past, successfully "resolving" the position and status of the bodies can destabilize the wider cause of historical redress. While exhumation may act as a catalyst to debate, the perceived "closure" which accompanies reburial may prematurely close a window of engagement with the past. The successful location, identification and formal reburial of human remains may be a paradoxical and highly ambivalent point in the narratives of these deaths. While recognizing the affective expression that may be enabled through acts of reburial, in the moment at which these bodies are rendered corporeally present and accounted for, their psychic and symbolic presence may become destabilised and even diminished. When a community normalizes these bodies and incorporates them into cemeteries, and the state formalizes the deaths, this may cause the dead to lose some of their particularity and power as an affective and political category of deaths outside the norm. A consideration of two different ethnographic contexts, Cyprus and Argentina, reveals the ambivalence that may accompany the rematerialization of long-sought bodies.

Paul Sant Cassia's (2007) detailed study of the question of missing bodies in Cyprus serves as an example of the ambivalence and disillusionment that can accompany the return of missing bodies. Especially since in divided Cyprus, the early exhumations were clandestine raids across the border the Greek and Turkish sides, highly dangerous and invested with the significance of rescue missions to liberate the missing, the eventual return of weathered and disintegrating bones provoked disillusionment in some of Sant Cassia's informants. Sant Cassia's ethnography shows the emotional catharsis achieved through return and reburial, but also hints at the sense of anti-climax that accompanies the closure of a long struggle, the confusion provoked in relatives by the affective re-classification of these bodies and the bitter realization of the long years during which life was "on hold."

In the Guardian newspaper's coverage of the exhumations and reburials in Cyprus (Chrisafis 2008), there was a report from one of these funerals of a Greek Cypriot who disappeared in the 1970s. One relative said "He was the giant of the village but we've just buried him in a child's coffin. There was nothing left." The dead man as a presence in his family's imagination has flourished during his body's absence but was diminished by the body's materialization.

Although there is a distinction between the absence of the person and the absence of their skeleton, in the process of searching for missing bodies, the two sometimes become conflated or superimposed on each other in the minds of the relatives, and also in the way archaeologists or forensic scientists conceptualize their own contribution, and the exhumation becomes a search for a person rather than a body. The weight of emotional instability caused by the loss of a person, and the political tension surrounding the exact circumstances of their death, can instead become transposed onto the search for their body. Thus, the absence of the dead body can become integral to the campaign for recognition and acknowledgement of the loss of a person. Once the physical remains are returned, the campaign can no longer be structured around presencing the dead, or focused around the clear-cut technical and practical demands for the bodies to be found and returned. The wider campaign for both knowledge and acknowledgement of the deaths may lose its force or potency, and the opportunity for the bereaved to negotiate a collective narrative of these deaths may be closed off.

The example of ambivalent exhumations that has most directly influenced my understanding of the Spanish Civil War exhumations is archaeologist Zoe Crossland's (2000; 2002) study of the different voices within the campaign for the disappeared of Argentina's dirty war. Global attention was captured by the campaign of the Mothers of the Plaza de Mayo who held vigils for their missing children in a central square of Buenos Aires, where they could not be ignored. A large-scale programme of exhumations and eventual reburials was triggered. While the bodies were missing, the category of the disappeared held a particular potency. The power of this category lies in the vacuum of information that surrounds it which the imagination fills in with greater horrors. The Argentinean writer Ernesto Sabato said "The dead die once, the disappeared die every day". It is an ongoing crime and this maintains a state of active tension between a population and its government. Robben's (2005) extended analysis of first person accounts from Argentina powerfully communicates the kind of purgatory experienced by those who had relatives disappear.

When the remains of the disappeared in Argentina began to be returned to their families, there was a breakaway from the Mothers of the Plaza de Mayo who started a new campaign. When their children's bodies were returned to them, instead of stopping their vigils they began a campaign with the slogan *"aparición con vida"* meaning "appearance alive" but expressing the demand to "bring them back alive," rejecting the resolution or closure that exhumation was supposed to bring them and maintaining a state of active tension against the government. *Aparición con vida* was an emphatic statement that the dead person was still absent and that the return of their skeletons had not resolved this absence.

This places the burden of responsibility on the perpetrators and on the current regime which inherited state power from the perpetrators to give a full account of the narratives around these deaths, rather than making the bodies do this work. It also rejects the responsibility for incorporating these bodies into the category of the normal or everyday dead by normative mourning and formal reburial; instead it asserts the ongoing exceptionality of this category of dead. The state cannot delegate the mourning and commemoration of these victims of structural violence onto individual, private families (Robben 2005).

> "Argentina is unusual within Latin America in having a large and vocal proportion of human rights organisations opposing the forensic recovery of disappeared human remains... The common disparagement of this position fails to grasp that it is part of a coherent political strategy calling for the admission of wrongdoing by those responsible." (Crossland 2002: 121)

The demand to "bring them back alive" is psychically complex and emotive. It is intentionally unsettling because it appears at first sight to be an irrational demand which rejects the reality of these deaths. Crossland (2002) has pointed out that the apparent paradox in this demand is in fact a rhetorically powerful call for accountability. The apparent confusion or "irrationality" in this slogan foregrounds a confusion between people and bodies, which recurs in the way states, expert practitioners and the media talk about acts of exhumation. It can be understood as a symbolic rejection of the idea that the return of physical remains is enough to achieve either an emotional or political resolution to the violence that was inflicted by the disappearance. *Aparición con vida* is a reiteration that it was a living person who was lost, not simply his body. Far from the campaigners being confused about the status of the missing, they are rejecting this conflation between the dead person and the dead body that may occur when confrontations with the traumatic past are structured around the exhumation of physical remains.

"The Disappeared" Versus "the Not Known of": Conceptualizing the Spanish Republican Dead

Since commencing my fieldwork in Spain, I have reflected on whether this kind of ambivalence or disillusionment with the forms of political and emotional closure associated with exhumation could emerge in my field sites, and I have looked more broadly for the points of comparison and divergence between Spain and Argentina. The comparison is primarily interesting due to the way in which the Republican memory campaigners refer to events in Argentina as a precedent for the current Spanish campaign, and draw analogies as a source of moral and symbolic capital. The Republican memory campaigners categorize the Republican mass graves as a site of unresolved emotion and of ongoing political tension, and call for a physical intervention in the graves as a catalyst to open a new discursive space on the Civil War and dictatorship. However, the characterization of the Spanish Republican dead as a site of unresolved political and emotional tensions is much more complicated, and potentially problematic than it might be for the Argentine *Desaparecido* or the missing in Cyprus. In Argentina, the disappeared came to be a publicly acknowledged category in national discourse, one which came to haunt the collective psyche. In both Argentina and Cyprus, social networks and collective identities formed around the memory of the dead. Outside the immediate sphere of bereaved families, a visual language or iconography of memory, as well as designated physical spaces, emerged to presence the dead amongst the living in a public and enduring way.

Conversely in Spain, the post-Francoist consensus on the past, the "pact of silence", has also been described as the pact of forgetting, or even the pact of oblivion, communicating the idea that to some extent, a genuine erasure of this category of the dead has indeed occurred. Up until 2000, this category of Republican dead had been successfully "disappeared" from the national narrative, and yet within individual communities, memory of the Republican dead remained very close to the surface. Spain is and has been characterized by a highly fractured picture of the degree to which the dead have been remembered or forgotten. The condition of atomization under a long-lived and highly effective dictatorship means that the ways in which the dead were perpetuated by the living were necessarily subtle, private and clandestine, and therefore the enduring presence of the dead has been very hard to discern. It is hard to characterize the strength of memory and forgetting in the Spanish context due to the discontinuity of experience between the post-war and the post-Franco generations, and a breakdown in any discernible mechanisms through which the memory of the Republican dead, and of the events of these deaths, might be transmitted between generations. Related to this sharp generational divide, are the different trajectories of memory found in urban versus rural communities, and the dissonance between the local versus the national narratives of the Civil War.

Given these different trajectories of memory amongst different sectors of Spanish society, it is very difficult to form a coherent picture of the degree to which forgetting or "oblivion" has truly taken place. This is illustrated by the Republican memory campaign's ongoing effort to find an apt collective noun with which to describe the Republican dead. From the onset of the Republican memory campaign, the term *Desaparecido* was used to highlight the similarities with Argentina, and by implication, highlight the shortfall in the Spanish state's response to the graves, as encapsulated in the founding act of the campaign, Emilio Silva's newspaper article with its inclusive claim, "My Grandfather, too, was a *Desaparecido*." From the start of my fieldwork in 2003, the local co-ordinators, Republican memory campaigners, and forensic and archaeological practitioners, were wrestling with the significance of alternative names. Despite the use of the term *Desaparecido* by the Republican memory activists and the co-ordinators of the excavations in my field sites, I did not hear local residents or any of the elderly relatives of the dead using this term autonomously, suggesting it did not have a resonance with the way they conceptualized the Republican dead.

The difference between Spain and Argentina was pointed out by an informant who was one of the memory campaigners. "In Argentina they have *Desaparecido* but here we are starting from a different point, here we have the *desconocidos*" [meaning the unknown, but more aptly, meaning the *not known of*, the unacknowledged or unrecognized]. However, it is problematic to apply this label of "the not known of" too broadly, as it assumes that different sectors and generations within Spanish society are equally oblivious to the fate of the Republican dead. Many of the highly committed Republican memory campaigners I encountered during fieldwork are young professionals or students of the post-Franco generation, and many are urban dwellers. Their demographic segment has never been exposed to the reality of Spain's mass graves, and therefore campaigners may assume that the existence of the mass graves is widely unknown or forgotten, but it is false to extend this general state of forgetting to the individual communities in which the graves are located. Within a community, there are different ways of knowing about a grave that are not immediately apparent, and a particular grave may be remembered, even though there is no overarching narrative with which to remember the hundreds of comparable graves across Spain.

During fieldwork within very small rural communities and particularly among the oldest generation from surviving Republican families, it is clear that the killings have immutably altered these communities. For many of the children of the Republican dead, these killings have been a defining fact of their lives, shaping the way they perceive the narratives of their lives, their relationship to their community and nation, and their individual identity. Many of my elderly informants were raised in the 1930s and 1940s and were brought up by mothers and networks of female relatives who were consumed by grief for the death of the men, making them psychically very present, even if they were never discussed. My overwhelming impression from elderly informants was that the emotional and economic repercussions of these killings reverberated through their childhood, and into adulthood. During more candid, uninhibited moments of interviews and life histories, most elderly informants from Republican families could reel off the names of other Republican victims, and other working-class or Republican families targeted at the same time. There was clearly an enduring awareness of the identities of the dead within these communities, and it is therefore a poor fit with this existing pool of knowledge to characterize the Republican dead as "the unknown of".

In contrast to these nuanced attempts within the memory campaign to situate the Republican dead on an axis of memory and forgetting, the collective noun that recurs repeatedly in my interviews with the oldest generation of informants in these field sites is blunt and direct. The elderly generation, including those who lived through the war and the direct descendants of the Republican dead, consistently refer to those in the mass graves as the "*fusilados*", which simply means, "those who were shot." The contrast between the "disappeared" and the "shot" is stark. Whereas the word disappeared contains the inherent suspense of an unknown fate, and implies a liminal status demanding resolution, "those who were shot" is a definitively resolved term, allowing no ambiguity over the fate of these people. It not only asserts that these people are dead, but defines them by their cause of death. It is baldly factual to the point of being matter-of-fact. The matter-of-fact description and characterization of the dead in these field sites require closer examination, as they coexist alongside layers of self-censorship and prohibitions on the verbal transmission of memory, which may seem paradoxical and difficult for the outsider to navigate. The factual description of "those who were shot" appears at odds with the near total prohibition on any verbal reference to the existence of the dead or the graves.

Scattered in the Mountains but Buried Near-at-Hand: Dissonance in the Location of the Dead

In both of my field sites, the middle-aged descendants of the dead (themselves born after the war but during dictatorship) took an initiative to seek out the burial places of the dead. The location of these two mass graves was unknown to them, and thus they assumed the burial location to be clandestine and highly controlled knowledge, with few, if any, witnesses at the time, and no verbal transmission of this memory. Starting out on the search, they were prepared that the location of the graves might be forgotten. In both field sites, tactful enquiries rapidly opened up a network of contacts, indicating who amongst the oldest inhabitants of the community might know, and might be prepared to confirm, the location of the mass graves. In both field sites, it rapidly emerged that there was no ambiguity surrounding the precise location of the grave, nor its physical dimensions, as in both cases eyewitnesses had observed the immediate aftermath of the killings and had seen the partially buried bodies. A few key elderly residents were thus able to guide the archaeologists in the exposure of the mass graves.

For those local residents still grounded in the physical locations in which these deaths and burials took place, the memories turned out to be near-at-hand and surprisingly accessible for those who seek them out. During the initial phase of the investigation, the archaeologists and campaigners referred to "eye witnesses" almost reverentially, as singular individuals, a unique resource of firsthand knowledge of these deaths. Over time, it became apparent that this was not an accurate reflection of how knowledge of the graves was disseminated throughout and collectively held in these communities. I noted that several of my interviews with the elderly relatives of the dead contained a characteristic arc of disclosure, starting with a complete disavowal of knowledge of the grave, or at least of any privileged or particular knowledge of the grave, and then as their communication gained momentum, several informants made reference to their visual memories of the mass graves, and childhood memories of the immediate aftermath of the killings. I observed a further paradox in the divergent accounts elicited during life histories and during more structured interviews about the mass graves. Structured, factually-oriented questions about the location of the grave, who was in it, or on the events surrounding these deaths called forth a disavowal of knowledge, and noncommittal replies. Yet in extended narrative accounts of life histories, the same individuals recalled firsthand memories of the graves in stark terms, as seen in the excerpts of accounts given by informants in their eighties, talking about the grave site in Villavieja:

"After my father died, my mother brought us out here, all the children. We came here to this spot and my mother made a cross, she made a flat space on the soil and she put a cross with some stones to mark where the bodies were. You could see the bodies and you could see their clothes. And my mother pulled out a beret from the grave, and we always kept that beret at home as a memento. We have it still, I don't know if it's really his."

"My mother knew from the first day that they were here buried in the grave, she came and saw them with her own eyes. And later came a sister of mine that now herself is dead. And a man from the village, who had buried my father, came and said "Do you want to see your father? Yes? Then come with me." And he took her walking out of the village until this spot; here where they have the very tall pines growing […] My sister had that engraved on her mind for the rest of her life."

The matter-of-fact description of "those who were shot" and the acceptance of this bald reality make sense in the context of informants' firsthand exposure to death and human remains in the aftermath of these killings. The two excerpts above show a familiarity with the distinct physical space of the mass graves, distinguished by the tall pines, and within walking distance of the village itself. But in interviews specifically about the grave sites, the graves seem to shift location, and instead informants make reference to what is the common pool of knowledge about these bodies, and refer to the bodies as being in *"los montes"*, or "in the mountains", a figurative place which recurs with frequency when talking about the Republican dead in these communities. Despite these encounters with damaged, decomposing bodies and their personal possessions at the grave site, some kind of transformation has taken place in the way the location of the bodies is conceptualized through the subsequent 65 years. Despite being experienced firsthand by members of the community, a structural distance between grave and village is established.

The majority of my informants routinely spoke of these bodies as being scattered or sown in *"los montes,"* often accompanied by an expansive gesture towards the horizon. At first, I was more struck by the use of the word *montes* in a fairly flat region of Castile Leon. This term is rich and evocative in the village, meaning literally the hills or the mountains, but in usage it referred more broadly to "the wild country", and in opposition to the village space as a generic way of saying "not here" or "outside the village". The land in which these graves were placed is very close to the village, inter-visible with its outskirts, completely flat, immediately accessible by road and bordering onto cultivated land. The classification of the bodies, as lying in *"los montes"*, communicates their figurative rather than actual distance from the village. They are in a liminal, undomesticated and unquiet space, especially in contrast to the familiar village cemetery.

The account above makes reference to the height of the pines, and the presence of these pine trees and the distinctive clearing in which the grave is located, surfaced in different ways during interviews about the mass grave, serving as a mnemonic for the location even in those accounts which seem hazy on the location. The pines are invoked graphically in accounts of the killing and its aftermath: victims tied to trees; bullet holes in trees; the trees providing cover for these acts. The pines anchor these acts to a definite spot, although whether these references can be described as memory or as imaginative projections inspired by the physical locale is impossible to say. At this grave site in the pine clearing, there was an eye witness who marked out the dimensions of the grave for the investigators prior to the exhumation. This was the *resinero* or resin-collector who had stumbled upon the grave whilst it was being dug in preparation for the killings. His discussion of the site exhibited an intimately detailed knowledge, as he had traversed the same stretch of pines for years afterward, collecting resin.

In his account of a visit to a community in Poyales del Hoyo in Avila, to witness the reburial ceremony of recently exhumed Republican dead, Giles Tremlett (2006) notes how the precise location of the grave was referred to by a kind of mnemonic that similarly made reference to the physical characteristics of land use and plant cover. The grave was located at the "asparagus turning." "The vuelta de espárragos or place where there is enough space to turn a vehicle." It is the same kind of designation of place used daily in agricultural communities, to arrange meetings, or situate stories of local events. These prosaic physical descriptions denoted not only the place, but what had occurred there and been seen there; the places were imbued with a particular meaning to the older generation who have shared experiences of the grave site and the immediate aftermath of the killings. For those who remained living in these communities post-war, the same spaces were necessarily encountered as part of daily life, and incorporated into an intimate knowledge of a micro-environment such as that possessed by the resin-collector. These mnemonics for specific sites somehow co-exist with the characterization of bodies in generic places, used by convention, "los montes" and often "las cunetas" (the roadside ditches). A structural distancing of the bodies as scattered and remote is perhaps a necessary measure to negotiate the near-at-hand nature of the graves in daily life.

A careful distinction between adult and child ways of knowing appears to be one of the primary ways through which the dissonance between knowing and not knowing about the graves can be reconciled, and thus maintained, by informants in these communities. Information about the grave is frequently offered with the preface that it is "Something I knew as a child..." or "round here, the children said..." There appears to be other ways of knowing about the past associated with childhood, and a category of remembered information gleaned as a child, either half-understood fragments from adults, or transmitted as a type of folk knowledge amongst children. In extended conversations on the past, when informants reflect not only on *what* they know about the grave, but *how* they know about the grave, informants often struggle to locate the transmission of this information, but the recurring sources cited are the games, invented rituals and rhymes developed amongst the children in the community in response to the mass graves.

The types of ritual and game revolved around taking longer routes to avoid the graves, or daring to run past the grave in an atmosphere of fear and excitement. At a mass grave exhumation in Asturias, an elderly visitor to the grave recalled how the older girls in her school would organize clandestine expeditions amongst the children to pick and leave flowers at the site. From these childish expeditions, she had apprehended the location of the grave and rumours of who lay inside and also apprehended its secret nature. These accounts suggest that the children formed a subculture in the community, formulating their own responses to the traumatic past in the vacuum left by adult silences. In an interview with Emilio Silva, he described how a local resident of his grandparent's village contacted him in response to his appeal for information on the location of his Republican grandfather's grave. The probable location of the grave was known from an oral tradition that persisted amongst the children of this village:

> "a few times we thought about opening the grave, its location is known because there is a spot that the children always go past running, they call it *'the place of the group paseo'*, and they say there are dead people there." (Emilio Silva, Madrid)

This type of prefacing of statements about the graves serves to locate the knowledge of the past in the childish state. It is highly effective in bracketing these statements off both by maintaining a temporal distance and a type of moral distance, as a child is less responsible for what he or she says and does. These things that are "known as a child" distance both the memories and utterances from the norms of adult knowledge and communication about the past which dictate that a silence about the past should be maintained, and that dangerous knowledge should be contained within the individual. A striking comment made by an informant, Pedro, during an interview reveals the degree to which the child's understanding of the traumatic past is unsocialized and fails to conform to the rules observed in adult ways of knowing about the past. This makes it potentially threatening and uncontrollable, unless it is bracketed off as childish:

> "My father never spoke of this, not much in the home, because we were young children, and they say children and idiots speak the truth." (Pedro, Villavieja)

Bodies as Seeds: Organic Metaphors for the Dormancy and Instability of Human Remains

The current work of oral historians and anthropologists in the field of the Spanish Republican experience, and the topic of Civil War memory in contemporary Spain is characterized by metaphors for the maintenance of dualist or dissonant states while living under dictatorship. These are often metaphors expressing acts of internal containment and of the suspension of truths or realities which did not fit with the present. Graham refers to a condition of "inner-exile" suggesting a retreat inwards, and the concealment of knowledge even from oneself. Richards (2002) refers to "life in parenthesis" which communicates a temporary or contingent suspension of reality. The different ways of knowing about the dead previously discussed, which allow them to be both near-at-hand and yet publicly denied, and permit these apparently dissonant or contradictory realities to exist simultaneously, can be related to this condition of containment or suspension. The identification of this condition of reality under dictatorship suggests that it is useful to look more closely at the state of burial and the status of buried bodies. Metaphors related to burial, sowing and planting recur in conversations about the Civil War in these communities. In conversations that referred to the bodies as lying in "*los montes*" or more generally in the landscape, the remains were often described as *"sembrada,"* meaning literally sown but more generally to be scattered or spread, for example: "They sowed crosses through the countryside." Other examples are the description of Republican values, or memories of the dead being sown or being planted within the living:

> "I read on a gravestone once *"we have only died if you forget us"*. We haven't forgotten them, we give them dignity, and they haven't died because their ideas have been sown within us." (Eulalio, Las Campanas)

Most frequently the references are to a state of fear being planted during war and dictatorship. This fear is described as deeply planted as part of explaining its enduring quality, long after the dictatorship has ended:

> "So you can see why here the people still have fear. It's that they sowed terror here in such a way that was dreadful." (Nestor, Villavieja)

There are also references to planting and depth which recur in a number of interviews when informants are striving to explain the long time frames over which events in Spain have unfolded, and the decades of delay between the coming of democracy and the exhumation of the mass graves. The use of these terms perhaps suggests the perception that these processes have their own organic time frame. Although this has never been explicitly articulated to me, I note informants trying to understand themselves and explain to me how the past can apparently be contained and then surface again.

A more striking example of a plant or organic metaphor, which emphasises this notion of moving from containment to an eventual re-surfacing, is the metaphor of the Republican dead bodies as *"semillas,"* meaning "seeds". The conceptualization of Republican bodies as seeds clearly plays on a particular understanding of their buried state, and an understanding of burial as a state or potentiality or dormancy. The use of the term *"semillas"* has attained a particular symbolic significance within the Republican memory campaign, and recurs in their campaign literature and commemorative acts. In this interview extract, campaign co-founder and leader Emilio Silva explains the genesis of this metaphor and the significance that the term holds for him personally:

> "We made a documentary called 'Seeds'. The name 'Seeds' comes from [...] an old post-card made by a Republican intellectual who died in exile, called Castelao, and it was an illustration from a series he made in 1937. In the drawing you can see civilians, villagers, who are putting bodies into a mass grave and you can read the legend below which says *"you are not burying bodies, you are planting seeds."* When that card was brought to the excavation it gave us goose pimples because this card represents what we believe we are doing, which is gathering these seeds. We don't know yet what the fruit will be, but I believe it's something better for Spanish society. It thrilled me, this drawing. That he imagined in 1937 that all this was going to happen. It's like a cosmic message." (Emilio Silva, Madrid)

This is a dense and figuratively rich extract but is clearly significant to understanding the contemporary Republican memory campaign, and more broadly the exhumation of Republican mass graves. As Emilio Silva terms it: "this card represents what we believe we are doing, which is gathering these seeds". The significance of this image as described here is multi-layered, in that the idea of burying a seed suggests that the dead bodies contain an inherent potential that will be activated at some point in the future. Furthermore, that the origins of the campaign metaphor, of buried bodies as planted seeds, can be traced to this 1937 Republican image, strongly communicates a sense of inevitability, or a pre-ordained quality about the re-surfacing of these bodies. It is this pre-ordained quality, as if the drive for exhumation emanates from the past, or from the dead themselves, that is communicated by the phrase: "It's like a cosmic message."

The less explicit organic metaphors that recurred amongst relatives of the dead, and members of the two communities I studied, referring to sowing, planting, depth and resurgence after dormancy, and the more emphatic image of bodies as seeds invoked in the Republican memory campaign, are important in that they highlight points of comparison with the other international and historical contexts of exhumation discussed at the beginning of the chapter. The Spanish Republican dead cannot be said to function as a site of active political tension in exactly the same way as the disappeared of Argentina or the missing in Cyprus. Their absence has not been made present in the same forceful, public way by the communities and the relatives of the dead. The image of the dormant seed allows these bodies to be buried but not resolved, and instead they are inherently unstable, containing the potential for change and resurgence. Their burial in mass graves can be conceived of as contingent or provisional, an equivalent to the "life in parenthesis" described by Richards (2002). The Spanish graves contain their own form of political and emotional tension which was not readily apparent for decades but has resurfaced in its own time frame.

Conclusion

To conclude, it is useful to consider the shifting status and interactions with the emptied mass grave, and the relocation to the new normative commemorative space created in the village cemetery through the act of reburial. A small handful of my most reflexive informants, primarily those closely involved in acting as local co-ordinators for the exhumation, as well as a few of the archaeologists and forensic practitioners who had returned to the community to attend the formal reburial ceremony, made a series of striking reflections, contrasting the thoughts and emotions elicited by the old mass grave site versus the new cemetery burial. At the old mass gravesite, the excavated grave had not been fully refilled, and the large depression and some smaller hollows where individual skeletons had been located were visible. The grave contained floral tributes and messages in varying stages of decay, suggesting sporadic but ongoing interaction with the site. An impromptu banner had been erected over the grave site detailing the massacre, and making the dual nature of the site as a place of both execution and clandestine burial explicit to the visitor. This made the wording of the banner more explicit and robust than the epitaph on the cemetery monument, which served a more normalizing function, integrating the names of the dead in amongst the other tombstones. Interestingly, the degree of permanence intended in the erection of this banner was unclear, as if the commemorative function of the site was still emerging.

One informant active in the Republican memory campaign of the region, but not native to the village told me how he found himself frequently taking diversions to the grave site, located as it was at the turn-off of a major road. He said "I stop here if I'm anywhere nearby. I feel I have to come and have a look." He characterized it as a space that was good for thinking about the past, but also thinking about the meaning of the exhumation itself. This observation, made amongst a group of campaigners and excavators, triggered spontaneous recognition and acknowledgement from others that they also had made solo trips to the grave, stopping en route through the region, but were unaware that others had done this. These impromptu, solo trips seemed to contrast with my observations of the often collective and highly performative nature of cemetery visits in Spanish villages. Other informants, who lived closer, described walking to the exhumation site, and even gravitating towards it. The emptied out grave site clearly retained a significance even without the bodies and objects that had been removed. I felt it had become a place to be close to these dead Republicans through their imaginary remains, rather than their physical remains, and it was in the realm of the imagined that the dead now functioned more potently as Republican "seeds". As an execution site and a place of clandestine mass burial, the emptied grave site was also the enduring physical trace of the specific acts of violence that had taken place in that community, and materialized the particularity and exceptionality of this category of the dead, even after the bodies themselves had been incorporated into the normative space of the cemetery.

My impression from the mass reburial ceremony held in my field site, and the shifting interactions with the now-empty grave site, is that exhumation and reburial may fulfill the expression of unresolved affective and familial bonds with the dead, but they do not enable the fruition of these bodies as Republican "seeds." For those members of the community, and of the Republican memory campaign who perceive the war dead as dormant seeds, as sites of a political tension and potentiality, the meaning of these deaths for contemporary Spain, and importantly, the meaning of having now exhumed them, were still being shaped and discerned. This reflective "work" upon the grave site continued after the physical work of exhumation and reburial had been completed.

Acknowledgements I would like to thank members of ARMH, and those who collaborate with them, whose openness and patience enabled me to undertake fieldwork. I thank my informants for speaking on these themes. Part of this fieldwork was undertaken with support of a doctoral grant from the AHRC, UK.

References

Aguilar, P. and Humlebæk, C. 2002. Collective Memory and National Identity in the Spanish Civil War, *History and Memory*, 14, 1–2, 121–164.

Chrisafis, A. 2008. Bones Don't Speak, *The Guardian* 15th April.

Crossland, Z. 2000. Buried Lives: Forensic Archaeology and the Disappeared in Argentina, *Archeological Dialogues*, 72, 146–158.

Crossland, Z. 2002. Violent Spaces: Conflict Over the Reappearance of Argentina's Disappeared. In *Matérial Culture: The Archaeology of Twentieth-Century Conflict*, eds. J. Schofield, W. Johnson and C. Beck, 115–131. New York: Routledge.

Desfor Edles, L. 1998. *Symbol and Ritual in the New Spain: The Transition to Democracy after Franco*. Cambridge: Cambridge University Press.

Fernández de Mata, I. 2004. The "Logics" of Violence and Franco's Mass Graves: An Ethnohistorical Approach, *International Journal of the Humanities*, 2(3), 2527–2535.

Ferrándiz, F. 2006. The Return of Civil War Ghosts: The Ethnography of Exhumations in Contemporary Spain, *Anthropology Today*, 22(3), 7–12.

Gonzalez-Ruibal, A. 2007. Making Things Public: Archaeologies of the Spanish Civil War, *Public Archaeology*, 6(4), 203–226

Graham, H. 2004. The Spanish Civil War, 1936-2003: The Return of Republican Memory, *Science and Society*, 68(3), 313–328.

Kovras, I. 2008. Unearthing the Truth: The Politics of Exhumations in Cyprus and Spain, *History and Anthropology*, 19(4), 371–390.

Preston, P. 1989. Revenge and Reconciliation, *History Today*, 39(March), 28–33.

Richards, M. 2002. From War Culture to Civil Society, *History and Memory*, 14(1–2), 93–120.

Robben, A.C.G.M. 2005. *Political Violence and Trauma in Argentina*. Philadelphia: University of Pennsylvania Press.

Sant Cassia, P. 2007. *Bodies of Evidence: Burial, Memory and the Recovery of Missing Persons in Cyprus*. New York: Berghahn Books.

Silva, E. and Macías, S. 2003. *Las Fosas de Franco: Los Republicanos que el Dictador dejó en las Cunetas*. Madrid: Temas de Hoy.

Thomas, H. 1990. *The Spanish Civil War*. London: Penguin

Tremlett, G. 2006. *Ghosts of Spain: Travels through a Country's Hidden Past*. London: Faber and Faber.

Verdery, K. 1999. *The Political Lives of Dead Bodies: Reburial and Postsocialist Change*. New York: Columbia University Press.

Chapter 4
A Sense of Absence: The Staging of Heroic Deaths and Ongoing Lives among American Organ Donor Families

Anja Marie Bornø Jensen

I know he is not dead. He is alive in other people that are out there today. He is just not with me, but he is out there in other people... And that for some reason has given me great solace, knowing that other people are benefiting from my son's death instead of just putting his body in the grave and saying goodbye. And that is the end of it. That is not the case.
(Donor Father)

Introduction

This chapter deals with particular human encounters of absence and loss as they are expressed by the families of American organ donors. After tragically losing a family member and saying yes to donation of the organs, many of the families of organ donors formulate perceptions of life, death, and organ donation that seem to insist on the continuing existence of the dead donor in different ways. These ideas are mainly structured and encouraged by the American organ organizations, supporting donor families in the time after the organ donation and wishing to transform the traumatic experience of losing a family member into positive sense-making stories about organ donation.

Suffering from a loss all the while finding a meaningful purpose in having given organs to others initiate peculiar paradoxes of grief and joy, death and life, and pointlessness and purpose among the involved families; paradoxes that call for anthropological investigation. Exploring these analytically through notions of presence and absence will be the purpose and challenge of this chapter.

According to Eelco Runia, presence is "'being in touch' – either literally or figuratively – with people, things, events, and feelings that made you into the person you are" (Runia 2006: 5). Dealing with commemorations, remembrance or the fascination with memory, Runia argues that when people attend the Vietnam Veterans Memorial or the reading of names of the dead at the World Trade Center,

A.M.B. Jensen (✉)
Department of Anthropology, University of Copenhagen, Copenhagen, Denmark
e-mail: anja.jensen@anthro.ku.dk

M. Bille et al. (eds.), *An Anthropology of Absence: Materializations of Transcendence and Loss*, DOI 10.1007/978-1-4419-5529-6_4, © Springer Science+Business Media, LLC 2010   63

it is not in search of meaning, but rather in search of "presence". Runia also claims that while presence is the denotative side of art, consciousness, and life, meaning is the connotative side (ibid), the point being that meaning is a specific way of defining or understanding presence. The point is also that presence is as important and foundational as meaning, and we have to recognize the "need for presence" which is not always (only) a struggle for meaning, but can be "an attempt to create an endurable and enjoyable intersection of both meaning and presence" (ibid). This chapter will embrace this understanding of the coexistence of presence and meaning, but at the same time discuss how meaning can also be the connotative side of *absence*. Specific interpretations and constructions of "being absent" can be as meaningful or sense-making as "being in touch", as we shall see from the case of American donor families interacting with an organ organization commemorating the organ donors. From this context, I will argue that "being absent" is not the opposite of "being in touch", it is a premise. Regaining or maintaining the presence of the organ donor would not be possible without the inevitable absence following death. What is central is how absence is staged, negotiated, and understood. From this empirical context, I shall therefore explore the intersections of absence and meaning, the ongoing dynamics of presence and absence, and learn how the organizational staging of organ donation can be understood as a search for specific sense-making domains of absence.

The chapter is based on anthropological fieldwork among donor families organized in the New York Organ Donor Network (henceforth NYODN or the organization). NYODN is the organ procurement organization of New York City. It has approximately 120 employees, and it covers all aspects of organ donation and transplantation such as PR and communication, encouraging the public to sign the donor registry, approaching families for consent, coordinating donation and transplants, cooperating with hospital intensive care units and transplant centres, offering support to families after the donation, and hosting a volunteer department consisting of both donor families, organ recipients and other interested parties that are trained to do public speeches about their personal experiences. My fieldwork was located at the Donor Family Services department of NYODN, referred to as "Aftercare" in daily speech. "Aftercare" is a concept that has spread across the entire United States after intense lobbyism over the last 20 years from American donor families active in the "National Donor Family Council". The council has worked intensively to put donor families and their special needs on the medical and public agenda, for example by writing a grief support book for donor families, making education programs for intensive care nurses, and by officially defining "The Donor Family Bill of Rights", making sure that families of donors are entitled to decent care, support, and information during and after the process of donation. The concept of Aftercare can be best described as an organizationally structured support program offered to families after their consent to donate.

In New York, the two-year program consisted of bereavement cards, letters of thanks from the President of the NYODN, phone calls to the families, information about the organs, invitation to social events and acknowledgement ceremonies. In addition, the Aftercare program offered options to communicate anonymously with the organ recipients and an ongoing opportunity for the families to call the Aftercare

Department with any questions or concerns whenever these may arise. The talks could concern doubts about whether brain death really meant dead, the wish to know what went on in the operating room where the organs were removed, the desire to hear how the organ recipients were doing, or they could express a mere need to talk to somebody who is there to listen and show understanding no matter what. In this organizational setting, it became evident that the purpose was not only to take care of donor families, it was also to create, shape, and stage certain stories of absence and link personal grieving with an organizational purpose.

Staging Absence: Organizational Sense-Making

Among the NYODN staff members, I often heard two foundational sentences expressing the organizational philosophy about donor family aftercare: The first was: "Donor families are our best advocates", and the second was: "If donor families have a good experience with organ donation, they will tell 50 people, if they have a bad one, they will tell 500". Hence, the organization had a great strategic interest in making sure that the positive family stories were promoted, and the negative ones were transformed into something else or silenced. To meet this goal, the organization provided donor families with a certain specialized terminology in order to help them speak about the donation and articulate the painful emotions of losing a loved one and making the decision to give the organs to others. According to the Manager of the organization, one of the major ways to support the family was to "provide them with terminology" to speak about it all. Over the years, the Aftercare Department had learned from donor families what worked for them, and hence they were not afraid to introduce that to newly bereaved donor families. This terminology would for example be statements such as "organs are gifts", that organs were "recovered" not "harvested", and that their loved one is "living on in the spirit", and will "never be forgotten". The specific use of words acted to provide families with the right value-laden terms to classify their actions. Anthropologist Michael Jackson argues that when people make words stand for the world, it is possible to manipulate ones experience of the world (Jackson 2002:18). Following this line of argument, organizational aftercare for donor families manipulates families' devastating experiences and transforms organ donation from being associated with tragedy into being a "gift of life". Language has taken over and manipulated and reinterpreted the experience into something sense-making, a much different perspective than the tragic devastating circumstances, usually preceding the decision to donate organs.

One major purpose of the Aftercare program is to present families with organizational values regarding organ donation and structuring and redefining their experiences from the hospital. In doing this, the organization not only provides families with rhetoric tools to describe death, the decision to donate and the outcome, it also structures families into a specific group defined by the term "donor family". A major part of the Aftercare program is to introduce families to this term and make them adopt their new organizational identity. Many families in the organization embraced their new category immediately, and they regarded and presented themselves as "donor families" first and foremost because it was a meaningful way for them to justify constantly talking about their dead family member. However, other families did not accept the term to the same degree, because it implicitly implied an acceptance of the organizational understanding of organ donation that was not shared by all families having gone through it. For them, however, there was no other choice than to remain outside the organization. The term "donor family" was organizationally created and not up for discussion. Coordinators openly stated that "donor family is our term, not theirs" suggesting that they were aware that families should be guided into this new identity that carried a tremendous aura of sympathy, respect, and acknowledgement. The staff at Donor Family Services made sure to communicate the organizational value that donor families had done something extraordinary and are considered very special while showing understanding, empathy, and respect through long conversations with families over the phone. During one of these phone conversations, I heard one of the staff members saying the following to a mother, who had lost her daughter:

> I can't imagine how it must be to lose a child. You always imagine that you go first. You should know your daughter is a hero to many people. She saved the lives of six people. You should be very proud that she was able to help these people. You did the right thing. I will send you a package with some stuff that might help you deal with the grief. Again, I want to offer you my condolences. It is an honour to be able to speak to someone like you and your family. (Donor Family Services staff, phone conversation with donor mother)

As shown in the above quote, expressing empathy and admiration was important elements in how the organization communicated with the bereaved families. The emphasis on doing "the right thing", the right thing being to save other people's lives, is an organizational value that lies as the foundation for all the work being done in the organization. While having as a goal to help and support grieving families, this aftercare work is also done strategically in accordance with the purpose and the values of the organization; to promote organ donation to the general public and encourage others to make the same decision "to save lives" because it is "the right thing". This particular organizational staging and understanding of loss and bereavement is what relates absence to meaning and what gives rise to a moral presence of the organ donor because it is his/her body parts that now inhabit the bodies of others. Absence and presence are the prerequisites of each other.

The organizational influence on the creation of donor family stories became evident to me during my participation in a Volunteer Training in NYODN, where donor families and recipients received training from two members of an organization called "Transplant Speakers" on how to build up and how to tell their personal story to the general public. The stories should contain an introduction stating who you were and where you came from, for example: "I am a donor mom from NYODN". After that, families should have "the body of the story"with the personal experience of loss and donation and perhaps some tactful humor. Thereafter, families should deal with "myths and misconceptions", for example by invalidating the myth that "doctors let people die to take their organs" or "donation disfigures the body and delays the funeral". Families were also told to use up to date statistics on the waiting list number. Finally, the story should have a "close" where the storyteller should personalize it to the audience, call people to action by encouraging them to sign the donor registry, and finally say thank you and invite people to ask questions. This event showed how families were taught to transform their individual experiences into shared organizational narratives with different content but following a shared structure. Almost exactly the same idea unfolds in anthropologist Vibeke Steffen's significant study of Alcoholics Anonymous in Denmark (1997). The stories have several functions: Creating a community among fellow sufferers, making stories recognizable to an audience, and reshaping and confirming the legitimacy and social existence of the organization.

However, in the stories of many of the donor families I spoke to, the statements of the organization had clearly overwritten their personal experience and dominated the families' public versions of their stories. But in more personal and confidential interview settings, both sides of the coin were revealed, and the coexisting understanding of organ donation as a triumph and a nightmare became evident to me. A donor father showed how the organizational slogan of "turning tragedy into triumph" was incorporated in the expression of his experience while later in the interview revealing that the visual idea of organ donation was tearing him apart and leading him to drug abuse.

> It [organ donation] has helped us to come to the realization that this horrible incident was unavoidable, that he was involved in. And we took that tragedy and we turned it into a triumph by making other people's lives better because of Joey.

> I had been drinking a lot, and I had been abusing legally prescriptive sleep medication, but I was not using it properly. And the reason I was using both, was because of the dreams I was having and the visions of Joey on the operating table that I could not get rid of (Donor Father).

The organizational orchestration of stories can therefore also be looked upon as attempts to stage certain perceptions of absence and presence. Joey should be remembered as a young man saving lives in death, not a maltreated body on an operating table. In order to have an acceptable organizational presence of the organ donors, they have to be absent in certain ways; preferably heroic and life saving, not as blood and flesh causing nightmares. The nightmare vision of organ donation, the doubts about brain death, the fear of having killed your family member by consenting to organ donation exist among many of the donor families I met. But the organization deals with this under private almost therapeutic circumstances and conversations, and in this process it emphasizes the brave and positive aspects of organ donation that some donor families find comfort in telling and retelling as we shall return to. A popular version of the story is the one of the "organ donor hero" that is able to transform senseless deaths into meaningful memories.

Transforming Absence: Constructing a Hero

> Then I went home to explain to my kids what had happened. And my daughter was only five and did not understand life and death, so when I told her, she cried, she begged and pleaded for me to take her to heaven just for one minute to say goodbye to Mom.

But my son was 13 and he understood what was happening. And when I told him that his Mom had died, he cried and cried and we hugged for a long time. In search for something to tell him, I started explaining organ donation to him and that she was going to be able to save somebody's life. Through his tears he looked up at me and said 'That makes Mom a hero, doesn't it'. And I said, 'I guess it does'. And from that day on, we think of her as a hero, as someone, who maybe ran through a burning building and pulled some people out before being overcome by the smoke and flames herself. And it is that, what has really gotten us through this whole grieving process. (Donor Husband)

In the NYODN, this idea of an organ donor being a hero was constructed or indulged with a therapeutic purpose for the donor family. Many donor families adopted this idea about the donor as "a hero saving other people's lives" because it reassured them that there was a purpose or a meaning to the death and it gave a socially accepted model for reinterpreting a tragic loss. For donor families in the New York area, the heroism of saving others often had a reference to the terror attacks on World Trade Center on September 11th 2001 (9/11) because the event still had a significant impact on them. They often incorporated their version of 9/11 into their stories about losing a family member and consenting to organ donation. This indicates a link between public disasters and personal traumas, as also touched upon by Jackson (2005) when comparing the loss of a public landmark to a loss in people's personal lives. After the attack, New Yorkers were in a state of shock, but at the same time they seemed linked closely together in what Jackson refers to as "reclaiming a sense of shared certainties and meanings" (Jackson 2005: 15–16). The hero stories of organ donation were often deliberately designed by the organization to relate organ donation to well known ideals of saving lives. By relating the idea of organ donation to 9/11, NYODN put its organizational agenda within this framework of the New York's "shared certainties and meanings" and thereby created a cultural truth about the hero-ism of organ donors that was nonnegotiable. This idea is similar to what anthropologist Glenn Bowman classifies as "identity reconstruction after trauma". His work on 9/11 explores the processes "which transform calamitous events into consensual narratives" (Bowman 2001: 17). I claim that the understanding of the organ donor as a hero could be seen as a "consensual narrative" within NYODN because it has the ability of trans-forming the family catastrophe of death into the social pride of organ donation.

Heroizing and focusing on the positive characteristics of a dead person is not confined to organ donation. However, organ donation adds new aspects to this post-mortal honoring because the death literally results in improving or saving other people's lives and in that sense it is a very tangible proof of the selflessness of the donor. The fact that some of the donors had actually taken an active decision to donate and talked to their families about it beforehand is what characterizes them as heroes in the eyes of the donor families and the NYODN who see them as role models for others. The heroic aspects of the stories represent what anthropologist and historian Peter Gibbon calls the "moral component of heroism": The hero serv-ing as a model or an example (Gibbon 2002: 4). In the case of organ donors, the purpose is to convince other people to donate. In American campaigns for organ donation, the term, "be a hero, be an organ donor" is very popular. Hence, the hero stories of organ donation act as yet another deliberate organizational tool to control the experiences of donor families and promote a general idea of organ donation as a way of being absent in a heroic way and thereby maintain or regain presence.

Looking at heroism in a broader historical and societal context shows that, in the USA, the hero has often been connected to military deeds, but the word has been tainted with bad connotations because of ambiguous attitudes toward American soldiers during the Vietnam War. After the 9/11 attacks, however, the word hero has been revived across the nation in descriptions of the courageous deeds of fire fighters, police officers, rescue workers, and the passengers on board flight United 93 who fought the plane hijackers (Gibbon 2002: 63–65; Skimin 2005: 305).

Writing about organ donation in an Israeli context, anthropologist Orit Brawer Ben-David claims that in Israel, a heroic death implies giving one's life for one's country. A heroic death is defined as the death of soldiers in war when the personal body becomes symbolically part of the national body. Other types of deaths such as suicides or traffic accidents do not have social significance and are therefore not categorized as heroic deaths. However, consenting to organ donation can transform an ordinary way of dying into a heroic death deserving national attention and recognition (Ben-David 2005: 128). Notions of transformation were also an element among American donor families. A father told me that his son was in the American Air Force when he died, training to be a pilot, like his father. Now the son would never serve his country and save American lives as he (or his father) had planned to, but he was able to "save lives in death". Thus, through the optic of organ donation, a teenager was suddenly a national hero because his body parts were helping "84 people in 24 different states". The father made sure to mention this constantly during public speaking as a very tangible and quantitative fact and a way of reassembling the whole body of the son and preserving his presence in spite of the fact that he was dead. Thinking about the organs still being alive, the father could create a heroic future for the son, even if it was not the one he originally intended. Looking at this through the optic of presence and absence reveals that this staging of heroic death creates a kind of "absence with a future", which in some cases is more glorified and socially accepted than ordinary life would have been. In life, father and son had their disputes, but by way of the specialized rhetoric of organ donation, all conflicts are forgotten, and the dead son becomes present in his absence in a way that is controllable and in accordance with the father's original goals and ideas about the son's future. Of course, the father is devastated by his son's death, but it can also be argued that he is able to be "in touch" with his son in certain ways because he is dead which exemplifies my initial point that in this context, absence is a premise for being in touch.

Commemorating the Dead: Objects of Acknowledgement

In order to meet the donor family's need for recognition, the NYODN made huge efforts to memorialize organ donors publicly and thereby acknowledge not only the decision made at the time of death but also the life of the organ donor. In the social interactions between donor family and organization, the way people engaged with certain objects played an important role. Families were presented and provided with organizationally designed objects to understand the concept of organ donation, to attach the organizational values to their personal experiences and to provide certain material

Fig. 4.1 Memory Quilt from New York Organ Donor Network. Photo by the author

means of remembering the dead. Such objects include specific brochures and pamphlets explaining organ donation, butterfly pins to symbolize ongoing life, coffee mugs, key chains, T-shirts and posters stating that organ donation is "the gift of life", and certificates of appreciation sent to donor families. Two of the most significant objects are the Memory Quilt (Fig. 4.1) and the Gift of Life Medal of Honor (Fig. 4.2).

Fig. 4.2 The Gift of Life Medal of Honor from New York. Photo by the author

The Donor Family Memory Quilt, a quilt where the patches are made by the various donor families to commemorate the donor, is always displayed at the ceremonies and events with NYODN. The patches of the quilt are created by the donor family and can show a picture or a symbol of the donor and are made in certain colors and styles families associate with the donor, according to his or her age, sex, religion, occupation, or hobbies as a way of representing their personalities. Occasionally, the patches are made out of the donors' favorite clothes. The memory quilt seemed to have a tremendous emotional impact on the donor families. The patches represent their loved ones, and the quilt is treated as a valuable symbolic object and handled with utmost respect. It represents the personal lives and stories behind organ donation and it represents the multitude and diversity among organ donors and their families. But it also serves as a valuable exhibition object for NYODN that uses the quilt as a powerful and visual PR strategy in its efforts to promote organ donation.

The other item is The Gift of Life Medal of Honor, which is handed to donor families at large recognition ceremonies by representatives from the organ organization or famous organ recipients, in order to publicly thank and honor the donor and the family. Families are asked to line up, and while solemn music is played and pictures of the organ donors appear on a large screen, families shake hands with a leading person in the organization and have their picture taken with the medal. Sometimes, families also get to say the name and age of their loved one when receiving the medal. The medal is a tangible symbol of the honor associated with being a donor family; families are almost rewarded for their efforts and donors are treated like war heroes serving their country by saving lives. The medal serves as a strong organizational tool and a symbolic way to structure the idea of organ donation and have families think of it as heroic and brave – an act similar to dying on the battlefield. American soldiers are honored by their city or their country and receive medals, and so should organ donors according to the philosophy of the organization. This need for national recognition was expressed by many donor families since the heroism in the stories of the families was not exclusively confined to the urban context of the terrorist attacks; it also acquired a national character as this donor father expressed when explaining why he used the word hero about his son:

> And I can think of nothing else other than standing in front of a bullet and getting shot for the President of the United States or something that a Secret Service agent will do that is more heroic than being an organ donor and having made that decision to let the medical team do whatever they need to do with their body to help other people to live. (Donor Father)

Families explained that it was a great honor to receive the medal, and it made them feel acknowledged by their country. This national acknowledgement can be a kind of relief for a family that may have had to answer many critical questions from their closest network of family and friends concerning organ donation. The national acknowledgement is materially manifested at the 10.000 square-foot National Donor Memorial in Richmond, Virginia (see Sharp 2006), and is acted out at national events where American donor families come together. At the recognition ceremony for donor families at the so-called Transplant Games in Kentucky 2006, guards in uniforms marched in carrying the American flag accompanied by a rendition of "Amazing Grace", and the audience pledged allegiance to the flag and sang the National Anthem. Thereby, the gratitude expressed toward donor families from the stage symbolizes the gratitude of their country and not "only" of the recipients or the organization staff. The national acknowledgement manifests itself in the fact that all American donor families are invited to Washington once every second year to the National Donor Recognition Ceremony. This ceremony includes the same elements as described above but, according to donor families, it has even more significance and a larger national context since it is held in the nation's capital with the National Guard presenting the flag and playing music. The medal therefore was a very important object because it reinforced a national attention to the life that was lost, served as a cultural and political approval of the idea of organ donation in spite of occasional personal nightmares about the procurement of the organs, and it communicated the need to make the donor and their families visible and present to the American public. Even though organ donation is more evident and visible in the American public media compared to other countries, the American organ donation community still demands more public attention and recognition in their quest for awareness.

Some American donor families also engaged actively in discussions on how to make use of and present these objects. During a meeting in the Donor Advisory Council in the NYODN, families discussed a suggestion posed by the organization to have the Gift of Life Medal sent by mail to all families instead of handing it out at the yearly Recognition Ceremony for donor families. All families agreed that it was better to present it to the families at the ceremony, the argument being that otherwise it would lose its value. This indicates that the value of the medal lies in the ritualised act of receiving it and not only in the object as such. A mother of a donor explained how she would not consider it an acknowledgement if she received it in her own home. The medal would never acquire its intended value by being sent by mail to a private home. To her, it was very important that the medal was presented to donor families in a public setting where the donors could be remembered. This discussion about the medal indicates the significance of the national state or the public to be present in the interactions with donor families. It also points to one of my main arguments, namely that it is in the social and ceremonial performances of the Gift of Life Medal of Honor and of the Memory Quilt that families are able to generate the feeling that their loved one is not forgotten, but still present in private, as well as in public memories (Jensen 2007). The presence of the dead donor has an important feature which will be elaborated further after having explored the significance of the organs living in others.

Living in Others: Durable Body Parts

The substantial attention given to what is often seen as an alarming lack of organs in many Western countries and the ensuing potential commodification and reification of human body parts worldwide have been widely discussed in the social sciences for decades. This has been described as a process of objectification, devaluation, or dehumanization and considered problematic by many anthropological authors dealing with both organ trade in third world countries, the concept of gift exchange in organ donation, and the problematic of brain death (Alnæs 2001; Appadurai 1999; Fox and Swazey 1992; Healy 2006; Kopytoff 1986, 2004; Lock 2002; Scheper-Hughes 1996, 2004; Sharp 1995, 2000, 2001, 2006). One can argue that the premise for the transplantation business is that the individual lives of donors are reduced into body parts. However controversial this might be, the transformation of personal subjects into desired objects (body parts) should not necessarily be looked upon as devaluating human life or as some kind of identity depreciation. Looking at organ transplantation through the optic of presence and absence illuminates something else. In the world of the bereaved, the transformation of a person into an object for transplantation is simply a necessary premise in order for the deceased to regain the subject status and for reclaiming a *particular kind* of presence in spite of death. Therefore, the categories of subject and object are not antipoles; rather, paraphrasing Latour (1993), they come together as hybrids, which can be an interesting way of looking at the body parts of organ donors.

In his influential book from 1986, Arjun Appadurai argues that things have social lives and can have different meanings and statuses according to context (Appadurai 1986). Lesley Sharp has developed this perspective in the realm of organ donation, claiming that an organ can simultaneously embody the essence of a loved one, be a gift for a recipient in need, and be a needed object of surgical desire (Sharp 2000). Therefore organs, like other things, contain a multitude of meanings according to shifting perspectives. From the perspective of the donor family, the meanings associated with organs change over time. At the bedside when trying to make the decision whether to donate, some families regard the organs as things that cannot be given away, or, paraphrasing Weiner, as "inalienable objects" (Weiner 1992). Other families regard the exchange of organs as a means to ensure the ongoing survival of their dead loved one. One donor mother told me that she found comfort in the fact that she did not have to bury everything when her son died. Knowing that his organs were still out there in other people helped her in her grief and gave her a sense that he was not entirely dead. For her, donation was a means of maintaining her dead son's presence and thus of surmounting absence and death. Another donor mother expressed the idea of ongoing body parts like this,

> I met Jenny's heart recipient. Her name is Alice. What a cute little lady she is. The first time I met her, she said 'I have this energy I have never had. When I wake up I have this urge to go rollerblading. I just have this energy. My husband has to sit on me and say no Alice you are not ready to do this'. Jenny rollerbladed all the time. Jenny was a karate expert. And I wonder. Do the characteristics, do parts of Jenny still live? It is a good feeling that a part of her is out there rollerblading or doing karate or whatever. (Donor Mother)

This focus on organs carrying personal characteristics and still living on appeared helpful to some families. The idea of a pounding heart functioning well in another body was perceived as solid proof to the families that death had occurred, but that the death was not to be understood as final. To grieving donor families, the organ recipients are the concrete evidence that the characteristics of the donor or the "life" in some peculiar way, goes on because of the use of their body parts. This corporeality seemed to be the most meaningful way for the bereaved to keep the idea of the donor still being "alive". Because of this focus on the body parts, many donor families feel that they are luckier when compared to other families who have lost kin. The knowledge that the organs are alive in other people is a tangible way to deny death and absence, and keep the idea of presence through a pounding heart or another organ. A donor mother explained it like this,

> I have people living today, who had that second chance in life that my daughter was able to give. It's the most healing thing to know that Mary's memory and her legacy will live on

through other people through years to come, through the woman who received her heart on to her children on to her grandchildren on to her great grandchildren. (Donor Mother)

Statements as these show the importance of looking closer at the notion of future lives and imaginations of kinship. By way of the organ recipients, the daughter and by implication her mother become a biological factor in reproducing their own family and the recipients' families, thereby creating new lives and new generations.

One father stressed the idea of the durable nature of the body parts of his late young son when he himself needed a bone implant in his back because of a spinal injury. He went to the tissue bank where the bone of his son was kept, only to find out that everything had been used. After at first being disappointed that this biological connection to his dead son could not be (re)established, it gave him a feeling of pride that the bones of his son were of high quality and in high demand. What this father did was to focus on the tangible materiality of the body and the high quality of the body parts, and the fact that they are functioning well in other people. This utilitarian perception of the late son's body is, however, simultaneously turned into a reinterpretation of the son's qualities and achievements when he was alive. Through his absence in death, the presence he had while he was still living was recreated.

However, organ donation can also create more disturbing notions of absence and presence that were not as widespread or directly spoken of in the organizational reality: What if the body parts were wasted and never transplanted into others? Families who chose to donate were often very sorry to hear if the organs were rejected by the recipient or if the recipient died right away. Some families were also told at the hospital that the organs could not be used because of hidden diseases such as cancer, HIV or hepatitis. These families were officially classified as donor families because, as the Aftercare Manager said, "we try to explain that the gift is real whether or not there is a transplant outcome". But even though the organization appreciated the intention to donate and not only the eventual outcome, it was the number of saved and improved lives that really made a difference for donor families alongside the notion that the organs had actually been transplanted into someone. A woman who donated the bone and tissue of her mother was very afraid the parts of her mother were not usable and were "stored in a freezer somewhere". This terrifying vision was rooted in the fact that she felt that families who donated organs got more organizational attention and acknowledgement than families like herself who "only" donated tissue and bone that were not considered quite as life-saving as solid organs, even in spite of the organizational attempts to neutralize this difference. This shows that along with certain notions of absence, there are also certain notions of presence that are more tolerable than others. Presence in other bodies and in other lives was sense-making to many donor families, whereas the idea of wasting organs could be understood as adding another painful level of absence on top of the absence caused by death. But yet another dimension needs to be added to the context and understandings of absence and presence within organ donation. In the performance of donor family stories, organ donors regain their presence not only in a bodily but also in a spiritual sense, and they are not the only ones having their presence reconfigured by way of organ donation.

Performing and Pursuing the Presence of the Dead and the Legitimacy of the Bereaved

> I always remember somebody saying, that a person is only dead when you stop talking about them. That has always stuck in my mind. (Donor Mother)

> I don't like the term 'lost'. I did not lose my daughter, she died. I know exactly where she is. To me, that is the only way that I can cope with this. (Donor Father)

The stories, the choice of words and the repertoire of expressions communicated by donor families help create what I call a "narrative presence" of the donor. And perhaps to some donor families, it is felt and experienced on stage as a more tangible presence. It is through the performance of the stories, what Edward Bruner calls "the expressions of experience" (Bruner 1986: 6), that the dead organ donors come to live and the family members feel they can still do something for their dead kin. Bruner argues that it is in the performance of an expression that culture is reexperienced, retold, and reconstructed and meaning is created (ibid: 11). Donor families are therefore able to regain various forms of meaningful presence of their relative, or to use Runia's definition, of "being in touch" with the deceased by performing the story of organ donation in the organizational context.

Hence, the organization not only shapes the structures and values for speaking about the organ donors; it also provides a stage on which the performance of presenting the deceased can be acted out without any questions. On this stage, there can be no such thing as the dead being lost or gone forever, to return to the quote above. The donors are dead alright, but they are still present because of the articulation of organ donation and their biographies. This seductive idea might be the reason why some donor families choose to speak about the death of their loved one over and over again. These stories and the strategic purpose they fulfill might not make sense outside the organizational context. But the particular context acts as a certain kind of social forum in which the dead can in fact become present through the revitalization of their spirit. Anthropologist Edward Schieffelin discusses something similar in his classic work *Performance and the Cultural Construction of Reality* (1985) where he examines the performance of nondiscursive spirit séances among the Kaluli people of Papua New Guinea. Scheiffelin's work focuses on a completely different regional, topical, and cultural context, but his argument about performance is still helpful here:

> Performance does not construct a symbolic reality in the manner of presenting an argument, description, or commentary. Rather, it does so by socially constructing a situation in which the participants experience symbolic meanings as part of the process of what they are already doing (Schieffelin 1985: 709).

In order for the absence of the deceased to become present in a meaningful way, a certain social situation must be established in which this performance is not necessarily perceived as a staging but as reality to families. And within the organizational context, the performance of the present dead is not a performance but experienced as a reality for families, marking a strong belief that the dead are present in spirit. It is part of their daily life in their involvement in the organization and to use the words of a donor mother, "the reason I get out of bed in the morning".

Although the sense of the dead continuing their lives is of course generated by the surgical transfer of organs, I argue that living on could also mean something else that goes beyond the biological substance of an organ and beyond materiality. The dead live on through the spirit, through the donor's legacy to use the words of the families. Statements such as "she was a very giving and caring person" provide families with a rational and logical way of explaining why organ donation was the right thing to do, and this could be a strategy of focusing on something other than and better than the tragic circumstances surrounding the death. Many families emphasize the altruistic character of the donor, by mentioning for example how he or she always cared for homeless people or made free wigs for cancer patients. Carrying out organ donation was a meaningful way for families to maintain this altruistic spirit and in a spiritual sense keep the donor present by constantly speaking about other positive aspects of their personalities that fit the narrative performance of giving.

Families maintained this spiritual presence of their late family members by constantly speaking about them. Speaking worked for the families as a way of easing the pain. It was therapeutic because it allowed families to experience a strong sense of the essence of the donor when speaking of him/her. They expressed how they felt the presence of their family member in the room while telling their stories. Some of them showed pictures of their loved ones while speaking and thereby ensured that the audience saw them too. To some, speaking about organ donation in the organization worked as a way of speaking with their dead relatives and addressing them directly. One donor father, for example, always said "this is for you, this is for you" to his late son when giving public speeches. The father meant, along with other donor families who chose to be involved in the organization, that his efforts of telling the story and promoting organ donation was what his son would have wanted him to do. And this fulfillment of what donor families chose to call the legacy reinforced the presence of the donor. A donor mother expressed how she felt the presence of her daughter,

> So I guess a good part of it, I do it [speaking] for her, even though I am helping other people. I always say Karen is sitting on my shoulder. When I used to say I could not do something, Karen's expression was always, 'Mom go for it'. You can do it. It did not matter what it was. It was always 'Mom go for it'. (Donor Mother)

Even though the public speaking reinforces the idea of an ongoing relationship between a donor family and the deceased, the dynamics of presence and absence were not only between life and death but also between anonymity and acknowledgement among donor families. Some of the families I spoke to stated that they did not want any remuneration for "the gift of life", but they wanted something else that the organization was able to give them:

> We want to be acknowledged, we want people to remember that if it were not for donor families, organ donation would not happen, so be gentle with us. (Donor Mother)

Looking back at the historical context of American organ donation reveals a struggle on the part of the donor families to be recognized as a group. The whole movement of American donor families has grown from a protest against being overlooked as a group. 25 years ago, donor families were not accepted as a group because they were a reminder that the transplanted body parts came from a living person, which could cause problems for the organ recipients who were told by doctors to consider the donated organ a mere spare part. The donor family involvement can be regarded as a way of defeating the anonymity of the organ donors in American society. Anthropologist Lesley Sharp (2001, 2006) shows that for many years, American donor families have chosen to make themselves and their dead family members visible and clarify to the public that organs do not grow on trees. They come from people with a life and a story and a family as is shown in the Memory Quilts mentioned earlier. American donor families show pictures, print T-shirts, tell stories, make quilts, plant trees, and lots of other activities to put a face on donation and keep the memory alive. Some donor families still recall participating in the Transplant Games the first year donor families were allowed to come, being housed several miles from the organ recipients and being ignored in the official program and in the social gatherings. Thanks to the effort of active donor family lobbyists over the last 25 years, this has changed. But some families still have an urge to point to their situation and remind us that they and their dead family member must be recognized. A donor mother made me realize this by referring to the concept of American heroes and introducing the idea of the silent hero which was how she looked upon her daughter.

> We have our war heroes and then we have silent heroes: People who gave that gift. People like Jenny and any organ donor. They are heroes. Very seldom do you hear their name, very seldom do you put a face to that person – you hear – oh someone received an organ oh how wonderful. Do people think that these organs are in coolers in a hospital room somewhere? We talk about the transportation of organs in coolers. This is what the general public sees. And this is what they see on TV – carrying that cooler. Do they put that with a human being with a face and say oh my God it came from a 4 year old boy who fell down the stairs....

> We honour our heroes every day. The war heroes. We hear how many are killed in the wars and I think – wauw you know – there are a lot more out there that need to be recognized. We cannot only hear the recipient side of the story. We have to hear the other side of the story and know that this is a good thing to do. (Donor Mother)

In conclusion, it can be argued that donor families struggle to maintain the presence of their loved one, but also their own presence as donor families as somebody who have lost the individuals providing the organs for the cooler. The position as donor family can be interpreted as a life transformation and new identity (Jensen 2007), and the families constantly reassure each other that they need to be heard and most importantly that the dead donors need to be recognized and memorialized. The paradox of the organ donors as being dead but alive in others; absent, but absent in a certain way so they regain presence, runs parallel with the justification of the donor family. Donor families are present as a category because of their absent family member. And they have become more visible as a group as a reaction toward others' ignorance of their existence. They have become present by way of their public absence. Some of the donor families have experienced a life transformation and now have their primary social lives in the context of the organization where they can be among fellow sufferers or professionals sympathizing with them. Therefore, it is not only the organ donors who regain a presence in absence or in certain meaningful notions of absence. The whole conceptualization of donor families, too, can be understood within the dynamics of presence and absence. As with the revival of organ donors, absence in its many forms is the premise of the donor family's sense of presence; a presence that is constantly staged and negotiated, confirmed and reconfirmed in the organizational context. Thereby through a premise of "being absent", a sense of "being in touch" is achieved that is embedding the desire for recognition in a nexus of memorialization, commemoration, and "herofication".

In this theoretical landscape of presence and absence, one must remember that finding sense or purpose of the tragic death of a loved one will never erase the pain of losing, no matter how many lives are saved by organ transplantation, how many medals are handed out or how great an effort is put in by organizations or fellow sufferers. But this chapter has shown that the pain is somehow eased when the American organ organizations strategically provide donor families with a highly specialized social platform in which absence is not silenced, rather reinterpreted, transformed and articulated into something that can be rendered meaningful in the context of organ donation. Looking at this particular social performance, attention and recognition, one might argue that there is not only an "enjoyable intersection of meaning and presence" as stated by Runia (2006), but also of "meaning and absence.

Acknowledgements I wish to thank Professor Lesley Sharp, Barnard College, Columbia University and Professor Miriam Ticktin, New School of Social Research for inspiring comments to an earlier draft of this chapter.

References

Alnæs, A.H. 2001. *Minding Matter. Organ Donation and Medical Modernity's difficult Decisions.* Dissertation submitted from the degree of Doctor Rerum Politicarum. Oslo: Department and Museum of Anthropology. The Faculty of Social Sciences. University of Oslo.

Appadurai, A. 1986. 'Introduction: commodities and the politics of value'. In *The Social Life of Things*, ed. A. Appadurai, 3–63. New York: Cambridge University Press.

——— 1999. Materiality in the future of anthropology. In *Commodification: Things Agency and Identities*, eds. W. Van Binsbergen and P. Geschiere, 55–62. Berlin/Munster: LIT.

Ben-David, O.B. 2005. *Organ Donation and Transplantation: Body Organs as an Exchangeable Socio-Cultural Resource.* Westport, CT: Praeger.

Bowman, G. 2001. 'Thinking the unthinkable. Meditations on the events of 11 September 2001'. *Anthropology Today* 17(6), 17–19.

Bruner E.M. 1986. 'Experience and its expressions'. In *The Anthropology of Experience*, eds. V. Turner and E.M. Bruner, 3–30. Chicago: University of Illinois Press.

Fox, R. and Swazey, J.P. 1992. *Spare Parts: Organ Replacement in American Society.* Oxford: Oxford University Press.

Gibbon, P. 2002. *A Call to Heroism. Renewing America's Vision of Greatness.* New York: Grove Press.

Healy, K. 2006. *Last Best Gifts. Altruism and the Market for Human Organs.* Chicago: The University of Chicago Press.

Jackson, M. 2002. *The Politics of Storytelling: Violence, Transgression and Intersubjectivity.* Copenhagen: Museum Tusculanum Press.

——— 2005. *Existential Anthropology: Events, Exigencies and Effects.* Oxford: Berghahn Books.

Jensen, A.M. 2007. *Those Who Give and Grieve – an Anthropological Study of American Donor Families.* Master Thesis Number 430. Copenhagen: Department of Anthropology, University of Copenhagen.

Kopytoff, I. 1986. 'The cultural biography of things: commoditization as process'. In *The Social Life of Things*, ed. A. Appadurai, 64–91. New York: Cambridge University Press.

——— 2004. 'Commoditizing kinship in America'. In *Consuming Motherhood*, eds. J.S. Taylor, L.L. Layne and D.F. Wozniak, 271–279. New Jersey: Rutgers University Press.

Latour, B. 1993. *We have never been modern.* Cambridge, MA: Harvard University Press.

Lock, M.. 2002. *Twice Dead: Organ Transplantation and the Reinvention of Death.* Berkeley: University of California Press.

Runia, E., 2006. 'Presence'. *History and Theory* 45(October), 1–29.

Scheper-Hughes, N. 1996. 'Theft of life: Organ stealing rumours'. *Anthropology Today* 12(3), 3–11.

——— 2004. 'Parts unknown'. *Ethnography* 5(1), 29–73.

Schieffelin, E.L. 1985. 'Performance and the cultural construction of reality'. *American Ethnologist* 12(4), 707–724

Sharp, L.A. 1995. 'Organ transplantation as a transformative experience: Anthropological insights into the restructuring of the self'. *Medical Anthropology Quarterly* 9(3), 379–389.

——— 2000. 'The commodification of the body and its parts'. *Annual Review of Anthropology* 29, 287–328.

——— 2001. 'Commodified kin: death, mourning and competing claims on the bodies of organ donors in the United States'. *American Anthropologist* 103(1), 112–133.

——— 2006. *Strange Harvest: Organ Transplants, Denatured Bodies and the Transformed Self.* Berkeley: University of California Press.

Skimin, R. 2005. *Footprints of Heroes: From the American Revolution to the War in Iraq.* New York: Prometheus Books.

Steffen, V. 1997. 'Life stories and shared experience'. *Social Science and Medicine* 45(1), 99–111

Weiner, A.B. 1992. *Inalienable Possessions: The Paradox of Keeping-While-Giving.* Berkeley: University of California Press.

Part III
Temporalities of Absence

Chapter 5
Derivative Presence: Loss and Lives in Limbo in the West Bank

Lotte Buch

Introduction: Voids

My endeavor to enquire ethnographically into absence – absence of words, of social categories and of human lives in discourse and imaginaries – seems to spur particular and significant reactions in the course of conversation. When I tell people, academics or NGO representatives based in Palestine, Geneva, or Amman about my study of politics and affect among wives of political detainees from the West Bank, the reactions are not as diverse as one might envision. Some say, with a shrug, *"Oh, I see, but do you also speak with the detainees themselves? Because, as you know, they are the ones who are truly suffering"*? Another response is *"Why don't you speak with the martyr's widows or their mothers instead, that will tell you what suffering is really about in Palestine."* Revealing what is taken to be a proper infliction and what is not these comments point toward the existence of a register of acknowledging suffering in Palestinian life. In this register, there are those whose ailment is ranked, yet there are also those whose place in the register is less a place than a void. These are the women who are married to Palestinian detainees, women who can be said to be present in that register exclusively by means of their detained husband's absence. The presence of certain forms of life and of suffering in the imaginary (Taylor 2004) of what is worth paying attention to discloses what Runia has termed "the stowaway to presence," namely a void, an absence that is invisible yet intrinsically there (Runia 2006b: 1). Conceptualizing the matter of absence in the lives of Palestinian women related to either martyrs or detainees is the object of this chapter.

L. Buch (✉)
Department of Anthropology, University of Copenhagen, Copenhagen, Denmark
e-mail: lotte.buch@anthro.ku.dk

M. Bille et al. (eds.), *An Anthropology of Absence: Materializations of Transcendence and Loss*, 83
DOI 10.1007/978-1-4419-5529-6_5, © Springer Science+Business Media, LLC 2010

Framing Absence

The living room is considered to be the most significant space in a Palestinian household; it is the room where guests are received. A lot of effort and resources go into decorating this room, since it serves as a representation of the family and its relative prosperity and not least its ability to receive guests. As elsewhere in the Middle East (Schryock 2004; Abu-Lughod 1986; 1993), hospitality is a key value in the occupied territories. The arrangement of the living room thus refers to how the inhabitants wish their guests to see and think of them.

For families who have lost a male member of the family, temporarily or permanently, it becomes even more significant to display their propriety and social values. The arrangement of the living room of a young female informant, Amina, will serve as a poignant image. The stylish décor of Amina's tidy living room is dominated by one thing in particular. A 100×80 cm poster in a gold frame occupies one corner. The photostat displays a portrait of a young man in profile wearing a combat uniform, holding an AK-47 rifle, the most common weapon in the occupied territories. The background of the photostat is a waterfall set among rocky cliffs and green pine trees. Almost unnoticed, the lower right hand corner of the big photostat holds a passport size photo of another man, a simple portrait, showing only the face of the man. The big photo displays Amina's first husband who was killed by Israeli soldiers and who is therefore considered to be a martyr (*as-shahid*). The smaller photo is of Amina's second husband, her late husband's brother, who is a political detainee (*al-azeer*), sentenced to spend 30 years in Israeli prison.

The stark contrast in size and ornamentation between the two photos of Amina's husbands is a material illustration of my overall aim in this chapter. I hope to show that in the occupied territories the absence of a husband is perceived in radically different ways depending on the permanency or temporal character of his absence. This, in turn leads to equally different acknowledgement in what could be called a hierarchy of suffering for the absentee's female relatives, to the extent that it is appropriate to introduce the term "derivative presence." Absence, in this paper, is thus framed through a concern with the materiality of human relations. I investigate this through an optic of loss; both material and intangible kinds of loss and absence that make themselves present in the world. I argue that this can be said to determine gendered social being in the occupied territories at present, understood here as both the occupied Palestinian territories and Palestine as a social imaginary (Taylor 2004).

This concern forms part of an overarching research interest in tracing the category of what is termed "the secondary victim" in the field of psychosocial interventions in conflict areas (cf. Hein et al. 1993; Kanninen et al. 2002; Salo et al. 2004). I set out to explore this by focusing on torture survivors and their families in the occupied territories, a place and a situation where it is predominantly men who are torture victims or survivors.

Because my main field context is the occupied territories, hesitancy is pertinent when applying the categories of "torture victim" or "torture survivor." The UN convention against torture (UN 1984) is quite unambiguous with regard to what counts as torture. However, from ongoing engagement with the rehabilitation sector for torture survivors in Gaza and the West Bank, I became aware that torture as a forensic term makes little sense to employ, since it is not uncommon among Palestinians to articulate themselves as a collective of torture survivors to varying and competing degrees, irrespective of the UN definition of torture. Rather, torture in Palestinian vernacular covers a range of experienced encroachments, including checkpoint abuse, the regime of permissions to enter or leave the occupied territories and most notably death and captivity of the Palestinian population due to *al-ihtilal*: the (Israeli) occupation.

These afflictions, however, are not considered equally torturous or worthy of acknowledgement in popular national discourse. This makes it appropriate to speak of a hierarchy of suffering (Farmer 2003, 1997), in which some infringements such as death or detention in Israeli prisons hold the pivotal place (Allen 2006, 2009; Butler 2004). The place of martyrs and the political detainees at the top of such a hierarchy mirrors the Palestinian situation, in which the most honorable activities a man, and to some extent a woman, can undertake are so-called operations of resistance to the Israeli occupation (Nashif 2008: 25; Peteet 1991; Allen 2008). This fact must be understood in the context of the historical and ongoing situation in the occupied territories, that Roy has termed "de-development" (Roy 1995, 2007). This term defines Israeli politics of closure and restricted access to export and infrastructure as a process aimed at causing a standstill of Palestinian economic growth. One result of this is poverty rates rising to 65% in the Gaza Strip and 38% in the West Bank in 2004 (Passia 2008: 349). With a lack of financial means of securing education or migration, social status and upward mobility are difficult to achieve unless one participates in activities that counter the Israeli occupation and its impingement on Palestinian economic, social, and political life (Allen 2006). Accordingly, in the hierarchy of people who have sacrificed their lives, hopes and personal well-being for the national struggle for a state, and who occupy the most important places, are primarily *al-shahid*, which coins the notion of the martyr and secondarily, the political detainee *al-azeer* (Nashif 2008: 19; Khalili 2007).

The difference between the two may be understood with regards to three aspects, namely religion, temporality, and the question of ambiguity. A martyr who has lost his life in the struggle for Palestine has made the ultimate sacrifice: his or her life. This sacrifice is both a religious sacrifice due to the meaning of martyrs in Islam (Allen 2006), and it is a national sacrifice in the effort to create a Palestinian state (Khalili 2007). The martyr and the detainee diverge also with regard to time and closure. For the martyr, his death finalizes his life and turns him into a martyr, whereas the detainee is still alive. The detainee has sacrificed his freedom but not his life, and his is thus not an ultimate sacrifice. These aspects render the martyr an unambiguous figure, whereas the detainee remains ambiguous in his captivity, where he according to Nashif is a liminal figure (Nashif 2008: 96). The ambiguity of the detainee in contrast to the martyr also rests on the uncertainty concerning what is thought to take place during captivity in an Israeli prison. This elusiveness allows people through the production of rumor to worry or guess whether the detainee has surrendered to Israeli pressure and has provided the prison managers with information, thereby potentially stooping to national treachery. As Das writes, the power of rumor lies in the way in which experiences can come to live through the act of telling (Das 2007: 208). Through rumor, the heroism of the detainee may be doubted.

These potential allegations notwithstanding, for many Palestinians, the martyr and the detainee epitomize the heroism of the agents in the national struggle for a Palestinian state in a double sense; not only are they praised in popular national discourse for having been willing to pay the ultimate price for a greater common good (Allen 2006; Nashif 2008; Khalili 2007). In the local and international discourse of conflict intervention, too, the martyrs and detainees are portrayed as the primary victims, because of the possible consequences of death, physical, and mental torment after prison or a failed, but wounding, operation against the Israeli occupation (Salo et al. 2004).

The so-called secondary victims, then, are the mothers, the children, and the wives of these perceived heroic men (Lau 2003; Sideris 2001). In order to fully grasp the meaning of being a secondary victim, I have done fieldwork among women married to detainees, widows of martyrs as well as among local and international NGOs offering services to these families. An underlying concern throughout the chapter is the notion of secondary victimhood as a lens through which to envisage suffering, and to investigate the absence in language or imagery it produces (Fassin 2008). As I put forward in this chapter, it is in the texture of these absences that the social capital of suffering and either primary or secondary recognition reside, defining in pervasive ways what counts as victimization.

Focusing on wives of detainees or widows of martyrs, this chapter highlights how different registers of absence have appeared, and have turned into significant vehicles of understanding gendered social being in the occupied territories. The absence of these women's husbands has proven important, because there is a tension between the absence experienced by wives of detainees and widows of martyrs respectively. Through these empirical voids, absence has thus emerged as an analytical prism, through which one can view the women's lives and their situation as gendered beings and the way they live and are looked upon, both locally and internationally. Analysing the intertwining of intangible loss and the texture of absence in Palestinian women's lives, I argue that the presence or absence of a husband is a significant marker of the women's presence in a social world.

This raises questions about why a situation in which *loss* defines a woman's social presence and existence, as in the case of the martyrs' widows, is different from a situation in which *absence* defines a woman's social presence and existence, as in the case of the detainees' wives. And, following from this, what is it about the materiality of loss that makes it legitimate to acknowledge some experiences as a loss, and others as mere absence? I suggest that we can only understand the difference between the respective ways in which martyrs' widows and detainees' wives are perceived through an optic that investigates the meaning of loss and sacrifice in a local and international context on the one hand, and by attending to the structural relationship between men and women in the occupied territories on the other.

At first glance, the obvious way of understanding what is at stake would be to consider analytically the classic anthropological concept of liminality (Turner 1967,

1974, 1986) in relation to loss and transformation of social status as experienced by the Palestinian women. But the question is what liminality means in a situation when the supposedly liminal transcends the temporally transitional and becomes permanent? Attempting to contribute to anthropological analysis of precisely these matters, I hope to use this chapter to move through but beyond liminality in the search for a viable mode of understanding the meaning of loss and absence in relation to gendered presence in the social world of the occupied territories.

Presenting the Loss of Palestine

Among historians and social scientists alike, Palestine seems to serve as crystallization of a place, in which the past is not past but present (Abu-Lughod and Sa'adi 2007). Every personal and collective story that is told about loss, violence, or death in present time is always already inscribed within the larger story of the Palestinians as a people defined by their losses, loss of a homeland, loss of family members, and loss of human dignity. The meta-narrative of all these stories is the 1948 event of "Al Nakba," which literally means the catastrophe. According to Israeli historian Ilan Pappé, more than 700.000 Palestinians were uprooted in the establishment of the Israeli state (Pappé 2006: xiii). This story is one that has affected generations of Palestinians in that the event turned them into the exceptional category of "Palestine Refugees" (Rubenberg 2003: 13), a term that determines first, second, and third generations of Palestinians' access to land, kin, and status as citizens in contemporary Israel and the occupied territories.

Rather than providing a currency of the drawn-out or even futile peace process, suffice it to say that loss, bereavement, coping, and making sense where there seems to be none, are not extraordinary events but part of everyday life and discourse (Das 2007). Events of sudden death, disappearance, and violence are found in all families. Households without a martyr or a detainee are few and far between. As such, images of widows and mothers mourning the loss of their sons or husbands in the struggle for a Palestinian state are highly present in local and international media (Allen 2009).

The public display of mourning is paralleled privately by the families and widows of martyrs. During my fieldwork, they too spoke willingly and extensively about the martyr. Often, the narrative about a martyr is a well-rehearsed story about the martyr's deeds, the detailed, visceral circumstances of his death (Allen 2009), and the emotionally straining loss of a father or a husband. In the majority of the life stories of widows and mothers of martyrs, the loss was framed as a narrative of meaningful loss, despite affective cracks in the stories, where religious and, in particular, national meaning did not really make up for the personal loss. This is somewhat contrary to what such a loss is supposed and assumed to do in Palestinian, national imagery and public discourse, and among international observers claiming to "know" Palestinian human losses to be incommensurable with loss of a life in Western cultural spheres, because of the alleged meaningfulness rendered to martyrdom in both religion and Palestinian nationalism (for discussion of this see Allen 2006).

In both national and international imaginaries of Palestinian suffering and in private conceptualizations of bereavement, some images of suffering and loss are more materially present than others. For example, there is a strong public awareness in Palestine of the 8,500 detainees (Btselem 2008) who are currently detained in Israeli prisons for the participation in political activities forming part of the resistance against the occupation (Jean-Klein 2003; Nashif 2008). And images of "a Palestinian mother" who mourns and suffers the loss of her sons to either death or imprisonment circulate and are recognized in formal as well as informal social fora. Significantly, the wives of the aforementioned political detainees are present only through the contours of their absence in this elaborate discourse. Through the following examples, I will describe what modes of affliction that define presence and absence in the occupied territories and how these are interwoven with notions of value, loss, and gendered being.

Lives in Limbo

Throughout my interviews, there is a void in explanations as to the qualitative difference between being the wife of a detainee and the widow of a martyr. This void in the data is not due to lack of questions about it on my part, but it can be explained by something apparently intrinsic to the situation of living with an absent husband while not having suffered an absolute loss. The wives of the detainees, I suggest, live with an absence that defies both verbalization and graphic materialization. The absolute loss experienced by a martyr's widow, on the other hand, marks a stark contrast to the elusive nature of absence that the wives of the detainees live with. The story of Samiah shows the difference between the two.

In the home of Samiah, a wife of a martyr, the relative splendor of the living room shows a stark contrast to the rest of the worn-down, sparsely inhabited concrete house. Samiah's damp, dark living room has as its main attraction two centerpieces standing on two pedestals. In one of the centerpieces figures a pair of men's spectacles together with a photograph of Samiah's deceased husband. In the other is his plastic digital watch. The clock is still running. *"I cannot bring myself to stop it, so it still has its alarm set for 8 o'clock in the morning. In that sense my husband lives on with me, may God be with him. I know, every morning that the clock will set off. You see, he is still part of my day,"* Samiah said.

The way in which Amina, whom we met in the beginning of the chapter, and Samiah's martyred husbands stay with them through artifacts as part of the women's lives, alludes to the ability of rendering materiality and presence to their losses and to the memory of the deceased martyr after his death.

The described objects serve as personal metaphors for the absentee. It is, however, not only through such manifest objects that the women's husbands stay with their families. In these particular families' interpretation of Islam, an interpretation that by other Palestinians is considered to be traditional and to a certain extent extremist, the martyr is believed not to leave his body; in a sense his bodiliness stays with him. Amina's mother-in-law explained this to me: "*A martyr is not a dead in the way we normally think of death. His spirit stays alive, and as Muslims we believe that he has a guarantee to enter paradise and that no one else has that guarantee. And, you know, the martyr's body stays warm and fresh; it does not decay or smell bad. That's why when I first encountered the sweet scent of a martyr, I prayed to God that one day my son will smell like the martyr.*" The sense in which the martyr's absence gives way to his eternal presence in the lives of his close kin figures clearly in Amina's mother-in-law's account of the martyrdom of her son.

Pointing to a possible difference between affinal and consanguine kin, the martyrs' widows spoke differently from Amina's mother-in-law. At the same time, as the martyr's presence is secured among his bereaved family through objects, imaginaries and sensual perceptions, the widows all underlined that their life with him was a closed chapter. His absence in the widow's life, even though his absence was what ensured his eternal presence, was certain and unambiguous. This is what renders a martyr's widow an honorable social presence (cf. Allen 2006 for discussion of this). A martyr's relatives know where he is, that he is dead, that they lost him, and this sense of closure allows them to mourn for him. The widows I spoke with all tried in different ways to move on, start their own life, finish their education and get a job. Apart, that is, from Amina whose second husband is still detained.

Amina only spoke about her husband in prison when probed by one of my direct questions. Showing more than a family resemblance to other interviews with detainees' wives, I would argue that this is because, as opposed to the widows, who could narrate a well-rehearsed story complying with popular templates of recounting sacrifice, Amina has no story to tell. The story of her imprisoned husband is not closed. It is a story without an ending; and thus a story that cannot legitimize proper mourning, a claim to suffering or a spectacular materialization of her loss. However, intertwined with a deeply embodied national discourse of loss and mourning, to Amina herself, lack of talk about her second husband, also had to do with her feelings toward him. Whereas her first husband became someone she loved very much, in her own words her second husband was "*nice, polite and a good father for the children.*" But it was never him she thought or dreamt about. But to talk about life as a wife of a detainee is to talk about a void: about places, times, and situations that were somehow not quite right because something was and continued to be missing.

Another person I talked to was Naima, a female employee of the council of the village of Dar Noura. I had talked to Naima about the occupation: "*People in Dar Noura were responsible for a lot of important stages of the Palestinian revolution. Important operations were done by people from here. Even though it was not good for the families, people from all over Palestine respect us because of it.*" Naima's comment was said with pride in having participated in the struggle against the occupation. However, at the same time Naima conveyed how the heroic deeds had not only affected the families of the men in a positive way. Her quote speaks of the complexity of knowing the limits of efficacy of national discourse in intimate spheres. Naima knows this not only from being a council employee. Her husband planned one of the operations she describes. As a consequence, he is imprisoned for lifetime, plus 70 years.

I participated in a three months' group therapeutic project for five detainees' wives in Dar Noura. The therapeutic project was initiated by an internationally funded NGO in Ramallah offering rehabilitation of torture victims. Alluding to the meaning of torture in local vernacular again, the centre's focus was the political detainees, and their families, the secondary victims of the men's captivity. When participating in the therapeutic sessions, the women in the group would talk at length about the way in which their neighbors and families were keeping their whereabouts under close surveillance, "*as if we are under a microscope*" as one woman put it. The aim of the therapists facilitating the group was to promote strength and empowerment, specifically in terms of telling the women to stay good but not to care too much about the comments and the gossip about them behind their backs. A formulated goal of this therapeutic group was the creation of a network of support among the women. In the beginning of the therapeutic project, the main therapist probed the women to speak about their feelings in relation to their husbands in captivity, their families, and "the village." This invitation was largely ignored, because of the potent forces of network and social relations. This points to a poignant difference between the actual significance of the social relations that make up the women's lives, and how these are imagined within a broadly defined Bion-inspired notion of group therapy which was the model employed in this instance. Within this idea of group therapy, it is the objective that the social relations of the groups' participants throughout the duration of the group make up a social forum in its own right; a forum where the participants can momentarily suspend their habitual social ties (cf. Bion 1996). For a number of reasons, this did not happen in the described therapeutic group project.

Because the village in question originates back mainly to one prominent family of the West Bank, the women in the group were related to each other either as consanguine or affinal kin. In the beginning of the therapeutic process, one of the women in the group, Layla, broke the news of her daughter's engagement. Layla is 39 years old and has four daughters. Due to her husband's key role in the aforementioned "operation", the Israeli authorities have demolished her house. Her husband has been sentenced to prison for 19 years, and he figures at the centre of one of many posters of the heroes of the second Intifada. Speaking about her daughter's engagement made Layla proud, yet also a bit sad. For one thing, Layla regrets the loneliness she will feel without her daughter in the house. But more importantly, perhaps, she was sad that her husband was not part of discussing the engagement, the suitability of the groom, the party, or any of the elements of a marriage that are thought to be the bride's father's responsibility. The other women in the group showed their understanding, saying that Layla had to do it anyway and should not worry about the gossip, telling her that she is still living even though her husband is in prison. Layla invited all of them to come to the wedding, as a wedding is considered a happy occasion for all villagers. The women, however, were all vague in their replies as to whether they were going to turn up on the night, and merely responded to Layla's invitation with an evasive *in shallah*, God willing.

On the actual wedding night, Layla looked stunning, wearing discrete make up and the exact same nice, subtle, and respectable clothes as her younger sister, with whom she shares the practical and moral responsibility of her household. Layla handled the role of the hostess for the women's party well, yet her usual air of quiet sadness lingered with her even on this night. After a while of dancing, she came over and chatted. Asking her if she was happy, she looked away and said, "*there is something missing*," alluding to her husband. Layla's husband though, was not the only one missing. None of the members of the therapeutic group project, who were also Layla's near and distant kin relations were there. The only ones from the group were the two psychologists and myself. When I later asked Layla where the other women from the therapy group had been, she said she did not know. The following days, I posed the same question to the women of the group, and each of them excused herself. The women's absence from Layla's daughter's wedding illustrated the practical voids in the otherwise strong discourses of support and network in the village.

Although Layla is the most "simple" among the women in terms of economy and education, she is well liked and holds a good reputation, partly due to her husband's perceived heroic deeds. According to the discourse of collective pride about the village's heroes promoted by the employee of the village council, a marriage within one of the most heroic and sacrificing families would have been an appropriate place to display support for Layla and her family. Before going deeper into the role of social networks in relation to absent husbands, another example will serve to nuance this.

The issue of public appearance and social presence was a returning topic of conversation among my informants internally and with me, when speaking about their lives after their respective husbands had been detained. People in the village, as well as the women's close and distant relatives kept an eye on them. As my informant Mervat said during an interview with her and Muna "*It is as if when her husband is in prison a woman has to kill herself and she must put herself in the prison too. And at the same time, my husband is saying if I tell him how I feel, about my sadness, why are you crying, you must be proud of me, that I am in prison.*" Mervat added that her husband was always calling the house from the prison to see if she was home or out of the house. If she was out he would say, "where are you", "where have you been", "why are you going out", "who are you with", and "what are you wearing". No matter whom she was with or where she went, there would always be someone who claimed to have seen her in the company of someone not proper, wearing something inappropriate. "*After my husband was detained, I stopped being a woman, now I am just a mother,*" she would say.

A few days after the conversation with Muna and Mervat, I called in on Mervat to see if I could stop by for a chat with her one morning. She welcomed me and when I turned up with my assistant Rawan, Mervat looked different. Usually when she was at home, she wore an old, casual track suit. On that day, she wore her gold jewelry and a transparent blouse with a low neck line. In fact, a neck line so low that it visibly displayed a lacy, red bra beneath her clothes. During our chat, she would shift between covering herself up and letting us glimpse her lingerie until her oldest daughter demonstratively entered the living room with a safety pin, which Mervat awkwardly used to collect her clothes and cover herself up with.

Clearly referring to our discussion about womanhood and feminine identity the week before, Mervat's materialization of her female identity was, importantly, for Rawan and my eyes only. Any sign of femininity, sensuality or the like was confined to the domestic sphere and could be displayed only for a close circle of female friends like Muna. This applied to all the women I knew. The first time I visited, the women were dressed up, but after the first visit they did not bother changing their clothes, since I stopped being a guest. If one of the women at a group meeting wore mascara, the others would comment. Some cheered and others exchanged glances. The disputed issue of wearing make-up even in women's closed fora elucidates how in this particular instance, a local discourse of social control, appropriate, and modest behaviour for women, and particularly women without their men, is not an abstract discourse but a lived orientation in the world, directed toward others and self (cf. Abu-Lughod 1986; 1993). It seems that social surveillance, even for someone who feels the effect of constant surveillance, forms a blind spot; a naturalization that comes with the stowaway to social structure.

Relating Mervat's display of her femininity to the event of Layla's daughter's wedding, I propose that to the detainees' wives, a wedding means something entirely different from the joyful event it is supposed to be. A wedding is normally the only event where women are allowed to let their hair down and wear festive, even sensual clothes and make up, and display femininity and womanhood in public. To the detainees' wives in Dar Noura, however, the wedding represented yet another occasion for villagers and neighbours to scrutinize the women's appearance. As such, the absence of the women's detained husbands, which is not considered to change anything because it is not recognized as a loss, proved instead to have caused a total transformation of self perception, life-world and gendered identity and of the women's social presence. The wives of the detainees seem to have become ambiguous figures, derivatively present through the absence of their husbands.

Ambiguity runs through the totality of the women's lives as illustrated in a conversation I had with Naima, the employee of the council over a Friday lunch in her house. I commented on her new short crop, in reply to which she said: "*I am so frustrated, I did not know what to do, so after my visit to Hatim's* [her husband] *lawyer I cut my hair short – Hatim can't see me anyway, so it does not matter what I look like or how I appear.*"

Speaking with her about her frustration she said "*It is not a loss, it is something else. It is living without my soul mate. We used to share everything but then I suddenly lost him, there is something missing in my life. No, it is not a loss, because loss is a negative thing, whereas missing someone is more romantic. And he does not want me to be lost. And I do not accept to have the feeling of loss in my life, because he has to be with me. Whenever there are important decisions around our new house, I postpone them until Hatim will be out of prison.*" Naima's frustration discloses the ambiguity of loss, absence, and not least the way in which temporality marks out the different spheres. Since Hatim is not dead, she has not lost him, yet her feelings of missing him are not merely romantic longing and desire. I suggest that we can think of her husband's absence, not only as a temporal suspension of his material presence in her life, but a suspension that does not make him as absent as a loss proper would. At a first glance, Victor Turner's (1967; 1974; 1986) term of liminality seems appropriate in emphasizing the temporal suspension of social being. However, as I will elaborate on below, the concept of liminality only goes some way in capturing the situation of the wives of detainees.

Ambiguous Absence

Moving away from the micro– and intimate level of gravely but invisibly distorted everyday lives of the detainees' families, I will discuss how to think more generally about absence, loss, and presence in the Palestinian context. For that purpose, I suggest we retrieve some of the introducing reflections of this book, aided by Runia's thoughts on presence (Runia 2006a; 2006b; 2007).

Runia argues that presence is not that which figures directly in a narrated story. Rather, presence can be conceived of as that which comes along as the stowaway (2006b: 1). Presence is difficult to access because of how it coincides with one of our blind spots – namely culture (ibid). This is significant here because apart from speaking about seemingly specific issues of loss and notions of suffering, victimhood and lives that get lost in the slipstream of these notions, the situations, the lives, and experiences I have described are not exceptions to the rule. Rather, these lives are molded not only by the violence of the Israeli–Palestinian conflict but through embedded structural relations between men and women.

By looking at these structural relations, it becomes clear that ideas of social presence are highly gendered. This was apparent in the situation of the wives of detainees against the backdrop of widows of martyrs. However, before the described women came to inhabit these categories, they were Palestinian women. And, in the occupied territories, women's presence, if not existence, is defined by the presence or absence of the men in their lives, depending on who at any point in time, is the primary, male relation to a woman. Understanding this social fact I draw on Suad Joseph's idea of "patriarchal connectivity" (Joseph 1999). Joseph suggests that the Western notion of self is ill at use in Middle Eastern countries because the ideal self in Arab societies is not a bounded unitary individual but rather a relational person, organized as patriarchal, with less than stable borders between self and other.

In the context of this paper's analysis of women related in different ways to heroic men, the patriarchal relationality can be inferred from the fact that the term used to designate these women was not "widow" but *zogat as-shahid* or *zogat al-azeer,* which means wife of martyr and wife of detainee, respectively. In the women's own speech, the issue of relationality figures in the way in which the women most often refer to themselves with the use of *wadi'* instead of *ana*, which refers to "my situation" (as married to detainee or martyr) instead of "I." However, patriarchal connectivity as a structuring principle pertains not only to the women in question, but equally to all women in Palestine.

The circumstances diverge between martyrs' widows and detainees' wives when it comes to the issue of the absence of a husband. When absence comes in the form of a permanent loss, it is different from when it is an allegedly temporary absence, with a duration equal to the prison sentence. This is partly because it is acknowledged that when a man dies, his family and his wife experience a loss. Consequently, because a widow to a martyr has derivatively sacrificed her own life through her husband's sacrifice of his life for a bigger cause, her loss is recognized. In this respect, religion plays a most salient part because of the meaningful frame of interpretation, justification, and legitimization of loss that their practice of Islam allows

(Allen 2006; Schulz 2003). Compared to the detainees' wives, to lose a husband in a way that complies with available religious parameters of meaning surrounding such a loss is, in fact, a gain. Of course, whether this applies on an emotional level varies from woman to woman, but socially losing a son, a father, or a husband to martyrdom is in official discourse considered to be honorable. It is a loss that has a designated place in culture and therefore makes sense, implying that the widow also inhabits such a place of recognition. This does not exempt the martyrs' widows from facing many of the same issues of public gossip, speculation, and surveillance, as do detainees' wives. But the acknowledgement of martyr's widows and their affliction, I suggest, has to do with the transformation in their social status that occurs when their husband dies, a transformation that through their close relation to the martyr places them nearer to the top in a hierarchy of people who have sacrificed their lives for the national struggle and for their faith.

Attempting to understand why such a hierarchization of suffering renders less recognition of the affliction of detainees' wives necessitates a return to temporality in relation to loss or absence. For the martyr's widows, their transformation in social status and the durability of their loss is permanent. The chapters of the widows' lives as wives are closed off and whatever remains of the husband/martyr's personal belongings and memorabilia ensures his eternal presence but, significantly, in a new chapter in their lives.

Detainees' wives, by contrast, live with an absence that is thought to be temporary, irrespective of the fact that it may last for the rest of the women's lives. Because of the hope that with a peace agreement with Israel, all the political detainees will be released, the issue of captivity remains within the realm of the temporary, no matter how many life sentences the detainees in question have been handed. Because of that, and due to the latent hope of a successful negotiation of "the detainees' question" with Israel, the absence of the detained husband is thought of as a pause, and therefore not as something that is perceived to cause the same permanent transformation as when a husband dies. We saw the ambiguity of this issue of losing versus missing in Naima's comments about the issue. Part of the ambiguity resides with the fact that a woman married to a detainee's social status is not supposed to change, or if it does, it does so allegedly to the better because of the honor of being married to a hero. Despite of this, nothing stays the same; the women's social status does change. From being treated as respectable housewives, the women become suspended between being married and yet dangerous and unrestrained because their husband is not there. This ambiguity or permanent limbo of their status brought about by their husbands' absence is what makes them slippery objects to handle for society, resulting in their being treated as if nothing and yet everything at the same time has changed regarding the women's presence in a social context. In contrast to such an ambiguous presence, a presence that is derived from the incarceration of their husbands, the widows to martyrs become something in their own right, namely widows, because of their loss and because of the absolute value of that very loss, namely a martyr who has sacrificed his life for Palestine.

The difference between the significance of a loss proper and a temporal absence is therefore due to the fact that absence of a detainee husband does not enter the realm of a loss proper, and thus the wives of these prisoners remain ambiguous. Whether a sentence reads 19 years in an Israeli prison or lifetime plus some, for the wife, her kin, neighbours, and villagers, this is not felt as an imprisonment with a definite end. This endlessness, however, rests on something else than the actual duration of the sentence: The indefinite absence and the way it defies categorization is entwined in cultural ideals pertaining to Palestinian women.

The situation of detainees' wives slips from the places of cultural recognition of sacrifice or loss, exactly because what they are living through is considered neither a loss nor a sacrifice. In the equation of the lives of the detainees' wives, the ones recognized as suffering the most are the detainees themselves. Significantly though, I noted earlier that the detainees themselves are also potentially ambiguous figures, even if perhaps not to the same degree as their wives. Ambiguity then can be said to unsettle the validity of a public, well-known discourse about relatives to detainees as subjects who gain in social status and honor derivatively through the acts of their relatives. In a sense, the double ambiguity of the wives of detainees is molded through how the wives' social presence is derived from the absence of their detainee husbands. The potential ambiguity, intrinsic to the figure of the detainee, seeps into this derivative presence of the detainee's wife.

Nonetheless, it is beyond doubt that the women, whether widows or married to detainees, are honored in their own perception and in the eyes of their social relations because of their men's activities. The concern of the chapter has been to point to some of the blind spots produced in the slipstream of such national discourses of honor, heroism, and derivative pride.

If we look beyond the intangible loss or material absence that detainees' wives live with indefinitely, we see that Palestinian culture is not the only place in which they do not have a presence. As stowaways to the Israeli–Palestinian conflict the detainees' wives are neither bereaved, nor have they lost, they are neither imprisoned, nor tortured or traumatized in the literal sense. However, these proxies are what the Western based or funded organizations set up as criteria for recognition of victimhood and suffering. Palestinian wives of detainees fail every single one of these proxies, and in that sense their presence in Palestinian society as well as in international psycho-social discourse is merely derivative, and in a hierarchy of sufferers they occupy a blind spot. For these women, derivative presence and secondary victimization merge and form lives at the margins of social visibility.

References

Abu-Lughod, Lila and Ahmad H. Sa'adi. 2007. *Nakba: Palestine, 1948, and the Claims of memory.* New York: Columbia University Press.

Abu-Lughod, Lila. 1986/2000. *Veiled Sentiments. Honor and Poetry in a Bedouin Society.* Berkeley: University of California Press.

Abu-Lughod, Lila. 1993/2008. *Writing Women's Worlds: Bedouin Stories.* Berkeley: University of California Press.

Allen, Lori. 2009. Martyr bodies in the media: Human rights, aesthetics, and the politics of immediation in the Palestinian intifada. *American Ethnologist* 36 (1): 161–180.

96   L. Buch

Allen, Lori. 2008. Getting by the Occupation: How Violence Became Normal during the Second Palestinian Intifada. *Cultural Anthropology* 23(3): 453–487.

Allen, Lori. 2006. The Polyvalent Politics of Martyr Commemorations in the Palestinian Intifada. *History and Memory* 18 (2):107–138.

Bion, Wilfred. 1996. *Experiences in Groups and other Papers*. London: Routledge.

Butler, Judith. 2004. Precarious Life: *The powers of mourning and violence*. New York: Verso.

Das, Veena. 2007. *Life and words. Violence and the descent into the ordinary*. Berkeley: University of California Press.

Farmer, Paul. 1997. On Suffering and Structural Violence: A View from Below. In *Social Suffering*, ed. Arthur Kleinmann, Veena Das, Margareth Lock, 261–283. Berkeley: University of California Press.

Farmer, Paul. 2003. *Pathologies of Power: Health, human rights, and the new war on the poor.* Berkeley: University of California Press.

Fassin, Didier. 2008. The humanitarian politics of testimony. Subjectification through trauma in the Israeli-Palestinian conflict. *Cultural Anthropology*. 23(3): 531–558.

Hein, Fadel A., Samir Qouta, Abdel A. M. Thabet, and Eyad El Sarraj. 1993. Trauma and mental health of children in Gaza [letter]. *British Medical Journal* (6885): 1130–1131.

Jean-Klein, Iris. 2003. Into Committees, out of the House? Familiar Forms in the Organization of Palestinian Committee Activism during the First Intifada. *American Ethnologist* 30 (4): 556–577.

Joseph, Suad. 1999. *Intimate selving in Arab families: gender, self, and identity*. Syracuse: Syracuse University Press.

Kanninen, Katri, Raija L. Punamäki, and Samir Qouta. 2002. The relation of appraisal, coping efforts, and acuteness of trauma to PTS symptoms among former political detainees. *Journal of Traumatic Stress* 3: 245–253.

Khalili, Laleh. 2007. *Heroes and Martyrs of Palestine: The Politics of National Commemoration*. Cambridge University Press.

Lau Ee Jia, Lisa. 2003. Equating Womanhood with Victimhood: The positionality of woman protagonists in the contemporary writings of South Asian women. *Women's Studies International Forum* 26: 4369–16.

Schulz, Helena Lindholm. 2003. *The Palestinian Diaspora*. New York: Routledge.

Nashif, Esmail. 2008. *Palestinian Political Detainees: Identity and community*. Abingdon, Oxdon: Routledge.

Pappé, Ilan. 2006. *The Ethnic Cleansing of Palestine*. Oxford: Oneworld.

Passia. 2008. Passia Diary 2008. *60 Years Palestine Nakba 1948*. Jerusalem: Palestinian Academic Society for the Study of International Affairs.

Peteet, Julie M. 1991. *Gender in crisis women and the Palestinian resistance movement*. New York: Columbia University Press.

Roy, Sara. 2007. *Failing Peace: Gaza and the Palestinian-Israeli Conflict*. London: Pluto Press.

Roy, Sara. 1995. (2001). *The Gaza Strip: The Political Economy of De-development*. Washington: Institute of Palestine Studies.

Rubenberg, Cheryl A. 2003. *The Palestinians. In search of a Just Peace*. London: Boulder.

Runia, Eelco. 2007. Burying the dead, creating the past', *History & Theory* 46: 313–325.

Runia, Eelco. 2006a. Spots of time. *History & Theory* 45 (October): 305–316.

Runia, Eelco. 2006b. Presence. *History & Theory* 45 (February): 1–29.

Salo, Jari A., Raija L. Punamäki, and Samir Qouta. 2004. Stress Associations between self and other representations and posttraumatic adjustment among political detainees. *Anxiety and Coping* 17 (4): 421–439.

Schryock, Andrew. 2004. The New Jordanian Hospitality: House, Host, and guest in the Culture of Public Display. *Comparative Studies in Society and History* 46(1): 35–62.

Sideris, Tina. 2001. Rape in War and Peace: Social Context, Gender, Power and Identity. In *The Aftermath. women in Post-Conflict Transformation*, eds. Sheila Meintjes, Anu Pillay and Meredeth Turshen. London: Zed Books.

Taylor, Charles. 2004. *Modern Social Imaginaries*. Duke: Duke University Press.

Turner, Victor. 1986. Dewey, Dilthey and Drama: An Essay in the Anthropology of Experience. In *The Anthropology of Experience*, eds. Victor Turner and Edward Bruner. Chicago; Chicago University Press.

Turner, Victor. 1974. *Dramas, Fields And Metaphors. Symbolic Action in Human Society*. Ithaca: Cornell University Press

Turner, Victor. 1967. *The forest of Symbols. Aspects of Ndembu ritual*. Ithaca: Cornell University Press.

Online Documents

Btselem. 2008 Detainees and Prisoners. Statistics on Palestinians in the custody of the Israeli security forces. Retrieved from: http://www.btselem.org/English/Statistics/Detainees_and_Detainees.asp

UNCHR. 1984. UN Convention against Torture and other Cruel, Inhuman or Degrading Treatment or Punishment. http://www.unhchr.ch/html/menu3/b/h_cat39.htm

Chapter 6
Materializations of Disaster: Recovering Lost Plots in a Tsunami-Affected Village in South India

Frida Hastrup

Introduction

The Asian tsunami that swept across coastal regions all around the Indian Ocean in December 2004 left innumerable affected communities at a loss. Thousands and thousands of people perished, many more were left homeless, personal and household belongings were washed away, and the afflicted populations' trust in their surroundings was seriously compromised. The South Indian village of Tharangambadi on the coast of Tamil Nadu was one of the places badly hit by the disaster (see F. Hastrup 2008, 2009). Out of the village's total population of about 7,000, the tsunami killed 314 persons, the clear majority of whom belonged to the 1,200 fishing households settled along the beach lining the Bay of Bengal.

In this chapter, I focus on the recovery process as undertaken by survivors in Tharangambadi in the wake of the tsunami. Anthropologists have recently noted that even seemingly disempowering experiences of disorder and fragmentation do not lead to passivity; in many societies, crises may simply constitute a context for subjective agency (Vigh 2008: 10–11). In times of trouble, people often display a remarkable talent for living and a degree of resilience, which prompts a need to rethink dominant models of trauma, as Nancy Scheper-Hughes has observed (2008). The capacity to act and exercise resilience in the face of overwhelming events was certainly apparent in the case of Tharangambadi, and on the basis of 10 months of anthropological fieldwork among men and women of the village's fishing community, conducted in 2005, 2006 and 2008, I explore how the villagers have worked over time to make their local world inhabitable in the face of a brutal and disconcerting experience.

More specifically, in the following sections, I analyze the conspicuous connections that the villagers of Tharangambadi made between ways of relating to the material residues of the disaster and ways of recovering from it. My main argument is that an important element of the survivors' recovery work has been to engage with

F. Hastrup (✉)
University of Copenhagen, Copenhagen, Denmark
e-mail: frida.hastrup@anthro.ku.dk

M. Bille et al. (eds.), *An Anthropology of Absence: Materializations of Transcendence and Loss*,   99
DOI 10.1007/978-1-4419-5529-6_6, © Springer Science+Business Media, LLC 2010

a complex material register, in which objects that have disappeared, been destroyed, or that have yet to materialize play a central role. Attending to these objects, I suggest, serve more generally as a means for the villagers of presenting, processing and ultimately alleviating the strong sense of uncertainty brought about by the disaster. Even at the time of my most recent fieldwork, survivors would jump at the sound of shouting or hurried movements in the beach area, and they would often comment on any shifts in the sea or surf seen from their habitual settlement along the waterfront. The ongoing shifts in and discussions about people's housing arrangements in the wake of the tsunami also testified to a widespread sense of unsettlement shared by many survivors. Consequently, in both a figurative and literal sense, the disaster was seen as threatening to displace the villagers from their habitual paths and dwellings. Thus, fieldwork amply showed that the tsunami had not yet been assigned to the past; to many survivors, the tsunami was still an unclaimed experience, the character of which had yet to be determined. In the light of this, I suggest, engaging in various ways with missing, broken or unfinished artifacts and their ambiguous nature as both present and absent, served as common materializations of loss and seemed to function as a means for the survivors to reclaim their everyday life in the aftermath of the disaster. As I will show, the survivors' attending to the physical materializations of disaster was an element in an overarching recovery process.

As an experience continuing to feature in people's lives long after its occurrence, the tsunami was not seen by survivors simply as an event of the past but equally as a threat to a durable present and an anticipated future. The absences that I deal with here are therefore not just the concrete material losses suffered by the villagers on account of the tsunami, but additionally, the attendant absence of the ability to act in the present habitual social setting and to plan ahead for a time to come. In other words, long after the tsunami, the villagers of Tharangambadi were suspended in a matrix made of the presence of disaster and the absence of certainty.

Recovery and the Realm of the Ordinary

As Veena Das has observed with regard to the effects of collective violence in India, recovery after disruption is often not accomplished through grand ritual gestures, as much as through an everyday work of repair (Das 2007). Taking my cue from this insight, I locate the Tharangambadi fishing community's effort to recover not in formal acts of healing or in official commemorative displays, but in an ongoing practical process of letting the disaster descend little by little into the realm of the ordinary. Following Das, I am interested in the ways in which the disaster has attached itself to the lives of people engulfed in it. This perspective entails a focus not on the disaster as a singular event, but as an experience that has seeped into the survivors' lifeworld. As Das has noted, disruptions in social life do not merely consist in the dramatic events as such, but also in an ensuing sense among survivors that their access to a habitual context has been blocked or threatened (Das 2007: 1–12).

The lacking sense of accessibility to an everyday social context was apparent in Tharangambadi, as was the steady work to restore it. The sense of displacement was often pointed out to me; when I walked around the affected areas in the company of villagers, they would continuously point to ruined houses and tell me who had lived there, or which activities they associated with the damaged structures. "This was Vijay's house, and over there was Latha's home", my field assistant Renuga would say, before indicating the destroyed house, on the porch of which she had often waited when she went to fetch water as a young woman. "Before the tsunami there were two rows of houses here with narrow paths between them. We used to play here when I was a child. Now the houses are gone, and the families have moved", my friend Arivu said on a walk through the northern and most heavily damaged part of the village where he had volunteered to show me around.

Interestingly, the material register invoked to encompass the sense of disruption and displacement from habitual context was not only apparent in relation to objects that had been damaged, but applied equally to unharmed buildings and structures that for some reason or other were connected to the tsunami. Survivors thus continuously used material constructions as points of orientation and as objects central to their experience of the tsunami when moving around the areas of the village once flooded by the waves. As late as 2008, the villagers would point out rooftops, staircases and tall houses to where they had hastily fled when outrunning the tsunami waves. Several times when we were walking by, Renuga would say:

> "See that building over there. I ran and ran as fast as I could until I could climb onto the roof of it. So many people were already there when I came. I was saved by the St. Theresa's Teacher Training Institute."

In these cases and on countless other occasions during my fieldwork, the villagers thus connected material objects and buildings to the tsunami and made clear that for better or worse the disaster still constituted a point of orientation in their lives, forcing them to re-enact relations to their well-known settings; to be sure, the scars from the tsunami had become attached to life in the fishing community.

The local use of these material manifestations of the tsunami is perhaps not just a result of the sheer enormity of the disaster, which in itself could force it to the centre of the survivors' attention, but also because, as Daniel Miller has suggested, human perception per se tends to comprehend through particular forms. According to this line of thinking, as human beings we have no way of perceiving except through specific form, and our access to the world is therefore always objectified (Miller 2005). In the light of this observation, the tsunami cannot be perceived of except through its material manifestations; or to put it simply, once the waves have withdrawn, to the survivors, the tsunami *is* its consequences. The villagers of Tharangambadi simply lived a life in touch with the disaster through its physical traces appearing in people's daily lives, and by actively pointing to these, the villagers testified to the disaster's encroachment on their everyday actions and movements.

In this light, recovery is not a matter of sealing off the disaster in an absolute past, but of restoring the accessibility of a habitual social context. In other words, rather than striving for a sense of closure after the disaster, which is necessarily a retrospective attempt at cleaning up in all senses of the word, the survivors seemed more concerned with recovering their sense of agency exercised in the present with a view to future prospects. To this end, the ambiguous material manifestations of disaster such as missing, damaged or incomplete objects seemed to lend themselves more easily to the task of reclaiming life than did symbolic and retrospective enshrinements representing the tsunami as an event of the past. Thus, as I show, the inherent human capacity of objectification notwithstanding, not any material object was apparently allotted a part in the recovery process. This became apparent through the villagers' reception of the official commemorative monument constructed in Tharangambadi during my fieldwork.

A Monument to Mourning

In many fishing villages along the coast of Tamil Nadu, monuments constructed in remembrance of the victims of the tsunami began to appear during my fieldwork in 2006. In Tharangambadi, a memorial monument to honour the deceased from the fishing village was completed and inaugurated on the second anniversary of the disaster in December 2006. The memorial, funded by the local council of elders governing the fishing community, is situated on the Kamarajar Road, the main street connecting the fishermen's part of the village with the busy market street of Tharangambadi, and the monument thus occupies a central spot in the village near the main junction, which most people from the fishing community would pass several times in the course of an ordinary day. The memorial is made up of a large black marble column with the names of the persons from the fishing village, who died on the day of the disaster, inscribed in Tamil on the sides at the base of the pillar. Around the column is a small grassy and neatly kept garden with flowers and figures of birds, all of which are enclosed by a fence with a large gate.

Even though the monument was decided upon by the local village council of fishermen, judging from my observations, the individual local villagers largely ignored the memorial in the course of their everyday routines. The central geographical location of the memorial did apparently not imply that the monument occupied an equally prominent position in the minds of the members of the fishing community. All through the construction phase in the end of 2006, and again during my fieldwork in 2008, I never once saw a local inhabitant of the fishing village stop to look at the memorial or even talk about it in any significant way, except to specify that this shop or that house was located near the monument. Save for an occasional gardener tending the flowers, I never saw anyone inside the fence encircling the column. The memorial, it seemed, had simply become a site on the map and not a station in people's everyday movement; the villagers could of course see the monument, but apparently they saw no point in actively engaging with it (Fig. 6.1).

Thus, even if the marble memorial provides a stone proof narrative of the tragedy caused by the disaster and thus testifies to a hugely important event in the lives of many, to the villagers such chiselled testimony of the tsunami seemed – as of yet – to

Fig. 6.1 The memorial monument to the right of a newly laid road. Photo by the author

play little role as a shared material expression of the experience of loss. As intimated in the above and as I will elaborate on in the following, the villagers made ample use of material objects and structures when they conveyed how the disaster had left its mark on people's lives. Hence, it is not the material quality as such of the memorial monument that caused the villagers to largely disregard it. Rather, the concept of monuments suggested by Michael Rowlands and Christopher Tilley might give a clue as to why the villagers in Tharangambadi paid little heed to the memorial. As Rowlands and Tilley have observed:

> "A monument is an object taken out of history, by history. Yet it stands for history in terms of what it has left behind, as a mnemonic trace that also separates it from the present" (Rowlands and Tilley 2006: 500).

Following this observation, memorial monuments are necessarily separate from the present by their inherent attempt at converting an event into something that belongs strictly to the past. Thus, by its very construction and design, the memorial represents the disaster as a concluded event, the lethal effects of which have once and for all been calculated, listed and engraved in stone. As such, I suggest, it does not mirror the villagers' experiences of still living in various ways and to varying degrees with the presence of the tsunami. If a sense of closure is still wanting, the tsunami cannot be taken out of history and turned into a monument; consequently, for the time being, the marble column somehow misses the point. Paradoxically, the monument is out of touch with the disaster.

What is essentially at stake here is the temporality of the experience of bereavement. In an effort to define the concept of loss, Eng and Kazanjian (2003), drawing on Freud, point to the role of melancholia and contrast this with mourning by distinguishing between how the two concepts imply different stances to the past. Melancholia as opposed to mourning entails an open relation towards history:

> "While mourning abandons lost objects by laying their histories to rest, melancholia's continued and open relation to the past finally allows us to gain new perspectives on and new understandings of lost objects (...) In this sense, melancholia raises the question of what makes a world of new objects, places, and ideals possible" (Eng and Kazanjian 2003: 4).

Indeed, at the time of my fieldwork, the bereaved were still in the process of recovering the ability to envisage a world of new objects and ideals, a world without what had been lost. The survivors were still engaged in restoring the access to everyday life; the effects of the tsunami were a source of melancholia featuring on a daily basis and were not mourned as a past story with a fixed design.

Insofar as the memorial monument symbolically enshrines the tsunami by representing it as a past event, it simply seems to fall short of encompassing an existing experience of having been displaced from a present habitual context and of being in a process of gradually reclaiming it. As I will substantiate further in the following, in their effort to present the prevailing absence of certainty, the villagers employed wholly different and much more complex materializations of loss than a purely retrospective memorial monument.

The Materiality of Loss

Even at the time of my latest fieldwork in Tharangambadi in the spring of 2008, the destruction caused by the disaster was still highly visible for all to see. Worldwide, the tsunami spurred the largest ever humanitarian emergency and rehabilitation response (Telford et al. 2006). Tharangambadi, too, was propelled into this massive relief effort, but the many reconstruction projects implemented in the village by numerous NGOs and other humanitarian actors have so far not entailed a simultaneous process of removing what was destroyed. Importantly, the villagers themselves have also done little to erase the marks of the tsunami from their local environment. As a result, broken and useless fishing boats, parts of ruined and abandoned houses, heaps of bricks and rubble, flooring and tiles and other such physical traces of the flooding lay scattered all around.

During all of my fieldworks, the co-presence of destruction and reconstruction was conspicuous. In the northern beach area of the village, which was most severely hit by the flood waves, the simultaneous presence of contradictory features in the landscape was particularly pronounced. Here, deserted and partly wrecked houses overgrown with shrubs and left to further dilapidate are crisscrossed by newly laid, straight and even "Emergency Roads" made during 2007 by the Tamil Nadu government in response to the tsunami. One explicit purpose of the roads was to facilitate evacuation from the coastal areas in the event of new tsunami alerts or floods – a function that by 2008 struck me as somewhat ironic given the seemingly permanent desertion of the neighbourhood ensuing from the tsunami and from the ongoing re-housing practices also authorised by the state. The newly constructed roads simply appeared to me as dead-ends on all accounts; not only do they end abruptly near the waterfront on the edge of the village; they also lead through ruined areas where no one lives anymore. As my friend Arivu, who had walked around with me in the deserted area, aptly remarked at some point during my fieldwork in 2008: "Sure, the roads are nice and even, but perhaps they would have been of more use if they had been made when people were still living here."

The ill-timed road project notwithstanding, although the ruined areas were deserted they were clearly not irrelevant to the villagers. As already intimated, rather than being merely a consequence of a delayed or failed effort to clean up, closer inspection revealed that all the material remnants of the tsunami left more or less untouched were, in fact, significant to the survivors. In contrast to the villagers' inattention towards the official memorial described above and as already illustrated, time and again the people I engaged with would point to the physical destruction apparent both outside the village and inside people's homes in an effort, it seemed, to locate or pinpoint the otherwise overwhelming experience of disaster and the losses it had brought about in terms of both destruction and disconcertion. The various material residues of the tsunami appeared to serve as landmarks of orientation and were by their very ruined nature somehow expressive of the experience of dislocation, whether figurative or literal. What emerged was a particular and ambiguous materiality of loss.

Even when I posed quite general questions about how the tsunami had affected people's lives, the survivors would at some point in the conversation almost invariably produce an elaborate and detailed listing of which household items and personal belongings had been washed to the sea. During a visit to Jayalathi's house in the summer of 2006, when the family had long since returned to their original and reparable house in the heart of the fishermen's settlement, she pointed out a blurred line on her living room wall indicating the water level at the time of the flooding. As Jayalathi said, while standing next to the neck-high mark on the wall:

> "Do you see this mark? Tsunami time, this is where the water was. All the way up to here, everything in the house was flooded. We can still see the line. The cupboard with all our clothes was swept from one end of the room to the other. When we returned to the house, the cupboard was upside down in the far corner over there. It was very bad. All the dresses were ruined. Too much cleaning had to be done before we could return."

Interestingly, the cleaning effort that Jayalathi talked about had not implied washing off the line of dirt marking the level of water on the day of the disaster. She kept pointing to the line and shaking her head; clearly to Jayalathi, the tsunami had left its mark in more senses than one.

On several occasions, Renuga would show me a neatly folded silk garment now stained with blurred shades of blue, green and gold, merging with the yellow fabric. While carefully folding the ruined silk sari and putting it back in the trunk under the bed from where she had taken it, Renuga would say:

> "Look at this sari. The colours are all mixed because of the tsunami water. Before, I only had it dry-cleaned. I used to wear it at weddings and other functions. Now it is of no use."

In yet other private homes, people would show me water-damaged family photos and school certificates, ruined and partly dissolved Hindu images, rusty and inoperative electrical kitchen machines, and other such items that they had either been able to salvage when fleeing the waves or, more often, that had been found in the houses when the owners had returned after the water had receded.

All these objects – literally watermarked by the tsunami – were kept neatly folded, wrapped, covered up and filed on shelves or in cupboards even in the cases where they would never stand a chance of being restored, cleansed or put to use again. Surprisingly, whether in the temporary shelters, where the many homeless villagers would have to camp for years, or in the permanent houses, the owners produced the items from among other household objects that had either come through the disaster unscathed or that had been acquired after the tsunami. The damaged objects were thus not confined to any kind of shrine or special display for purposes of commemoration, nor were they being flaunted at the visitor for me to help the villagers replace them. Rather, the artifacts bearing the signature of the disaster were kept as integrated parts in a composite pool of domestic objects furnishing people's homes. Even during my latest fieldwork in 2008, it was apparently out of the question for the owners to just dispose of these ruined belongings in an attempt to exorcise the disaster from memory. What was lost in terms of functionality or aesthetics was seemingly conceptualized very much in terms of what still remained (cf. Eng and Kazanjian 2003; Hetherington 2004). To survivors, even if these objects had been rendered unusable for their original purpose, they had clearly acquired a different but apparently just as significant function. The very brokenness of the objects had transformed them into mundane mementoes of the disaster and seemed to be the reason the objects were valued.

At first, the meticulous listing of household items that had disappeared in the tsunami and the careful preservation of useless belongings struck me almost as inappropriate, not least because it contrasted starkly with the economical ways that people would talk about deceased relatives who were usually recalled only through laconic remarks, stating that a missing son would have been a good fisherman, or that a lost daughter studied well. In the face of such tragic bereavement, I was surprised that anyone bothered to even mention that a water vessel or some other replaceable household item had been washed away to the sea. A closer look at recent anthropological understandings of materiality, however, suggests that the prominence of the material losses is something other than a superficial and materialistic approach to human tragedy. What becomes clear is that the objects marked by the event of the tsunami formed an "ontological tool" of social remembrance and knowledge in everyday life (cf. Pedersen 2007).

Breaking with a long tradition within anthropology to see sociality and materiality as two distinct and opposing categories, the former of which constitutes the proper analytical object of the discipline, it has recently been suggested that the material world cannot be separated from the social world. According to this line of thought, rather than seeing materiality as a frosting on sociality, the two concepts ought to be kept in simultaneous view as equally integral to humans' engagement with the world. The point is that subjects and objects, concepts and things, meaning and its materialization cannot be clearly distinguished from one another but should be understood as mutually constitutive. In short, material culture is not merely the expressive mode of culture (for recent examples see Henare et al. 2007; Miller 2005; Olsen 2003).

In consequence, the significance allotted by the survivors in Tharangambadi to objects gone, damaged and replaced should not be taken to imply that material losses are the most hurtful. If, in fact, the material world is constitutive of any social world, engaging with the things affected by the tsunami might be just a way of conveying the pervasiveness and reality of the disaster rather than a symptom of a superficial approach to human tragedy. The absent and scarred objects were no longer of any practical use, but had become tokens by which past, present and future had become folded into one compound setting encompassing the experience of the tsunami.

For the argument at hand, what is important in the recent anthropological discussions of materiality is the revision of a merely representational view of material culture as the overt expression of underlying immaterial ideas, symbols or cultural structures (Miller 2005; Olsen 2003). Fieldwork made clear that to the villagers of Tharangambadi, the continued presence – indeed preservation – of the material traces of the tsunami all around the village, whether in the guise of lost property, damaged belongings, lines of mud, ruined clothes, or buildings that provided a safe haven on the day of the flooding, did not serve as representations of the disaster pointing backwards in time to an overcome past. To the contrary, the various traces of the disaster were elements in a general framing of everyday life in the wake of the tsunami; they encompassed a living history rather than a fixed legacy such as that chiselled into the black marble of the memorial. When the villagers showed me a blurred wedding photo damaged by water, it was definitely expressive of something more than the wedding as a past important occasion, just as a partly dissolved school diploma was illustrative of more than an educational accomplishment. As David Parkin has observed:

> "While art, artefacts, and ritual objects are conventionally located in predictable contexts of use, items taken under pressure and in crisis set up contexts less of use and more of selective remembering, forgetting and envisioning" (Parkin 1999: 304).

Accordingly, as parts constitutive of an unpredicted world, the items partly surrendered to the pressure of the tsunami or the structures that had saved the fleeing villagers served a purpose of pointing both back in time and ahead, and showed how the disaster had attached itself to everyday life. For my present analytical purpose, what is most important in Parkin's observation is perhaps that objects in times of crisis may become part of a changed context of envisioning. As I will further substantiate in the following, in the case of the tsunami survivors in Tharangambadi the issue of being able to envision a future and thus counter the newfound absence of certainty, emerging as a threat of comprehensive displacement from one's life course, was a vital element in the recovery process.

Interrupted Trajectories

In the course of my talks with the villagers, I repeatedly came across expressions of a sense that future planning had been impaired by the tsunami. In addition to washing away people's belongings, in the eyes of many survivors the waves had also flooded and sucked away the ability to make plans for a time to come. One fieldwork observation made this particularly clear. Towards the end of my stay in the village in 2006, I went with Renuga for a walk around the northern and severely damaged part of the village. At some point, we got to a rather large house, which had been under construction at the time of the disaster and which the owners had abandoned and chosen never to complete. Renuga froze at the sight. "Look at this", she said, "someone had carefully planned for this house. They saved up money, designed the rooms and everything, and then it was of no use". Amidst ruins, heaps of rubble and broken fishing equipment, the sight of an unfinished, but unharmed, building was apparently what most dramatically materialized the experience of having been robbed of the capacity to make plans for the future.

Furthermore, looking closer at the ways in which the bereaved parents usually talked about their deceased children, it struck me that although the children, as mentioned above, were often quite perfunctorily characterized, they were almost invariably presented by qualities that somehow pointed to their future lives that had sadly been cut short by the tsunami. The parents thus focussed on what the children could have become, for instance a capable fisherman, an educated bread-winner, and a caring adult for elderly parents and so on, and lamented the fact that these potentialities would never be actualized because of the untimely deaths of the children. By verbalizing memories of their children in terms of broken or at least interrupted life trajectories, the parents grieved for a confused present and a lost future as much as for a past tragedy to be looked back on. To go back to Eng and Kazanjian's distinction between different stances towards the past quoted above, in these cases, too, a sense of melancholia rather than mourning prevailed. While the remarks about lost children and destroyed things respectively differed very much in level of elaboration, both of these idioms maintained the disaster as a presence in the everyday lives of the survivors – as an unhealed event spurring a pervasive melancholia due to broken future promises.

Anthropological studies of disaster often focus on the affected communities' level of adaptability when faced with calamity. This is obviously crucial to understanding disasters because it points to the fact that existing patterns of social, economic and environmental vulnerability influence people's chances of recovery, or indeed of survival, and it emphasizes the need to see disasters as processual phenomena rather than singular events (Hilhorst and Bankoff 2007; Hoffman and Oliver-Smith 1999; Oliver-Smith 1999; Oliver-Smith and Hoffman 2002). Nonetheless, the notion of adaptability as the greater or lesser capacity to cope with disaster seems to me to imply a somewhat crude notion of a reaction as the mere outcome of a simple one-to-one relation between an occurrence and the ensuing activities. In the case of Tharangambadi, it became clear to me that we need an idea of reaction to disaster that is not exclusively retrospective. In fact, it can be said of all human agency that it necessarily entails a view to the future. As Kirsten Hastrup has observed:

"Action is never simply a *re*action to what has already happened; it is also a mode of acting upon anticipation. Agency, in this sense (…) is closely tied to a vision of plot, to the antici- pation of a story, a line of future development" (K. Hastrup 2007: 199).

Following this, living with the presence of disaster in everyday life and striving to recover the access to a habitual social context necessarily implies the restoring of a vision of plot. In that sense, as Sandra Wallman has observed, the future is always in some sense contemporary, in that present actions are undertaken with a view to realizing an expected course of events (Wallman 1992).

My observations during my fieldwork from the newly established construction site where the majority of the displaced fishing families have been offered re- housing substantiate the view that future plans are an inherent feature of human agency. As I will show in the concluding part of the chapter, yet other material manifestations pertaining to the newly built houses performed a central part in restoring a sense of plot in the wake of the tsunami.

Conclusion: On New Plots

By 2008, many of the new houses built to accommodate the affected families had been completed and handed over to their owners. This meant that at the time of my most recent stay in Tharangambadi in 2008, most of the temporary shelters where many displaced villagers had camped for several years had been vacated. Interestingly, contrary to people's old homes in the abandoned fishing village, the deserted barracks were not just left to wither away through the wear and tear of time. Usually within days of being vacated, the shelters would be dismantled, often by the former inhabitants themselves who would gather the building materials and bring them to their new houses in the tsunami village, which was the common col- loquial name for the site where the fishing families were offered resettlement. Outside many of the houses in the new village, the house owners had thus piled up the bricks that had made up the flooring in the temporary shelters and collected the bamboo sticks that had held the roofs of the barracks and other such building materials. Quite literally, then, the villagers planned to incorporate the effects of the tsunami into their future lives. When I inquired about these stocks of building materials, the stated aim of this informal recycling practice was to enable the villagers to make future extensions to the donated houses. Invariably, the new house owners emphasized the possibility of adding future expansions to the houses as vital, and they praised the houses as much for what they might become as for what they were to begin with. As Tim Ingold has observed, to dwell somewhere is to actively engage with the world, whereby it attains significance (Ingold 2000: 153). As the resettled villagers in Tharangambadi amply demonstrated, it takes a practical effort to transform a building into a dwelling. The plans for extensions should not merely be seen as a matter of square metres. Rather, what seemed to be at stake for the survivors was an effort of appropriation, whereby the incomplete nature of the houses was seen as a token of an opportunity to regain a sense of agency; the attention directed at the features of the houses that had yet to materialize illustrated the effort of restoring an accessible social context and an ability to make plans for the future (Fig. 6.2).

Certainly, as the chapter has shown, the recovery of a life based both literally and metaphorically on a new foundation takes some time, and an experience as overwhelming as the tsunami is only gradually folded in to the everyday lives of the survivors. If the tsunami was at first an unclaimed experience spurring a comprehensive sense of displacement reaching way into the future, the gradual appropriation of the new houses seems to be a very literal illustration of the villagers' overarching effort to reclaim plots – in every sense of the word.

Instructed by my fieldwork in the Tharangambadi fishing community, I propose in conclusion that to the survivors the recovery work has been aimed not so much

Fig. 6.2 Extensions and building materials in the new tsunami village. Photo by the author

at overcoming a dramatic event of the past as at restoring a present room to manoeuvre within a recognisable horizon of expectation. As I have demonstrated, among other things by way of the remarks from parents about what deceased children could have become, by the distress spurred by the fact that people have had to give up planned-for houses in the original fishing village, and by the widespread practice of appropriating the newly built houses, what has been at stake for the villagers in post-tsunami Tharangambadi has been to recover their future trajectories, which were brutally intersected by the disaster. To this end, the survivors' acute attention towards destroyed, missing or incomplete objects seems to have been a key component. The practice among the survivors of leaving rubble scattered around the village, of carefully listing missing and replaced household items, of pointing out and preserving damaged belongings, lamenting the physical destruction of projected building plans, and of emphasizing the incompleteness of buildings was ubiquitous exactly because it testified to the *process* of dealing with the presence of disaster in the everyday life and of countering the perceived interruption of plots for the future. Whatever their guise, the villagers in Tharangambadi used these ambiguous manifestations of disaster as a practical means of engaging with the presence of disaster and the attendant absence of certainty in the wake of the monumental event of the tsunami.

References

Das, V. 2007. *Life and Words: Violence and the Descent into the Ordinary*. Berkeley: University of California Press.

Eng, D.L. and D. Kazanjian, 2003. 'Introduction: Mourning Remains'. In *Loss*, eds. D.L. Eng and D. Kazanjian, 1–25. Berkeley: University of California Press.

Hastrup, F. 2008. 'Natures of change: weathering the World in post-tsunami Tamil Nadu'. *Nature and Culture* 3(2), 135–150.

Hastrup, F. 2009. *Weathering the World: Recovery in the Wake of the Tsunami in a Tamil Fishing Village*. PhD Thesis, University of Copenhagen, Submitted in January 2009.

Hastrup, K. 2007. 'Performing the World: Agency, anticipation and creativity'. In *Creativity and Cultural Improvisation*, eds. E. Hallam and T. Ingold, 193–206. Oxford: Berg.

Henare, A., M. Holbraad and S. Wastell. 2007. 'Introduction: Thinking through things'. In *Thinking Through Things: Theorising Artifact Ethnographically*, eds. A. Henare, M. Holbraad and S. Wastell, 1–31. London: Routledge.

Hetherington, K. 2004. 'Secondhandedness: Consumption, disposal, and absent presence'. *Environment and Planning D: Society and Space* 22(1), 157–173.

Hilhorst, D. and G. Bankoff. 2007. 'Introduction: Mapping vulnerability'. In *Mapping Vulnerability: Disasters, Development and People*, eds. G. Bankoff, G. Frerks and D. Hilhorst, 1–9. London: Earthscan.

Hoffman, S.M. and A. Oliver-Smith. 1999. 'Anthropology and the angry earth: An overview'. In *The Angry Earth: Disaster in Anthropological Perspective*, eds. A. Oliver-Smith and S.M. Hoffman, 1–16. London: Routledge.

Ingold, T. 2000. *The Perception of the Environment: Essays in livelihood, dwelling and skill*, London: Routledge.

Miller, D. 2005. 'Materiality: An introduction'. In *Materiality*, ed. D. Miller, 1–50. Durham: Duke University Press.

Oliver-Smith, A. 1999. 'What is a Disaster? Anthropological perspectives on a persistent question'. In *The Angry Earth: Disaster in Anthropological Perspective*, eds. A. Oliver-Smith and S.M. Hoffman, 18–34. London: Routledge.

Oliver-Smith, A. and S.M. Hoffman 2002. 'Introduction: Why anthropologists should study disasters'. In *Catastrophe and Culture: The Anthropology of Disaster*, eds. S.M. Hoffman and A. Oliver-Smith, 3–22. Oxford: James Currey, School of American Research Advanced Seminar Series.

Olsen, B. 2003. 'Material culture after text: Re-membering things'. *Norwegian Archaeological Review* 36(2), 87–104.

Parkin, D. 1999. 'Mementoes as transitional objects in human displacement'. *Journal of Material Culture*, 4(3), 303–320.

Pedersen, M.A. 2007. 'Talismans of thought: Shamanist ontologies and extended cognition in Northern Mongolia'. In *Thinking Through Things: Theorising Artifact Ethnographically*, eds. A. Henare, M. Holbraad and S. Wastell, 172–204. London: Routledge.

Rowlands, M. and C. Tilley. 2006. 'Monuments and memorials'. In *Handbook of Material Culture*, eds. Tilley, C., W. Keane, S. Küchler, M. Rowlands, and P. Spyer, 500–515. London: Sage Publications.

Scheper-Hughes, N. 2008. 'A Talent for life: Reflections on human vulnerability and resilience'. *Ethnos* 73(1), 25–56.

Telford, J., J. Cosgrave and R. Houghton. 2006. *Joint Evaluation of the International Response to the Indian Ocean Tsunami: Synthesis Report*. London: Tsunami Evaluation Coalition.

Vigh, H. 2008. 'Crisis and chronicity: Anthropological perspectives on continuous conflict and decline' *Ethnos* 73(1), 5–24.

Wallman, S. 1992. 'Introduction: Contemporary futures'. In *Contemporary Futures: Perspectives from Social Anthropology*, ed. S. Wallman, 1–20. London: Routledge.

Part IV
Materializing Remembrance

Chapter 7
A Saturated Void: Anticipating and Preparing Presence in Contemporary Danish Cemetery Culture

Tim Flohr Sørensen

Introduction

It may appear rather straightforward to connect cemeteries with the notion of absence. After all, a cemetery is most often seen as a place for the dead, who are frequently conceived as absent, gone, missing or lost (e.g. DuBose 1997; Durkheim 1915: 339; Freud 1984 [1917]; Rubin 1985). The state of being – or non-being – of the dead is otherwise poorly defined, and may simply be considered a form of "no-moreness" (Sheets-Johnstone 1986: 50). At the same time, the cemetery can be said to contain the absent, because it is ordinarily a place where prolonged spatial and material relations to the deceased are allowed to exist as opposed to e.g. a mass grave, where the dead are meant to disappear (Rugg 2000: 260).

In recent years, a number of scholars have emphasized how relations persist between the bereaved and the deceased, despite the rupture posed by death (e.g. Bennett and Bennett 2000; Hallam et al. 1999; Howarth 2000, 2007a, b; Kellehear 2002; Klass et al. 1996; Miller and Parrott 2007). This perspective sheds light on the continuing bonds between the living and the dead that evolve through grief practices and commemoration, and contrasts views on grief that argue that the bereaved should "move on" in order to free themselves from the dead (e.g. Freud 1984 [1917]).

This chapter explores how the continued bonds between the bereaved and the deceased are articulated through the material practices unfolding in the context of contemporary Danish cemeteries. By emphasizing that relationships between the living and the dead are forged through material practices – as well as through mental processing – I offer a view of cemeteries as places of highly complex incorporations of presences and absences. The evidence from the cemeteries under investigation suggests that absence is articulated and perceived as an emotional

T.F. Sørensen (✉)
University of Aarhus, Højbjerg, Denmark
e-mail:farktfs@hum.au.dk

M. Bille et al. (eds.), *An Anthropology of Absence: Materializations of Transcendence and Loss*, 115
DOI 10.1007/978-1-4419-5529-6_7, © Springer Science+Business Media, LLC 2010

rupture but also as concrete and material voids. Likewise, presence is articulated both as the physical being-there and the feeling of nearness and immediacy in the midst of the fragmentation posed by the death of a relative. As will be demonstrated in the chapter, these intersections of presence and absence issue forth through *practicing* anticipation: i.e. the creative orchestration of graves along lines of more or less prescribed futurities, which – I argue – allow the deceased longevity in the lives of the bereaved.

The cemeteries and their grave plots are part of a larger network, in which social differentiation, moral expectations, ethical obligations and ideological contestations are at play (Sørensen 2009), but the focus in this chapter is on the generative absences that unfold here. A number of absences are at work at the cemeteries, belonging to rather dissimilar yet interrelated and imbricated regimes. The first and most obvious absence at the cemetery concerns the persons who have died and who embody a gap in the lives of the bereaved. The second form of absence is perhaps less conspicuous but just as significant to the understanding of the cemetery and assumes the shape of temporary textual voids, incomplete inscriptions, and the disappearance of prior representational formality on gravestones. These absences are all imbricated with and achieve presence through the sensuous engagement of the bereaved in particular commemorative forms (see also Sørensen 2009; Sørensen and Bille 2008).

A further aspect of this chapter is to explore the qualities of an archaeological study of contemporary material culture (Buchli and Lucas 2001). An archaeological approach to contemporary cemeteries may appear limiting in the sense that it would be easier and more productive to simply ask the users of the cemeteries about their aims and aspirations in the choice of specific material idioms. However, an archaeology of contemporary material culture does not so much pursue the intentions and perceived strategies of contemporary individuals. Its strengths instead reside in taking material forms seriously and allowing them to formulate implicit as well as explicit agendas, taking its point of departure in the affective agency of materials rather than the verbalized or written narratives of human agents.

This mode of exploration is what we may term the *archaeology of contemporaneity*, attempting to capture the fluidity of an archaeology that does not necessarily approach material phenomena through excavation, chronology and typology. The archaeological perspective forces us directly to think what and why something is not there. As a result of the often incomplete nature of the archaeological record, the discipline is forced to tackle that which is not there, what has been destroyed in the passing of centuries or millennia, is still unexcavated, or what was never left behind. Archaeology always faces the basic question, if an absence is the expression of lack of a given element in the past, is that lack intentional, or has the given element vanished through time. In this light, we may appreciate material culture as an agent that has the capacity to capture the unsaid, the non-discursive, and that which exceeds words. This is not necessarily an archaeology of "us" (Gould and Schiffer 1981), because an archaeology of contemporaneity does not necessarily share an identity with those or that which it studies. It is instead concerned with the presences and absences that are not revealed by verbalized or written statements by informants or historical sources. While the identity of the informant and the researcher may not be the same, the researcher instead shares a contemporaneity with the research material.

Absence and Commemoration

The affective power of the absent has been addressed by sociologist Kevin Hetherington's notion of an "agency of absence" (2004: 168), which he identifies in the context of consumption and disposal practices. He argues that disposal is not simply a matter of getting rid of objects considered to be waste. Instead, disposing of objects is an ongoing process that centres on an inherent potency of absence to constitute social relations.

Following this, I suggest that the cemetery, its grave plots and gravestones may be seen to comprise a continuum of social and material presences and absences. This continuum challenges the common view of gravestones as memorials created by the bereaved to represent the dead. The graves and the practices at the cemeteries thus reverberate between the living and the dead, and may entirely omit the representation of the deceased. This perspective prompts a need to take issue with the materialization, articulation and dissolution of commemoration and commemorative practices. Commemoration is frequently taken to denote the ways in which persons, things, events or places of the past are venerated, signified or represented (Gumbrecht 2006: 323–324; Hutton 1993; Tarlow 1999). Commemoration may also be treated as a mnemonic device for stating the meaning of those very persons, things, events or places (Hallam and Hockey 2001; Rowlands 1993; Tilley 1994). In this way, commemoration is most often understood as a means of pointing back in time to deceased individuals or to past events and experiences.

However, as became apparent through my exploration of contemporary Danish cemeteries, absences and voids in commemorative practices have the capacity to instantiate an amalgamation of past, present and future (see also Calow 2007). The understanding of graves as alluding to or being containers of memory falls somewhat short of grasping the full magnitude of commemorative potentials, in that it reduces memory to the identity of the deceased or to being iconic of the deceased. Commemoration and memory of the deceased may instead be linked to the emotional *immediacy* of the deceased as felt by the bereaved, e.g. a spouse sensing the presence of a husband or wife with varying intensities: "At its weakest this is a feeling that one is somehow being watched; at its strongest it is a full-blown sensory experience" (Bennett and Bennett 2000: 139).

At the cemetery, memory and commemoration may thus be connected to other sensuous qualities, establishing nearness and immediacy between the deceased and the bereaved through a material culture that may be seen to capture precisely these qualities. As I will substantiate below, the presencing of the absent in Danish cemetery culture occurs through the creation of affective materialities and aesthetics that reach

beyond mere representation. Rather, new sensuous immediacies are forged between
the bereaved and the deceased through which commemoration, disposal and social
relations are continually enforced, thereby defying distinct and final closures.

Design Idioms in Danish Cemeteries

Over the past 50 years, Danish cemeteries have been subject to numerous changes
in their overall design (Kragh 2003). These changes are defined by the cemeteries'
administrative bodies (The Ministry of Ecclesiastical Affairs, parochial church
councils, cemetery consultants and cemetery staff) as well as by the people organiz-
ing the individual grave plots, and their maintenance and use of the cemetery.

The traditional sections, typically surrounding a church, have developed gradually
from the late nineteenth century. They are characterized by rows of grave plots,
encircled by low hedges and framed by a grid of gravel or pebble paths. The most
prominent material change in the structural design of the cemeteries has been the
development of the lawn sections. These sections, which originated in the 1960s
and are still being constructed, are typically expansions to the older cemetery
sections rather than refurbishments. They are created within the framework of a
minimalist design idiom that only permits a flat grass lawn with simple flat gravestones, a limited number of taller trees and perimeter hedges.

The two types of cemetery sections are defined by different sets of regulations.
The grave plots in the traditional section are constructed as allotments that can be
decorated and used largely to the plot owner's choice, as long as they are not considered offensive by other users or by the cemetery administration. Ordinarily, the
grave plots are adorned with plants and shrubs, pebbles and stone arrangements,
and visitors traditionally decorate the grave with cut flowers and wreaths in addition to the more recent and increasingly popular trend of placing candlelight at the
grave. It is normally the closest of kin – the widow, widower, parents or children of
the deceased – who take care of the grave plot, planting, pruning, trimming and
watering the plants, weeding and raking the gravel, while more distant relatives,
friends and acquaintances of the deceased leave temporary decoration such as a
bouquet of flowers.

The typical gravestone in most traditional Danish cemetery sections is either a
natural stone or a stone carved from granite with inscriptions that are either
engraved or added in metal letters. The stones stand upright or are slightly tilted and
may be of very different sizes. The gravestones in lawn sections, to the contrary, are
almost always subject to a more strict set of regulations defined locally at the
cemetery. Some cemeteries allow small upright stones in different stone materials
and shapes, while most cemeteries require that the stones are flat, made of granite,
conform to prescribed size (e.g. precisely 40 cm × 60 cm), and lie horizontally in
the grass carpet. Sometimes, one or two hollows are fitted in the corners of these
stone, functioning as vases to allow for cut flowers, which are the only permitted
form of adornment. Each of the grave plots in the lawn section is restricted to this

simple, flat concrete slab, surrounded by level grass. This design idiom requires little or no action by the bereaved in terms of maintenance, as the individual grave plot is restricted to the gravestone itself.

The gravestone in traditional cemetery sections typically carries the name of one or two individuals, accompanied by their date of birth and their date of death. In many cases, the profession of the deceased may also be inscribed on the gravestone, in particular if the deceased was a man. Frequently, the text also states the place of birth or the place of residence of the deceased. Especially on gravestones older the 1980s, the maiden name of the wife would also be stated as a kind of female equivalent to the inscription of the husband's profession. These older gravestones also often carry a psalm verse or a Biblical quote, whereas relatively standardized and short greetings recently have become more popular, for example "Thank you for everything", "Beloved and missed" or "Rest in peace". Poetic lines that do not conform to such standardized phrases or derive from the Bible or psalms have become increasingly common within recent years. In addition to the textual statements on the gravestones, a variety of images, such as a crucifix, roses, pigeons and hearts also frequently decorate the more recent stones. In other cases, professional iconography may be present on the gravestone, for example the farmer's plough, the bricklayer's trowel or whatever tools signified the trade – or occasionally the hobby – of the deceased. Altogether, these texts and images constitute a rather comprehensible data log for the deceased, normally formulated by the bereaved shortly after the death of their relative. Through the text and images on the gravestone we may thus compose a narrative that includes personal names, age, gender, marital status, professional careers, geographical belonging, and religious and emotional references.

Inscriptions on gravestones have generally changed since around the 1980s in the sense that an increased number of expressions are now accepted. These novelties are found in the traditional sections as well as in the lawn sections, and in general they tend to be more pronounced at urn burial plots than coffin sites. In terms of the identity of the deceased, inscriptions on these types of stones are often very personal, giving only a first name, or a nickname, such as "Dad" or "Granny". In other cases, the stone does not even state the name of the deceased, but simply carries a greeting, a quote or a poetic phrase (for a discussion of these historical changes, see Sørensen 2009).

Absences at Danish Cemeteries

In many ways, contemporary Danish cemeteries assume the role of a place for absence, as outlined previously, harbouring the people who have vanished and thereby substantiating the social void that they have left. As such, the cemetery may be seen as a material and spatial proxy for a void that can be difficult to deal with, because of the abstract and immaterial character of the deceased, their death, and decomposition. Part of the ambiguous character of the dead may stem from the fact that while the deceased can be perceived as absent, the bereaved may at the same time experience them as socially and emotionally present, for example through the memory of the dead person or an ill-defined yet intimate feeling of nearness to the deceased (Simon-Buller et al. 1988–1989). In this way, absence is interwoven with the emotional presence of persons or things, and therefore also their potential immediacy; i.e. the emotional or sensory experience of "being in touch" (Runia 2006: 5).

Temporary Voids: Death As Completion

Many gravestones in Danish cemeteries pass through a phase where they carry only partial inscriptions. At this point, the name of the deceased is engraved on the stone, but a gap remains between her or his name and the greeting at the bottom register of the stone, reading for instance "Beloved and missed". The fact that this void is provisional has been attested through several observations at various cemeteries, where the gap on a gravestone has been filled in after a few years when the spouse of the person who had died first passes away.

A statistic fact which has had a concrete consequence for the normative spatial organisation of gravestone inscriptions, is that women on average have had a life expectancy of about five years longer than men since the 1940s (Plovsing and Østergaard 2008: 8). As men generally die younger than women, and as the wife is typically the youngest of the couple, most of the textual gaps on gravestones are in fact for the wife of the deceased, which also means that the name of the husband most ordinarily is placed at the top of the stone (yet this may also be seen as an expression of gender hierarchies). This condition has had some implications for the development of a normative design of gravestones. From time to time, we may thus encounter gravestones of couples where the wife has died first, but her name has been inscribed at the lower register of the gravestone, respecting the convention that her husband's name is expected to occupy the uppermost register of the stone.

In some cases, the gravestone seems to spell out that the separation of a deceased man and his wife is merely a matter of time. Some gravestones carry the names of both the deceased husband and the surviving spouse, indicating her date of birth and leaving a space for the date of her death to be inscribed after her burial. This form of temporary constellation of text and void appears to testify to the wife's devotion to her husband (or vice versa), that love and fidelity will last even beyond death. The death of the widow or widower is thereby the event that completes their separation from one another (Fig. 7.1). The void on the gravestone thus also excludes the possibility that the surviving spouse might remarry at a later point in life – or at least this appears to be the sincere intention at the time when the inscription was made.

Thus, these textual gaps are created with the intention of being interim absences, which are to be completed when the spouse dies and her (or sometimes his) name is added to the gravestone. The intervening void is a solid statement of "forever yours", and it thus represents a strong anticipation of the reunion of the married couple in death.

Fig. 7.1 The temporality of separation. Fårevejle cemetery, July 10th 2007 and August 3rd 2008. Photo by the author

Incomplete Information: Death As Continuation

In addition to temporary voids on gravestones, the inscription of formal data has been completely abandoned on several stones, fashioned along the lines of a more recent design idiom. As described earlier, these types of gravestones gradually began to appear in the 1980s, favouring first-names, nicknames, quotes, greetings or poetic statements at the expense of data and formal identification of the deceased. Previously, the use of only a first-name or a nickname and a greeting was almost exclusively applied to children's graves, which would frequently address the deceased in individualistic and personalized terms, such as "Memory of Frede and Baby Brother/Sleep tight dear children"[1], "Hanne/Our sunshine girl"[2] or "Sleep tight Little Jette/Gone but not forgotten"[3].

While these gravestones were created at a time when other idioms were normative, their way of addressing the dead have become entirely customary in recent years. The highly personalized statements and modes of referring to the deceased are no longer restricted to children's graves, but may be encountered at graves of people of all ages and seemingly also regardless of social positions. These gravestones lack formal

---

[1] Nykøbing Sjælland auxiliary cemetery; Frede 1917–1920, Baby Brother 1921.
[2] Nykøbing Sjælland auxiliary cemetery; Hanne 1942–1944.
[3] Højby Sjælland cemetery; Jette 1948–1955.

Fig. 7.2 Anticipating presence. "See you". Nykøbing Sjælland auxiliary cemetery, July 12th 2007. Photo by the author

personal names, but often carry another form of text, which offers more imaginative characteristics as the deceased is narrated through literary citations or very intimate references. This may for example be in the form of the stone slab at a grave plot at Egebjerg cemetery, stating "The Sun Also Rises"[4]. At other times, the statement on the gravestone is restricted to an informal greeting, for example "See you"[5], or "Sleep tight"[6], leaving out all other forms of text on the stone, even the name of the deceased (Fig. 7.2). In most cases, these texts indicate some sense of continuity beyond death, that the dead sleeps tight, that the deceased and the bereaved will meet again, or simply that life goes on, and the sun continues to rise despite of one's death.

It is sometimes possible to distinguish between gravestones addressing the deceased and those that cite her or him. The more conventional gravestones are usually addressing the deceased in the sense that the character of the inscriptions describes the loss felt by the bereaved; they may testify to the nature of the experienced absence of the deceased or address the hope for an afterlife. Some articulate appeasement and acceptance of the death, while others carry statements of great sorrow and emotional rupture. The gravestones that cite the dead often belong to the category where there is some form of agreement with death or where the death is surrounded by acceptance. Citing the deceased seems to invoke her or his voice, e.g. "You know"[7] or "Eddy was here",[8] which may be a way of articulating or creating a sense of presence and continued immediacy to the dead.

---

[4]Egebjerg cemetery, Kirsten Jacobsen 1920–2008.

[5]Nykøbing Sjælland auxiliary cemetery; no date.

[6]Nykøbing Sjælland auxiliary cemetery; no date.

[7]Egebjerg cemetery; no date.

[8]Bispebjerg cemetery; no date.

These statements are moreover characteristic of a tendency in the articulation of the grave plots to emphasize a private form of communication, which requires a certain degree of intimacy between the sender and the receiver of the statement. It is not immediately possible to decode the meaning of the message on the stone for the reader who is not familiar with the jargon or the frame of reference. The communicative aspect of the text on the gravestone thus does not seem to revolve so much around the memorialization of the person to a wider community, but is focused rather on a private communication to a more restricted social group with immediate ties to the deceased, wishing to sustain or prolong the sense of intimacy. These ties make it possible for the bereaved to decode the almost cliquish character of the text, while at the same time also setting the gravestone and the experience of the grave plot aside from other graves in the cemetery, emphasizing the individual personhood of the deceased.

Contained Absence: The Textual and the Material

In this way, the texts and the textual and material voids found in contemporary Danish cemetery culture represent a strong sense of commemorative subjectification. The subjectified character of the gravestones serves as a means of vitalizing the personhood of the deceased, and of articulating her or his personhood's perseverance and continuity. However, as a communicative device, the gravestones downplay or neglect the social convention of representing the deceased's formalized ties to the wider social community, which used to be signified by profession, place of birth and so forth. Instead, the subjectified gravestones create a statement of the personhood of the narrator of the text and the desired mode of commemoration by leaving out more formalized information of the deceased. By leaving out certain elements in the formulation of the grave plot, the commemorative aspect of the grave also comes to function as a mirror, reflecting not only the identity of the bereaved, but more importantly their feeling of presence and absence in light of the death of the relative. The void may thus generate a pre-mediated emotional sense of nearness to the deceased, which need not be objectified or verbalized. It is rather the elements, which are not represented that have the capacity to stimulate a feeling of presence, which may at the same time be rather ethereal and difficult to specify.

Textual Gaps

The different forms of textual voids are characterized by emotional, spatial as well as literal discontinuities. We may be used to thinking of death in terms of disruption, and the cemetery may in this perspective be conceived as a place that literally and figuratively contains absence (Meyer and Woodthorpe 2008). Along these lines, absence may be actively suspended in the social lives of the bereaved by being situated and framed. At the same time, the voids on the gravestones – the textual and literal gaps – create renewed and continuous social and material relationships that forge intimate bonds between the bereaved and their experience and memory of the deceased. These "incomplete" gravestones can – due to the literal voids as well as the cliquishness of their formulation – be difficult to read due to the scarcity of formal information. This is of course also a clue to understanding this form of design: the formal and factual information about the deceased is not intended to constitute the main message of this type of memorial marker. Instead, the deceased is portrayed through a different kind of commemorative practice, which appears to issue forth as sentiments, emotions and internalized memory, rather than matter-of-fact social data.

The various forms of textual absence can be interpreted as a narrative incompleteness without a predetermined conclusion, but may at the same time function as prolific voids that allow and require the reader to fill in the gaps by way of imagination. German literary scholar Wolfgang Iser (1978: 182) argues that the act of reading is structured by the reader's reception of the text, whose indeterminacies and blanks provoke the reader to reassemble the meaning of the text by composing and constituting its narrative, making the act of reading a "kaleidoscope of perspectives, preintentions, recollections" (ibid: 284). This approach to the text deemphasizes the literal meaning of the text as it was preconceived by the author, and instead focuses on the reader's reception of the text, and what the text *does* to the reader (ibid: 53).

While the inscriptions on gravestones may not be literary texts, it is evident that their gaps and indeterminacies nevertheless stimulate the same kind of creative continuity between text and narrative, yet this may unfold in widely different ways depending on the reader and her or his frame of reference, or on the reader's "repertoire" (ibid: 69). Put simply, there are insiders and outsiders in the reception of a gravestone; the immediate family and people who were not familiar with the dead. The widow of a deceased individual, for example, may primarily respond to the husband's gravestone through memory, and the lack of her name on the stone may indeed be seen by herself as "her" space, stimulating a sense of reunion or future presence. The same void may be seen by other relatives as an unfinished story of the mutual belonging of the widow and her husband, because they presumably also largely know what is embedded in the void. An outsider, on the other hand, would be forced to use the void on the gravestone to create a narrative that has other qualities; at the most basic level, the story of a man who has died and whose wife is to be buried in the same grave, but the specific orchestration of the text, the void and the textual indeterminacies may also offer perspectives on the marital institution and gender roles.

The missing texts and the lack of factual information thus establish a social and emotional continuum, the prospect of reunion with the deceased and the anticipation of return. This is established not by what we can read from the text on the gravestone, but from what we literally cannot read. The textual void on the gravestone thereby becomes the material intersection of the present and the absent, of life and death, which allows for a transcendence of the finality of death in favour of a continuum between the living and the dead. The lacuna is, thus, not a "nothing" but a creative interval and a suspension of continuity.

Material Gaps

In some cases, the literary voids are paralleled in the very lay-out of the grave plot, whereby the textual absence intersects with the material practices and spatialities created on the grave plot. A material element that frequently occurs on Danish cemeteries is the bench, which may be fashioned in a variety of ways. Ordinarily, it assumes the form of a downscaled version of a park bench, often made of granite rather than wood. The benches are often just ornamental devices and therefore remain empty seats, but occasionally they are used by the bereaved when they visit the grave. Unlike the textual gaps on the gravestones, the bench is characterised by offering a different kind of temporal void as it may be filled in by the presence of the visitors regularly and on a short-term basis, whereas the textual voids disappear upon being completed. The bench is interesting in the sense that it has the potential for changing the pattern of activities at a visit to the grave, which often focus on the maintenance of the grave plot, and it may instead offer the potential seat for quiet contemplation. A bench at a child's grave at Odden cemetery is thus being used every evening throughout the year, according to the cemetery personnel, when one or both of the parents of the deceased come to read their dead child a bedtime story. The bench may thereby be more than a decorative or functional installation, but is instead an item that suggests return, presence and continuity, as it basically anticipates an atmosphere of emotional association, and an active practice of nearness.

Likewise, another child's grave at Nørre Asmindrup cemetery has been laid out on a grave plot that is remarkably large when compared to the usual size of children's graves in Denmark. It covers the space that would ordinarily give room for three adult graves (Fig. 7.3). The child has been buried in the middle of the grave plot, which is adorned with toy figures, a statue of an angel and plants. The spaces that flank the central part of the grave where the child is buried are left un-worked, only covered with pebbles. These gaps are not mere ornamental spaces, but are, according to the cemetery administration, reserved for the parents of the dead child in the belief that this is where they will some day be reunited with their daughter.

Thereby, the voids at the graves do not only concern the social absence of the deceased, but are just as much active material gaps encompassing widely different practices of presence with varying temporalities. While the empty seat on the bench is being filled in repeatedly and suggests continuous presence, the empty spaces on the grave plot offer the anticipation of completion when the family is reunited. These two temporalities of absence offer widely different scenarios for the articulation and transmission of the emotional loss of the deceased, but have similar qualities with regard to their capacity to instigate anticipation and prolonged relationships with the dead.

In a similar fashion, the anticipation of a mended gap is exemplified by a recent and still rare phenomenon in Danish cemetery culture (Fig. 7.4). Thematically, it lies in direct continuation of the large grave plot for the deceased child in the above example, offering a place for a future burial. The regulative at the lawn section at the cemetery in Asnæs does not leave space for family graves *per se*, yet up to four individuals can have their ashes interred in the same urn burial plot. As a response to this relative limitation, an increasing number of people at this particular cemetery

Fig. 7.3 Reserving futurity. Nørre Asmindrup cemetery, July 15th 2008. Photo by the author

Fig. 7.4 Mending an emotional gap. Asnæs cemetery, July 24th 2007. Photo by the author

have recently begun to buy unused burial plots, reserving a specific burial place often next to close relatives. While wives and husbands frequently have their urns interred in the same burial plot, the children of the deceased seem to anticipate an independence from their parents in death, planning future burial with their own wives or husbands. Others again lose a dear friend, and as friends are not conventionally buried in the same grave, they buy plots in the vicinity to have a burial place close to the person who was emotionally close in life. The practice of reserving burial plots has assumed the material form of "temporary gravestones" in the lawn; plain cement slabs with no name or any other inscription, but apart from the entire absence of text, they are shaped within the exact same design idiom as the other gravestones in the lawn under which urns have been deposited.

Conclusion: Generative Lacunae

The material culture of absence in the context of contemporary Danish cemeteries forms one of several bonds between the bereaved and the deceased, and the world of the living may intersect in materially contingent ways with the abstract absence of the deceased. Cemeteries and commemorative practices are thus not merely about creating memorials and retrospective memory, but may also be a way of generating nearness for the bereaved, and therefore about moving closer to the dead in aesthetically experiential ways. These practices and materializations offer the bereaved a number of avenues for discovering and articulating their emotional situation. The loss is thus mapped out in acts of preparation and anticipation, which forestalls a central claim to emotional continuity between the bereaved and the nearness of the deceased.

At this level, we may distinguish between preparation and anticipation in the sense that preparation articulates the spatial movements and performances undertaken by the bereaved, while anticipation signifies emotional movement. Distinguishing analytically between anticipation and preparation – yet they overlap materially and experientially – adds a further level to the archaeological analysis of the presence of absence at the cemeteries. We may identify the preparation of presence in a number of instances, where social expectations and moral obligations account for a number of these; the grave plot is prepared in order to signify the moral obligation to maintain a dignified grave plot for the deceased. To the extent that these duties are intelligible to an archaeological approach, such preparation lies in a performance of sociality at the grave plot, setting up material markers of bodily presence for other users of the cemetery to recognize that social obligations to the deceased are being fulfilled. Anticipation, on the other hand, issues forth through the affective agency of the grave plot, and the ways in which the bereaved may achieve a sensory feeling of nearness and presence at the cemetery. In other words, acts of preparation dictate the bereaved to move in space, while acts of anticipation unfold because the bereaved has been moved emotionally.

Anticipating presence is thus not so much about materializing the memory of the deceased, but rather about the continuous bonds between the living and the dead, and about the continuity of past, present and future that may be established if the dead are permitted to remain active components in the biographies of the bereaved (Howarth 2000: 127, 2007b: 23). In this way, the practices and material culture of cemeteries offer several horizons of aesthetic, sensuous engagements that reverberate in the present and the absent. This suggests a turn from focusing solely on the meaning of graves and cemeteries, and what they represent, towards appreciating the emotional and affective presence in the material registers employed there.

The bonds between the absent and the present may be bridged by the practice of anticipation and the prescription of futurities (Jones 2007: 52–53). Anticipation is thus part of the void in the cemetery through which the bereaved may seek or experience atmospheres of emotional presence, and create futurities through the prolonged material engagements, such as maintenance and visits. Basically, the voids offer the bereaved the anticipation of a re-assemblage of fragmented emotional and social lives. The immateriality of the deceased – which constitutes both the problem and the ontology of their being – may thus be re-formulated and achieve sensuous immediacy and presence by being internalized, subjectified and not least materialized. Put simply, the deceased become embedded in the mental and material anticipation of a visit to their graves through the practices that the voids on the grave plot inspire.

As we have seen, the design of grave plots varies greatly at contemporary Danish cemeteries, whereby the means of recognizing sensibilities and immediacies within this form of material culture are highly personalized and depending on individual relations to the deceased as well as on the materiality of the grave plot. The code for designing a grave plot or a gravestone has gradually lost the standardization that used to be rather pronounced, and the cemeteries are now characterized by less idiomatic continuity than previously. Pursuing the notions of absence and presence not as separate or opposite but as entangled phenomena, demonstrates a number of complex and dynamic relationships between the bereaved and their mode of commemoration. Their experience of presence and their reception of seeming absences may consequently be rooted in the active creation of anticipation – or even providence – in the face of death and bereavement. The roles of present and absent are therefore not merely reversed; rather, they are entangled through the continuum of the living and the dead.

To expand, when arguing that the cemetery is a place for presencing the absent, we should also acknowledge that the one who is absent does not necessarily have to be the one who is deceased. It may just as well be the bereaved, who experience themselves as absent from their beloved parents, children or spouses. This is particularly apparent in the light of Runia's definition of presence as "a desire to share in the awesome reality of people, things, events, and feelings, coupled to a vertiginous urge to taste the fact that awesomely real people, things, events, and feelings can awesomely suddenly cease to exist" (2006: 5).

In some cases, the presence is characterized by a sensuous and subjective immediacy between the bereaved and the deceased; in other cases, it is an assurance of belonging and fidelity; it can be the promise of future, the enunciation that the absence of a loved one is temporary, and it can be an affirmation of the perseverance of love and affection. In other words, the voids apparent in the cemeteries become saturated with the feeling of nearness and immediacy through a practice of staying in touch.

References

Bennett, G. and K. M. Bennett, 2000. The presence of the dead: an empirical study. *Mortality*, 5(2): 139–157.

Buchli, V., and G. Lucas, 2001. "The absent present: archaeologies of the contemporary past," in *Archaeologies of the Contemporary Past*. Edited by V. Buchli and G. Lucas, pp. 3–18. London: Routledge.

Calow, J., 2007. Memoria, memory, and commemoration. *Mortality*, 12(2): 103–108.

DuBose, T., 1997. The phenomenology of bereavement, grief, and mourning. *Journal of Health and Religion*, 36(4): 367–374.

Durkheim, E., 1915. *The Elementary Forms of Religious Life*. London: Unwin.

Freud, S., 1984 [1917]. "Mourning and melancholia," in *On Metapsychology: The Theory of Psychoanalysis*, vol. 11, *The Pelican Freud Library*, pp. 245–268. London: Penguin.

Gould, R. A. and M. B. Schiffer. Editors. 1981. *Modern Material Culture: The Archaeology of Us*. New York: Academic Press.

Gumbrecht, H. U., 2006. Presence achieved in language (with special attention given to the presence of the past). *History and Theory*, 45(October): 317–327.

Hallam, E. and J. Hockey, 2001. *Death, Memory and Material Culture*. New York: Berg.

Hallam, E., J. Hockey, and G. Howarth, 1999. *Beyond the Body: Death and social identity*. London: Routledge.

Hetherington, K., 2004. Secondhandedness: consumption, disposal, and absent presence. *Environment and Planning D: Society and Space*, 22(1): 157–173.

Howarth, G., 2000. Dismantling the boundaries between life and death. *Mortality*, 5(2): 127–138.

———, 2007a. *Death & Dying: A Sociological Introduction*. Cambridge: Polity Press.

———, 2007b. "The rebirth of death: continuing relationships with the dead," in *Remember Me: Constructing Immortality – Beliefs on Immortality, Life, and Death*. Edited by M. Mitchell, pp. 19–34. London: Routledge.

Hutton, P. H., 1993. *History as an Art of Memory*. Hanover: University of Vermont.

Iser, W., 1978. *The Act of Reading: A Theory of Aesthetic Response*. Baltimore: John Hopkins Univerisity Press.

Jones, A., 2007. *Memory and Material Culture*. Cambridge: Cambridge University Press.

Kellehear, A., 2002. Grief and loss: past, present and future. *Medical Journal of Australia*, 177: 176–177.

Klass, D., P. R. Silverman, and S. L. Nickman. Editors. 1996. *Continuing bonds: new understandings of grief*. London: Taylor and Francis.

Kragh, B., 2003. *Til jord skal du blive... Dødens og begravelsens kulturhistorie i Danmark 1780–1990*. Sønderborg: Aabenraa Museum/Skrifter fra Museumsrådet for Sønderjyllands Amt.

Meyer, M. and K. Woodthorpe, 2008. The material presence of absence: a dialogue between museums and cemeteries. *Sociological Research Online*, 13(5).

Miller, D. and F. R. Parrott, 2007. "Death, ritual and material culture in South London," in *Death Rites and Rights*. Edited by B. Brooks-Gordon, F. Ebtehaj, J. Herring, M. Johnson, and M. Richards, pp. 147–161. Oxford: Hart Publishing.

Plovsing, J. and L. Østergaard, 2008. *60 år i tal: Danmark siden 2. verdenskrig*. Copenhagen: Danmarks Statistik.

Rowlands, M., 1993. The role of memory in the transmission of culture. *World Archaeology*, 25(2): 141–151.

Rubin, S. S., 1985. The resolution of bereavement: a clinical focus on the relationship to the deceased. *Psychotherapy*, 22(2): 231–235.

Rugg, J., 2000. Defining the place of burial: what makes a cemetery a cemetery? *Mortality*, 5(3): 259–275.

Runia, E., 2006. Presence. *History and Theory*, 45(February): 1–29.

Sheets-Johnstone, M., 1986. On the conceptual origin of death. *Philosophy and Phenomenological Research*, 47(1): 31–58.

Simon-Buller, S., V. Christopherson, and R. Jones, 1988–1989. Correlates of sensing the presence of a deceased spouse. *Omega: Journal of Death & Dying*, 19(1): 21–30.

Sørensen, T. F., 2009. The presence of the dead: cemeteries, cremation and the staging of non-place. *Journal of Social Archaeology*, 9(1): 110–135.

Sørensen, T. F. and M. Bille, 2008. Flames of transformation: the role of fire in cremation practices. *World Archaeology*, 40(2): 253–267.

Tarlow, S., 1999. *Bereavement and Commemoration: An Archaeology of Mortality*. Oxford: Blackwell Publishers.

Tilley, C., 1994. *A Phenomenology of Landscape: Places, Paths and Monuments*. Oxford: Berg.

Chapter 8
Bringing Home the Dead: Photographs, Family Imaginaries and Moral Remains

Fiona R. Parrott

This chapter is based on interviews and home visits with households participating in a project on loss, memory and material culture.[1] Of one hundred individuals and households accessed through door-to-door recruitment on a lengthy South London street, it was not surprising to find that almost half of those people had experienced a bereavement of a close relative, partner or friend in the last ten years. The bereaved ranged in age from young people in their twenties to elderly residents in their eighties and formed a relatively heterogeneous group with diverse ethnic origins and class background though white English, middle class home owners and renters predominated. It was evident from our conversations and their homes that displaying photographs of deceased members of their intimate social circle was important to the bereaved. Specifically, 34 households displayed photographs of parents and children who had passed away. While parent–child relationships were privileged, those more frequently pictured also included grandparents, siblings and to a lesser extent partners.

Unlike studies of bereavement which have accessed participants through counseling or self-help groups, this fieldwork found people in their homes and established working relationships with them over an 18 month period. This included my own residence on the street in a graduate house share for several months. As a result of the method of recruitment, this research into bereavement examined the way the absence of the deceased was felt at different points in the life course, beyond the immediacy of initial grief. Only two participants experienced a close bereavement during fieldwork and six experienced bereavements within the previous year, yet in all cases it was essential to work sensitively with participants as time elapsed was not necessarily a guide to its emotional resonance or feelings of loss and anger. What I will argue is that most participants experienced an urge to display some photographs of deceased relatives in their homes, and I will show that this feeling

[1] The fieldwork was conducted in collaboration with Professor Daniel Miller (See Miller 2008). It includes PhD material gathered independently between 2003 and 2007 (Parrott 2009).

F.R. Parrott (✉)
London School of Hygiene and Tropical Medicine, Keppel St, London WC1E 7HT, UK
e-mail: fiona.parrott@lshtm.ac.uk

could develop in response to specific events and situations, other than the initial experience of bereavement. These are not static displays that define the remembrance of the deceased as a one to one relationship of looking between mourner and picture of the deceased, in the present and of the past, but dynamic assemblages, objects cognizant of obligations, judgments, love and respect, that mediate relationships between the living.

This chapter subscribes to the view that it is not only the content of any one image that matters but their integration into domestic space. I will show that it is important to analyze what such photographs do, as part of the material culture of the household and its effects. Thus, it could be the absence of photographs in domestic space, which was felt or noticed at particular times, as much as the absence of the person from their lives. These doubly articulated absences impose themselves upon the viewer. But it is not only inclusions and exclusions but the selection, framing and arrangement of pictures that matters. This draws one into an exploration of the judgments and obligations as well as the comfort and longing brought by the portrayal of the faces of dead "loved ones." I will suggest that through their relationship to photographic objects, people deal with the moral remains of the deceased and shape their family imaginaries in complex ways.

An extensive literature on popular photography considers the family as an ideological and historical construct and the mutual relationship this construct has with photography (Wells 1997). According to this literature, taking and posing for a photograph is a performance, part of the myth-making structures that stage ideal (photographic) families as happy, unified and leisured (e.g., Gillis 1996; Slater 1983). This repetitive aspect of family photography was confirmed to an extent in my own work, including the observation that pictures of parents and children are more common than those of the extended family in the postwar era (e.g., Sontag 1977; Wells 1997).

However, although the subject matter was narrow, it was also possible to observe a cultural and historical mélange of classed and familial genealogies of style. In part, this was because of the mix of residents encountered on the street, but it also draws attention to the way participants often had old photographs on display. This resulted in a range of hues, styles, and even surface additions in the case of hand-tinted Jamaican and Cypriot studio portraiture of the fifties that helped viewers organize and relate to these decorations. Studies of non-Western photographic portraiture have explored the social significance of these surface aesthetics as well as their arrangements more thoroughly (e.g., Pinney 1997; Buckley 2001), but few have engaged with the temporal aesthetics of Western popular photography in the same way (see Samuel 1994), or their additions and framing (Drazin and Frohlich 2007). Already, with a view to family photography as a decorative and ritual art (Batchen 2004), one can suggest that there is more to family photography than conformity to narrow ideals.

Some authors have emphasized how illness and death, as well as divorce, are cut out of these conventional family narratives, from displays and from the archetypal biographical object, the family photograph album (Stewart 1984; Slater 1983; Spence and Holland 1991). Yet, this is also somewhat of a simplification. In fieldwork, it became clear that people did not stop taking photographs in anticipation of a person's death. Rather, the process of anticipatory mourning often prompted them to take more photographs not less. Several informants had photographs they had taken of the family stood around the hospital bed, marking these moments of togetherness. Those who had lost loved ones to long degenerative illnesses had whole albums of photographs of this time in their lives. This tells us as much about the practice of photography as death and dying. What value or status would the act of ceasing to take any further photographs give to their relationship with that person? The rituals of family life go on but because photographs are about remembering in the future, every act of photographing the dying articulates their anticipated absence.

These albums remained painful to view. One elderly mother, Ruby, showed me photographs of her adult daughter who had died after suffering from multiple sclerosis. These included photographs taken with family and friends on her last birthday and others taken in her home. The sequential arrangement could not help but show her deteriorating condition. While this album was kept with all the others in Ruby's living room cabinet, she told me she did not like to look at these photographs often. Our viewing of the album prompted Ruby to give a narrative of her daughters' death, of the final phone call from her daughters' ex-husband, how Ruby had stayed by her side lifting water to her lips and her ongoing anguish at being out of the room at the very last. The viewing of these photographs, despite or even because of the pictured smiles, involved conflicting emotions and the telling of unpictured moments and histories.

It is certainly the case that more unblemished and nostalgic images are selected for central display in the home[2]. These portraits stand in relation to painful images, remembered scenes, and narratives of illness and death. Thus, an important role for these unblemished photographs is that of reinstating a desired and comforting image of the person (Parrott 2007). One of the goals of this chapter is to demonstrate the complex integration of these seemingly non-confrontational images within domestic space.

The literature on death and photography went some way towards elevating the mundane family photograph by examining the intense emotional charge involved in viewing particular photographs, the now classic forerunner being Barthes' (1981) *Camera Lucida*. In this essay, his grief over his mother's death and response to a photograph of his mother as a young girl standing with her brother in the winter garden becomes a central part of his theory of the "punctum" of photography. This refers to an appreciation of the effects of a photograph that pierce the viewer beyond meaning. According to Rose (2004) in a study of English mothers with photographs of their young children, this experience lies in the corporeality of these photographs, and the bodily proximities involved in acts of seeing (2004: 560).

---

[2] I only found one exception to this rule. In a participating home, a grandmother had recently put photographs of her ill and premature grand-twins on display. This was when one of the twins who she still had guardianship of was around ten years old. She liked to have them because they showed "how far they had come." These photos were displayed as part of a narrative of progress over time. Of course, photographs of those who are dying do not fulfil this criterion.

Put another way, these photographs present their referents but do so through conversions of the materiality of faces, bodies, clothing, objects and places. Framed photographs, which continue to decorate domestic spaces, are held in hands, located in spaces. Part of the problem with much of the literature on family photography or death and photography, including Barthes' (1981), is the isolation of photographs from domestic practices (Rose 2005), though there are notable exceptions (e.g. Drazin & Frohlich 2007, Edwards 1999, Halle 1993). This links to a recent and increasing body of work on "the importance of the material and sensory in the communicative power of photographs" (Edwards 2005: 27). This chapter situates its analysis within this tradition, extending its insights to death and the display of photographs within the home.

One of the characteristic attributes of domestic photograph practice is the time investment involved in realising the value of photographs. This was often the reason that participants gave for "not getting around to doing the photographs" by which they meant ordering, sorting, framing, sending photographs to others and making albums. It also takes time to sit and look at photographs, alone or with others. But an appreciation of this time investment draws attention to the way doing the photographs can become a way of doing mourning. Remembering involves investing in producing a presence for the deceased.

For example, Mrs. Stone, a mother in her sixties put considerable effort into collecting photographs that included her daughter from other members of the family and making copies of them. Her daughter had died suddenly and unexpectedly from an infection connected with a routine operation. This activity extended years beyond the event of her daughter's death. In six homes, including Mrs. Stone's, special albums were planned and made that sequenced the life of the deceased that were available to show to others. Time was spent just looking at photographs. Julie, an English housewife, kept her photograph albums beneath her sitting room coffee table. She liked to sit on her own looking through different albums of "happy times" that included photographs of her deceased father. In six homes, including Mrs. Stone's, special albums were planned and made that sequenced the life of the deceased and were available to show to others.

Other activities included sending photographs to relatives and to others known to the deceased. This wider distribution happened most frequently around the time of the funeral. I observed how the parents and close friend of a young man who died in an accident emailed a portrait photograph, a close-up of his face, to an extensive circle of people. Another woman, Beryl, posted prints of her mother's portrait to their relatives in Jamaica who could not attend the funeral. These photographs provided a focus for contemplation, the reproduction of the images establishing a form of corporeal proximity shared between the photograph and mourners (See Rose 2005; Seremetakis 1991). This evidenced the work of those close relatives who bore most of the responsibility for doing mourning. Importantly, it situated them as the producers of the presence of the deceased and stimulators of appropriate remembering among an affective community.

Members of this extended circle of mourners were not expected to keep these photographs permanently on display. This practice defined the homes of those closely related to the deceased. Some relatives inherited photographs from the deceased. I found that many of these photographs were kept in their original frames, providing a good example of the way particular photographs may have biographies as objects (Edwards and Hart 2004). These photographs do not simply stand for memory in the sense of the photographic technique as imprint or metaphor (e.g. Forty 1999). Rather, remembering involved embodied memories of domestic spaces and narratives that could not be read from the content of the picture.

One portrait of my own grandmother, who died six years ago now, shows her in her twenties with waved shoulder length brown hair, wearing a yellow silk blouse. The picture is black and white. It used to be on her bedroom dressing table in the last two houses she lived in, and I looked at it many times, standing next to her, when I used to go and stay. She described the yellow silk blouse; I used to tell her she looked like a film star. I knew she liked to hear this then, and I smile when I see this desirable image in its new place on the window ledge at the house of my uncle, her youngest son. These photographs link chains of familial memory among close relatives. However, over time these biographies may be forgotten. Thus, "ancestor" portraits, of long dead relatives, that were also inherited and hung in some participating homes are very different objects of family imagining.

Looking at photographs in this way, as part of domestic practices, provides an alternative perspective on the maintenance and production of the presence of the deceased. It is not so much about the portrayal of the singular individual, the deceased, but about their integration within photographic practice. So far we have seen how this involves investment in doing things with photographs and memories of the things that were done with photographs, which combine to shape the feeling of the presence of the deceased in the home.

This perspective also helps to explain why the pictures of the dead within the domestic interior are dominated by images of deceased parents and children, where they have predeceased their parents, followed by siblings and grandparents. Parent–child relationships are central to family photography. Practices of taking, storing, giving and receiving photographs establish and maintain the identities of parent and child over a lifetime. For example, when taking photographs of babies and young children, parents think about storing them for the future. When adult children had left home, I found that it was common for parents to give old photographs to them, including "their" Baby albums.

From the beginning, by giving the relationship a history one commits to an anticipated future. This is one of the ways that people materialize the idea that "the lifelong nature of relationships with one's family of origin mark them as distinctive and different from all others" (Finch 1989: 241) into existence. It also pre-empts parents' anticipation of their own death and thus their future absence in their children's lives. The endings that are being described in this chapter are therefore part of this story. Photographs are used so frequently in life to objectify relationships between parents, children and grandparents. It is not surprising that they are a source of mementos in response to death. Displaying photographs is to do with parenting, with being children and being part of families (Rose 2005; Parrott 2009).

If we consider parents who participated in the study who had lost their children, these losses were overwhelmingly defined by lasting trauma. While the initial shock of grief might fade, the sense of loss endures for a lifetime, for it is this expectation of a lifetime relationship that is lost. The presence of other siblings or grandchildren was not necessarily an ameliorating force as children were considered precious and unique. Nothing could replace the loss of this particular child, whether this was among mothers who had lost young or adult children. By no particular design, I interviewed more mothers than fathers.

Ruby, the elderly participant who had lost her adult daughter to multiple sclerosis, had many photographs on display in her home, which showed all the members of her large family, grandchildren and great-grandchildren. Collage styles allowed her to place many pictures and people together. However, the dominant subject of the framed single portrait photographs in both the kitchen and the sitting room was her deceased daughter. This set her daughter apart. Specifically, these photographs allowed her to continue mothering and be seen to mother in her absence. This did not simply involve hanging photographs on the walls, but in her case included material-izing her continued attention to these photographs. Figure 8.1 shows how the frame of the photograph had become the focus for elaboration with a paper angel and angel pin, prayer cards and poems. Some of these prayers included those that her daughter had sent to Ruby, which she had later found when going through her letters. Batchen (2004) has shown that the sensory and symbolic enhancement of photographic frames is an important constituent in the experience of photography. This particular framing was central to the way Ruby recalled the religiosity of her daughter.

Fig. 8.1 Photo framed with angels and prayer cards

It seemed as if Ruby idealized this daughter in her relation to her other children. But it was not a straightforward idealism; it was part of a narrative where she acknowledged what she perceived in hindsight to be her failings as a mother. This was her failure to appreciate her daughter's goodness and daughterly affection during her life. Ruby would describe the little surprising discoveries she made after her daughters' death, of letters her daughter had sent containing newspaper cuttings and prayers that Ruby had not taken the time to read, of gifts she had given Ruby and also the letters of thanks she was sent by people her daughter had helped. Thus, photographs were part of this larger relationship to mementos and revelations, where their display provided one way of showing and viewing her delayed devotion.

If we compared Ruby's home to Lavinia's, we would count far fewer photographs of the young daughter Lavinia had lost. Here, the one portrait of her daughter produced a particularly, materially located confrontation with the experience of loss. This school portrait was hung on the sitting room wall, and it was a poignant example of the biography of a photograph. Lavinia had lost her daughter in a house fire. The council flat itself had been gutted, though they still lived in the same block, and it transpired that the photograph she had on display was part of a bundle of things that her daughter's school had given the family. These papers and photograph were absences that figured greater absences. The interview itself was stilted and short for it was even more difficult to ask and to talk about mementos of the deceased than usual.

Photograph displays help to maintain the preciousness of children over a lifetime. Being a respectful, caring child also often involves attention to photographs of parents. This helps to explain the sense of obligation to remember one's parents and the frequent display of their photographs. Some participants put up a photograph of their parents even when they otherwise displayed very few or no photographs throughout the house. Other homes placed these pictures within groups of other framed photographs. These pictures formed communities of living and deceased through the proximity of pictured and present bodies. Homes are the place to display "togetherness", in such a way that actual experiences of absence and separation may disturb but do not break its cohesion (Rose 2003:5).

My study corroborates others' observations that houses are not homes unless they bear witness to peoples' sociability and connectedness. As studies of the material culture of Industrial societies have established, the accumulation of photographs, other decorations and particularly gifts, establish domestic space as a site for the production and display of relatedness between the household and others (Chevalier 2002, Drazin and Frohlich 2007, Parrott 2009, Rose 2003). It was therefore the absence of photographs that could impose itself upon the viewer rather than or as much as the absence of the people the photographs depicted. There is a moral dimension to these displays; a moral home is one that remembers others and photographs make this intention to remember explicit (Drazin and Frohlich 2007). This helps explain the sense of obligation to display photographs.

Three participants who had lost either parents or siblings had recently bought their first houses. In these instances, it was possible to observe the way each made a space for the dead in their home. The formation of a new independent household, with display space of its own for which they were responsible, was an

Fig. 8.2 Cupboard with memorial photographs and flowers

important prompt for the creation of memorials. Hannah's brother had died the previous year after a long illness and she wanted to put up a photograph of him. The space that seemed appropriate for a photograph was what seemed to be a rather generic pine cupboard in the sitting room, shown in Fig. 8.2. In fact, this cupboard was a piece of her old home brought to form the new; it was taken from her parents' house and had formerly stood in her brother's room. Hannah links a vivid memory of her brother to the tactile experience of leaning against the cupboard when she was a child,

> I mean one of my earliest memories was lying next to that cupboard, watching my brother play on his computer, and he went downstairs and came back with this big spider in his hands, which I didn't realize, and put it on the pillow, next to me, and then first thing I knew about it was when it crawled onto my cheek and I screamed blue murder, my mum came running up the stairs and it was me with a dead spider cos I'd gone like that [*smacks cheek*], and him laughing at me…and that memory - the cupboard is very much in that.

Hannah selected a photograph of her brother that showed him before he looked ill. Both objects together produce a feeling of the presence of the deceased, which also allows for their appropriate remembrance in this new home. The cupboard drew the photographs to it, and the photographs complemented the bodily memories associated with the cupboards' solidity. She also put up a photograph of herself, her brother and her grandmother who had also passed away. The lamp, flowers and green houseplant were placed behind, to light and animate the display with living things.

As with all these displays, the whole arrangement is significant. It shifts easily between a genre of furnishing and decoration and personal memory; the two are intertwined (Kwint 1999).

The second participant, Jenny, selected a black and white wedding portrait of her parents to display in her living room on a side table. She and her mother had lost her father two years before. While the photograph brought the presence of her father into the new house, it was in painting and fixing up the house that Jenny felt his absence. This should have been a time where they could have worked together as father and daughter. Few words were used to articulate why she had chosen this photograph, she "liked it." It had come from her parents' house, and it showed them at a symbolic moment of unity. It was having it there that mattered, not the articulation of its significance.

This was in contrast to Ian who had also lost his father several years previously. When Ian bought and moved into his first house, he did not want to put up a photograph of his father in the front room. However, Ian wanted an object that would do the work of a photograph in remembering his father. For example, the memento he chose was placed in the sitting room, like many of the photographs of the deceased (Parrott 2009). He selected a cricket bat that had belonged to his father. This seemed to him to be a more appropriate and personal memorial, "less formal and ostentatious than a full length portrait in the room!" He collected it from his parents' house and by removing it from ordinary use, turned it into a revered and lasting object.

> I remember thinking it would be nice to have that as a memory because it was very him in a way, even though I've hardly ever played cricket in my life…I keep thinking of getting it lacquered or whatever, get it done properly…I know cricket bats are supposed to last forever aren't they?

But Ian also has to create the conditions for its acknowledgment as a memorial by others who visit the house. If a friend notices it and picks it up to swing it, Ian has to gently point out that it is "his dad's." This action creates the required atmosphere around this object through its handling and shares the knowledge of Ian's commitment to remember his father. This example suggests that while photographs are not always the memorial object of choice, they achieve something important in the eyes of others. Ian also had to carefully stage and "frame" the presence of his father in the home in the absence of a photograph.

It is not only when setting up home that the absence of parents and other close family members is felt and the urge to display photographs is acted upon. Perhaps, one of the most significant events to define the change in status of a home is the birth of children. Children create parents and grandparents; they are often a pivot around which extended family relationships are articulated. The display of photographs helps to maintain some aspects of these identities when those people have passed away, just as they do when family members are geographically separated and living in independent households. However, photograph displays can maintain complex family imaginaries through the precise material integration of the pictures of the deceased. This shapes the way their presence is experienced in the home and the continued impact they have in mediating relationships between the living.

Fig. 8.3 Displaying solidarity between generations

Helena and James' house is full of photographs. James' mother died before Helena and James were married three years ago, and she never witnessed the birth of their son. Her photograph is displayed in two important places in the living room of their house, which envision her inclusion within these events. Two wedding photographs were displayed side by side, shown in Fig. 8.3. The recent photograph on the right, taken at Helena and James' wedding was deliberately selected for its replication of the hue and pose of James' parents' wedding photo on the left. Both were framed in silver, honouring their status and reiterating the relationship between parents and son and daughter-in-law. The aesthetics of the arrangement displayed solidarity between generations. This was an imagined solidarity yet one with real effects. It gave James' mother a presence, which placed her in the relationship of mother-in-law to Helena and a part of James' new family home. Helena arranged the display herself after James received the original photograph.

In a second area of shelving in the room, this time dominated by colourful photographs of their young child, another picture of James' mother was included. This sepia photograph portrayed her in a relaxed manner, seated, smiling on the lawn. It was set in a thick, transparent acrylic frame like some of the other framed children's photographs. Again, it is important to understand what the staging and the viewing of these photographs achieve. This display explicitly positioned James' mother as a grandmother to her grandchild. When Helena and James show their son the photographs, they explain and help him learn who she is, though the little boy will never meet her.

In Layne's (2000) study of miscarriage and neo-natal loss in North America, she shows how the personhood of the lost child is established through consumer goods prior to and after the loss. Recognition of their status as parents may be developed through gift-giving on behalf of the lost child to the extended family, for example, giving angel decorations at Christmas. Relationships to goods establish the humanity of the lost child (Miller and Parrott 2007). This study extends Layne's insights. The example from Helena and James' home highlights the way relationships to photographs and their display not only keep identities from disappearing but are the form through which identities for the deceased and the living are recognized and established through relationships to photographs. This was the case even where James' mother had never known her son's wife and child.

One of the reasons why James has inherited these original photographs of his mother, including their wedding photograph, is that his father remarried and passed them onto him. Specifically, James' father has young children of his own and does not have time for his grandson. In this respect, Helena and James' child was seen to be "missing out" on having grandparents in two ways. Helena and James also felt a greater sense of responsibility to remember James' mother in the decoration of their own home because of the absence of her explicit presence in his father's. Photographs were displayed in such a way as to acknowledge this less than ideal family.

This suggests that Rose's (2005) insights are applicable to the experience of photography in bereavement. She writes, "Photos are felt to fill homes with the presence of those they picture," but their viewing also establishes a space in which the "complications of closeness" are articulated. (2005: 231). While she considers the placement of photographs to a degree, this chapter suggests that it is in the selection, framing and location of photographs that the complications of closeness are articulated.

Complex arrangements may express some of the ambivalent emotions experienced in deciding to display certain photographs. For example, when I visited Margaret in her large council flat, she had displayed portraits of her father and her mother separately at either end of a shelf in the living room with many objects in between. This distance was deliberate and was intended to allow her to honour her mother appropriately. She described how her father had betrayed her mother through a long term affair that he revealed to them only after her death. Her father then lived with his mistress until his own death. Originally, Margaret had only chosen to display a photograph of her mother, but the absence of a commemorative portrait of her father was then continually brought to her attention by the lack. She assuaged her sense of unease and put up a portrait of her father, but by placing it she also preserved some of the resentment and anger that distance implies. While she felt an obligation to display a photograph of her father, this example illustrates how frames and arrangements are selected to grant moral authenticity to displays at different levels of personal knowledge and feeling.

Conflicting emotions were also evident in Rachel's home display. She also found it difficult to permanently display photographs of her father in the house she shared with her husband. She used photographs in a slightly different fashion to Margaret, positioning them within a more temporary arrangement for three weeks around the first anniversary of her fathers' death. Three unframed photographs were arranged around a poem about loss on her desk. The two at the bottom were old black and white photographs with white borders, showing Rachel as a baby held in her fathers' arms and as a toddler feeding the ducks with her father.

Feeding the ducks was a fatherly activity that Rachel remembered him enjoying. As a long-standing alcoholic, he was on many occasions a more than unsatisfactory father. At the top was a colour photograph showing Rachel sitting rigidly in the centre supported by her two brothers with whom she is holding hands at the time of her father's death. Both types of images made the emotional charge of remembrance visible but also helped to make them manageable. It was significant that Rachel set this up in her personal study rather than the living room, not least because the remembrance of their father drew fraught lines of tension between the six siblings. These material choices in whether and how to display photographs were an important part of dealing with grief and obligations. As with Margaret, these displays objectified judgments as well as ideal aspects of relationships and roles.

We have already seen how it sometimes fell to children to pick up the responsibility of maintaining the photographs of a deceased parent when the other parent remarried. Photographs in particular could become an inappropriate presence in homes set up with new partners, where the ideal is one of serial companionate monogamy. It was not the need to make space for the dead that was highlighted but the need to lessen the degree to which the presence of the dead was felt in order to make space for the living. In general, photographs of the faces of ex-partners were an ambivalent subject. They were rarely displayed in the front spaces of the house though they were often kept as old albums or more intimate photographs put away in boxes or attics or more recently, in personal computer files and folders. It was not necessarily that a person wished to forget his/her former partner, but that photograph displays in particular established too great a presence for the deceased, for they portrayed the dead one's face and features within the domestic circle.

Among those who had children with their partner, it was convenient that they were able to pass these photographs on to them. Marjorie and Gregory for example had met on a holiday cruise and when they moved in together, Marjorie who was widowed gave the entire family photograph archive to her daughter. Other objects and practices that may have been a part of their previous relationship however were less problematic. For instance, the memory of an object, such as a piece of furniture, was recalled quietly and implicitly, unknown to others.

Some people did display photographs of their deceased partners. Miriam was in her thirties and had three children, one of whom was the child of her partner who had been killed in a motorbike accident three years before. His photograph stood on top of the television set. When we pointed to it, she talked about how she still visited his grave, but she spoke both with a sense that she ought to stop and a reluctance to do so. She implied that she ought to take down his things if she wanted to think about finding a new partner. But she was also ambivalent about how a new partner would fit into her family and children's lives when the man she had lost had been a father to them all. Like in many of the previous examples, the photograph had become a pivot for mixed and contradictory feelings about relationships.

Miriam implied that she was too young to focus her life on this loss. Of course, there were several widowed elderly participants who did display devotion to the portraits of their husband or wife. Often, their portrait was one of many photographs of the dead displayed in the home. Martha's photograph of her husband in her front room recalled a previous absence in their lives, which had become articulated with her final separation from him. Centrally displayed on the dresser was the portrait he had taken in his uniform before they both went off to do their respective duties in the Second World War. Yet even among the elderly and devoted, there was uneven remembering, it seemed as if it was inappropriate to display more than one deceased marital partner though each might now be remembered fondly. One participant, Lizzie, only displayed a photograph of her second husband for example though both men were part of her life history taking her from England to Spain and back to England again. What these choices show is that this type of display space must be an integrative relational space of future remembering, of which the boundaries may continuously be redefined.

These domestic photograph displays were also a restricted type of display space, largely devoted to constructing family imaginaries. This study encountered only one home, in which photographs of deceased friends were displayed, belonging to the home of Irish ex-publicans. This seems to concur with observations that domestic photograph display is dominated by the depiction of kin (Halle 1993). Young people's homes did display photographs of friends, but they were less likely to have experienced their loss. Where friends were displayed as part of the close circle of kin, their roles were more likely to be suffused (Pahl and Spencer 2003), such that one might describe them as fictive kin, though, there were too few encounters of the inclusion of deceased close friends to make further observations on this count.

These residents of South London whose photographs and homes I have described formed a relatively class heterogeneous group of British citizens of mixed migrant histories. For example, Ruby and Beryl had been born in Jamaica, while Miriam had been born in London to Chinese and African parents. Margaret and Rachel who were born to parents of English origin had grown up on local council estates, while Hannah and also Ian had moved to London from wealthier parental homes in the Home Counties. What was so clear from this approach was the wide relevance of displaying photographs of deceased members of their intimate circle in their homes. Houses were not homes without memorial objects, or put another way, without love and respect for the dead. But photographs are specific types of memorial objects. It was evident from our conversations that these images that captured faces, features and bodies were felt to bring the presence of the deceased into the home in a specific, transmittable way. Indeed, because of the significance of faces in establishing recognition, some features have been blurred in their reproduction as research images for this chapter.

Some clarification ought to be made with respect to the gendering of photograph work in the home, noted by other authors (Rose 2004, 2005). What I have argued was that most bereaved participants experienced an urge to display some photographs of deceased relatives in their homes. Photographs, however, are important decorative objects as well as memorials. Home decoration and memorialization as a gendered practice was illustrated by my account since it was biased towards the narratives of women who had taken responsibility for carrying out this work on behalf of the couple or the family. What I have not argued however is that domestic memorial practices or the display of photographs in the home are the prerogative of women, as some authors, including Rose, have tended to assume. For example, many single or non-cohabiting men displayed photographs of deceased parents. Elsewhere, I have explored the gendering of photography in comparison to other types of domestic memorial practice further (Miller and Parrott 2007). As Miller and Parrott argued, flexibility was observed in practice.

What this chapter has shown is how the desire to give the deceased a photographic presence developed in response to specific life events. This included displaying photographs of deceased parents, siblings and grandparents as part of the process of establishing a new independent household. Establishing a home as a young adult nonetheless depends on manifesting links to family within the new space. The desire to make a presence for the deceased could be connected to the event of making a new home, as much as the event of bereavement or the time that had passed since the death. Elsewhere, the desire to make the presence of the deceased a part of the house interior included displaying photographs of parents in response to feeling their absence from the event of marriage and even more so in the event of the birth of grandchildren. Houses and homes are inseparable from such life transitions (Pink 2001). Domestic photograph displays like the feelings of loss they respond to and manifest are not fixed but are the dynamic outcome of changing circumstances.

Similarly, when a participant had experienced the loss of a partner, it was not necessarily the case that their photograph was displayed in the long term. Unlike photographs of deceased parents, children, siblings and grandparents, photographs of deceased partners are more likely to be superseded by new photographs of a current partner, where photography participates in imagining a companionate model of serial monogamy. As this chapter showed, the point at which a photograph "should" be taken down was a problematic moment. For widowed parents who remarried, passing these objects to children, along with the responsibility to memorialize that person, helped to mitigate this transition.

By contrast, parent–child relationships were expected to last the lifetime, and the photographic presence of children maintained this sentiment and obligation even after death. In this respect, photographs among other objects are a significant part of defining this parent–child bond as a lifetime relationship. Elsewhere, I have also shown the importance elderly parents give to the preparation and gift of their children's childhood photograph albums in anticipation of their own death (Parrott 2009).

The positioning and viewing of photographs and the authoring of the boundaries of remembering through display also respond to ambivalent aspects of parent-child relationships. In Helena and James' home, his deceased mother took centre stage as mother-in-law and grandmother through the hues, styles, framing and grouping of photographs, whereas his father's second wife and children played no role in this articulation of generational togetherness. Margaret's unfaithful father's portrait was set apart from her mother's and Rachel's temporary display of poem and unframed photographs of her father who suffered from alcoholism were arranged in her personal study away from the eyes of visitors. The closeness of family is articulated as conflicting and ambivalent in the precise selections, arrangements and viewing of photographs on display. Staging the presence of the deceased plays a key part in the negotiation of the moral remains of the relationship. Thus, though photographs are involved in the controlled creation of the deceased's presence in the home according to what is felt to be personally and socially appropriate, this does not necessarily mean these things are less affective in the emotional lives of the bereaved.

At first, it may seem as if the hidden photographs and albums of sickness and sadness are involved in more painful and complex processes of remembrance when compared with the unblemished and nostalgic portraits on display. This chapter has sought to show that each takes their place in long-term remembering in the homes of the bereaved. These are not static displays that define the remembrance of the deceased as a one to one relationship of looking between mourner and picture of the deceased, a bridge between the present and the idealized past. These are dynamic assemblages of things and bereaved persons, in spaces that make grief and family imaginaries real. These affective objects, and the absent subjects and pictures they call to mind, are cognizant of obligations, judgments, pain, love, and respect. As dynamic and sometimes contested memorial objects, they continue to mediate relationships between the living in ways that allow the bereaved people to represent their feelings of loss and perpetuate their memories of absent loved ones.

References

Barthes, R. 1981. *Camera lucida: reflections on photography*. London: Flamingo, 1984.

Batchen, G. 2004. *Forget me not: photography and remembrance*. New York: Princeton Architectural.

Buckley, L. 2001. Self and Accessory in Gambian Studio Photography. *Visual Anthropology Review* 16(2), 71–91.

Chevalier, S. 2002. The Cultural Construction of Domestic Space in France and Great Britain. *Signs: Journal of Women in Culture and Society* 27(3), 847–856.

Drazin, A., and D. Frohlich. 2007. Good Intentions: Remembering through framing photographs in English homes. *Ethnos* 72(1), 51–76.

Edwards, E. 1999. Photographs as Objects of Memory. In *Material memories*, eds. by M. Kwint, C. Breward and J. Aynsley, 221–236. Oxford: Berg.

———. 2005. Photographs and the Sound of History. *Visual Anthropology Review* 21(1/2), 27–46.

Edwards, E., and J. Hart. 2004. *Photographs objects histories: on the materiality of images*, *Material cultures*. London: Routledge.

Finch, J. 1989. *Family obligations and social change, Family life series*. Cambridge: Polity.

Forty, A. 1999. Introduction. In *The Art of Forgetting*, eds. A. Forty and S. Küchler, 1–18. Oxford: Berg.

Gillis, J. R. 1996. *A world of their own making: myth, ritual, and the quest for family values*. New York: Basic Books.

Halle, D. 1993. *Inside culture: art and class in the American home*. London: University of Chicago Press.

Kwint, M. 1999. Introduction: The Physical Past. In *Material memories*, eds. M. Kwint, C. Breward and J. Aynsley, 1–16. Oxford: Berg.

Layne, L. 2000. He was a real baby with baby things. *Journal of Material Culture* 5(3), 321–345.

Miller, D. 2008. *The Comfort of Things*. London: Polity Press.

Miller, D., and F. R. Parrott. 2007. Death, Ritual and Material Culture in South London. In *Death Rites and Rights*, eds. B. Brooks-Gordon, F. Ebtehaj, J. Herring, M. Johnson and M. Richards, 147–162. Oxford: Hart Publishing/Cambridge Socio-Legal Group.

Pahl, R., and L. Spencer. 2003. *Personal communities: not simply families of 'fate' or 'choice', ISER working papers*. Colchester: Institute for Social and Economic Research.

Parrott, F. 2007. Mais où a-t-on donc rangé ces souvenirs? (Now where did we put those memories?). *Ethnologie française* XXXVII(2), 305–312.

Parrott, F. R. 2009. *The Transformation of Photography, Memory and the Domestic Interior: An ethnographic study of the representational, memorial and ancestral practices of South London householders*, Unpublished PhD thesis, Department of Anthropology, University College London, London.

Pink, S. 2001. *Doing visual ethnography: images, media and representation in research*. London: Sage.

Pinney, C. 1997. *Camera Indica: the social life of Indian photographs*. London: Reaktion Books.

Rose, G. 2003. Domestic spacings and family photography: a case study. *Transactions of the Institute of British Geographers* 28(1), 5–18.

———. 2004. "Everyone's cuddled up and it just looks really nice": the emotional geography of some mums and their family photos. *Social and Cultural Geography* 5(4), 549–64.

———. "You just have to make a conscious effort to keep snapping away, I think": a case study of family photos, mothering and familial space. In *Motherhood and Space: Configurations of the Maternal Through Politics, Home, and the Body*, eds. Hardy, S and C. Wiedmer, 221–240. Basingstoke: Palgrave MacMillan.

Samuel, R. 1994. *Theatres of Memory Volume 1: Past and Present in Contemporary Culture*. London, New York: Verso.

Seremetakis, C. N. 1991. *The last word: women, death, and divination in Inner Mani*. London: University of Chicago Press.

Slater, D. 1983. Marketing Mass Photography. In *Language, Image, Media*, eds. H. Davis and P. Walton, 245–263. Oxford: Blackwell.

Sontag, S. 1977. *On photography*. New York: Farrar, Straus and Giroux.

Spence, J., and P. Holland. 1991. *Family snaps: the meanings of domestic photography*. London: Virago.

Stewart, S. 1984. *On longing: narratives of the miniature, the gigantic, the souvenir, the collection*. Baltimore ; London: Johns Hopkins University Press.

Wells, L. 1997. *Photography: a critical introduction*. London: Routledge.

Part V
Ambiguous Materialities

Chapter 9
Absent Powers: Magic and Loss in Post-socialist Mongolia

Lars Højer

Introduction

When Mongolian villagers and nomadic pastoralists left socialism behind in the early 1990s, they were filled with the certainty that something had now changed – *post*-socialism had become an ethnographic reality rather than merely an academic invention. Socialism had profoundly altered the cultural and religious conditions prevailing in pre-revolutionary Mongolia, and with the passing of socialism Mongolians confronted the fact that something had been lost and an unbridgeable gap between pre-socialist and post-socialist times had emerged (cf. Humphrey 1992). It is this perception of gap and loss that is the focus of this article. However, rather than seeing it as lamentable loss, I will be concerned with the creative aspects of absent knowledge.

Speaking in the most general terms, anthropology has been obsessed with comprehending, understanding, and accessing culturally constructed knowledge and alternative ways of knowing. These, it is assumed, exist and can be comprehended, understood, and accessed by the culturally adept person as well as by the anthropologist. The anthropologist claims – explicitly or implicitly – that either it is possible to access this knowledge by using the right methods, or alternatively such knowledge cannot be accessed, thereby still presupposing its existence. The anthropology of knowledge, often indiscernible from a general anthropology of culture or meaning[1] (Boyer 2005; Crick 1982), then, is concerned with an assumed *presence* of cultural knowledge that can, at least in principle, be accessed, even if such knowledge is dynamic (i.e. it is still there to be followed), unevenly distributed

---

[1] Crick's review of the anthropology of knowledge is, by his own admission, indistinguishable from a review of anthropology in general (1982: 287). In the same vein, Barth defines knowledge in very general terms as 'what a person employs to interpret and act on the world' (2002: 1), although he claims that knowledge, as opposed to culture, is less 'embracing' and not just diffusely shared (2002: 1).

L. Højer (✉)
Department of Cross-Cultural and Regional Studies, University of Copenhagen,
Copenhagen, Denmark
e-mail:lhoejer@hum.ku.dk

M. Bille et al. (eds.), *An Anthropology of Absence: Materializations of Transcendence and Loss*, 149
DOI 10.1007/978-1-4419-5529-6_9, © Springer Science+Business Media, LLC 2010

(i.e. some still have it), or based on embodied competence and experience (i.e. it can still be learned). As such, the *presence* of cultural knowledge might have different roots and dynamics, but it is there to be grasped.

Within the past few decades, a number of discussions concerning the construction of knowledge, culture, and cosmology, on the one hand, and the revival, reinvention, or memory of tradition, on the other, have repeatedly addressed this question of cultural knowledge (see e.g., Barth 2002; Hobsbawm and Ranger 1983; Jing 1996; Keesing 1987; Watson 1994). It has been shown that traditions of knowledge – or, alternatively, culture, or cosmology – are not easily detachable from their pragmatic and performative transmission through social relations (Barth 1987, 2002), and it has been "revealed" how cultural traditions are constructed, that is, made up or transformed, in line with power structures (Bloch 1989a, b; Keesing 1987) or according to the (instrumental) agenda of elites or a present concern with national or other collective identities (Kaplonski 1998; Trevor-Roper 1983). Alternatively, it has been argued that cultural structure is not a side-effect of politics, but a potent and invisible presence in human endeavors, and, hence, that one should substitute "invention of tradition" with "inventiveness of tradition" (Sahlins 1999). For instance, a number of recent studies focusing on Mongolian and Inner Asian cosmologies and practices have shown them to contain their own specific cultural-cum-regional ontology, in one instance labeled as "transcendental perspectivism" (Holbraad and Willerslev 2007) and in another as "totemism" (Pedersen 2001). Apart from assuming the omnipresence of culture/knowledge, such discussions demonstrate that the sociology or anthropology of knowledge (Barth 2002; Boyer 2005; Crick 1982; Keesing 1987) – or, more generally, an epistemological anthropology of what and how we are made to know – has been the focus of much attention, as has the study of (cultural) ontologies of unique (and existing, i.e. *present*) ethnographic realities (Holbraad and Willerslev 2007: 330).[2] The fundamental agreement behind the disagreements – politics versus tradition or function versus culture – is that the *presence* of culture, knowledge, or ontology is not to be questioned.

Less attention, however, has been paid to the *absence* of knowledge as an elusive but effective agent in people's actions and as a proper anthropological (non-)object of investigation. This does not *contain* cultural presence – whether in the form of ontology, cosmology, or knowledge – at its center. The construction of knowledge loss in socialist historicity, for example, and the constructiveness of absence of knowledge in magical practices, as well as the intimate and mutually encouraging relation between the two, is a case in point. It is the aim of this article to remedy such disregard for absence, because certain magico-religious practices in Mongolia (and elsewhere), it will be argued, can only be understood if absence of knowledge – and, more precisely, knowledge of absence – is treated as a powerful presence gaining effects exactly by not being fully known.

---

[2] The debate on the transmission of culture (see, e.g., Ingold 2001; Sperber 1985) also seems to be concerned with *presence*: that is, the presence of psychological dispositions or the presence of a non-detached practical engagement with the world. In contrast, my argument concerns the creativity of engagement with absence or detachment.

The argument will proceed as follows. First, the problem about loss of knowledge in the Mongolian post-socialist context is briefly addressed. Next, attention turns to the socialist understanding and fabrication of history. It will be argued that, apart from having literally made persons, things, and religious knowledge disappear, socialism has also made people imagine a radical disconnection between the past and the present and served to empower what it was meant to suppress. Such radical disconnections with both the past and the imagined enemies of socialism have now become a powerful but also muddled and confused space for magical agency in post-socialist Mongolia. Third, it will be shown how a particular magico-religious object is constructed in order to defer full comprehension and thereby highlight the presence of a compelling absence. It is further argued that this mode of empowering is, if not identical to, then at least analogous to the unintended effects of socialism described in the earlier section. Finally, the two strands – magic and socialism – will be brought together in a case study from Ulaanbaatar, the capital of Mongolia.

Unknown Spirit Powers in Contemporary Mongolia

On the surface of it, the unknown, or simply the lack of knowledge, is a problem in present-day Mongolia.[3] Although Tibetan Buddhism was popularized and insti-tutionalized in Mongolian areas in the sixteenth century and emerged as the stron-gest institution in Mongolian society at the beginning of the twentieth century, when the Manchu Qing dynasty collapsed, all this came to an abrupt end during socialism. While some people secretly continued to carry out rituals at home and kept religious objects in the bottom of their household chests, away from public view, and even though knowledge of religious persons and texts was sometimes retained in ambiguous semipublic discourses (see Humphrey 1994), it is hard not to conceive of this as a historical rupture and detachment from the past. Most reli-gious practitioners were executed or forced to abandon their religious practices and a huge number of religious objects and buildings were destroyed during the Stalin-inspired purges of the 1930s. Combined with a general ideological campaign against "superstition" during socialism, such destruction has led to a major loss of canonical magico-religious knowledge. One lama[4] explained to me that socialism changed the mind of the young generation, who learned to destroy old religious objects with ease. Certainly, the transmission of religious knowledge was risky in socialist times, and now (people say) the old, wise Buddhist lamas have all died. If any potential students of magico-religious traditions were present during socialism, the teachers were – quite understandably – reluctant to accept them, and religious

---

[3] Present-day Mongolia refers to 2000/1 and 2006, when the material presented here was collected.
[4] Whereas a lama in the Tibetan context is a religious teacher, the term is used here for the Buddhist clergy in Mongolia, although many present-day lamas are not technically proper monks in the sense of having been ordained according to the canonical Buddhist monastic rules (Bareja-Starzynska and Havnevik 2006). Accordingly, the term is often used in a vague sense.

practices in the post-socialist era have often been constrained by the shortage of lamas, at least in the countryside.[5] People are therefore acutely aware of "loss" and consider this particular loss of knowledge as a hindrance to the contemporary practice of religion, often claiming not to be strong believers in anything. In addition, people imagine the past as a time when this loss was absent; back then, they would say, people knew all those things. So a common concern among Mongolians seems to be: how should one practice religion in the face of this loss, when one does not know how to do it, or what kind of powers one is dealing with?[6]

By turning this concern on its head, I will argue that such loss has a productive side to it, and that it is exactly from – and in – this loss that magical technologies and powers emerge. The concern with loss and absence as productive categories necessitates a reconsideration of the native Mongolian assumption that the amount of magico-religious knowledge and the magnitude and extent of religious practice correlate with people's strength of belief, as in the often heard conflation of lost knowledge with lost religion. This quantitative conflation implies that the more you worship and know, the more you are thought to believe, and the more you believe, the more you are thought to worship and know. A further implication is that people will cease to believe if they lose the knowledge of how to worship. Obviously, this suggestion is not easily dismissed. Some people do reject religion, at least on certain occasions, and people in rural areas often avoid relating to spiritually charged places and objects precisely because they do not know how to do it. Many people in Northern Mongolia, for instance, do not worship Dayan Deerh, a famous cave cult site, because they are unacquainted with the correct procedures. Similarly, it is not uncommon for people to hand over religious items to a temple (cf. Bareja-Starzynska and Havnevik 2006: 212), simply because they do not know how to treat them properly and, as a result, consider them dangerous (which, it should be noted, gives a novel and thought-provoking perspective on the trade in religious objects in post-socialist Mongolia). Yet, it is immediately clear that it is not because they do not believe in spirit powers that people avoid such places and items, but rather they avoid them, and avoid relating to them *because they do believe*.[7] Hence, the issue is that avoidance arises from a belief in the erratic power of such agencies.

---

[5] This picture is now changing in certain areas with the education of a new generation of young Buddhist lamas in Ulaanbaatar and abroad.

[6] It should be stressed that most of the ethnography presented here is based on my field experience from Chandman'-Öndör district, Hövsgöl province, in northern Mongolia, where religious practitioners are still few and so elaborate religious knowledge of cosmological ideas is rare and has a strikingly fragmented form. Anthropologists like Shimamura, Buyandelgeriyn, and Swancutt have worked among Buryat Mongols in the easternmost regions of Mongolia, where a particularly strong revival of elaborate shamanic practices can be observed. A similar revival of shamanic practices has not taken place in other parts of Mongolia (see also Shimamura 2004: 198–9). While this might account for my stress on "present absence" and the lack of references to coherent and elaborate cosmologies, I still believe that most points made in this article, even if slightly more pronounced in this region, are still highly relevant for studies in other parts of Mongolia.

[7] In this sense, loss is not opposed to belief but is rather its precondition. It is not implied, however, that people keeping religious objects are nonbelievers; rather, in this case, the loss or absence has taken enough shape for it to be dealt with safely.

They are erratic and uncontrolled because they have come to be imagined as lost objects and places – lost to present-day people, lost to the present (in that they belong to the past), and lost to the past (in that they survived into the present); yet very present *as lost*. They are what one might call a present absence because they point to an absence by virtue of their presence[8] (and hence, it is also an absent presence in that it is a shadowy, enigmatic, and incomplete manifestation [cf. Delaplace and Empson 2007: 2009; Holbraad and Willerslev 2007: 331, 337]).

Socialism and the Labor of the Negative

Before proceeding along these lines, it is useful first to explore the context of Mongolian socialism. During the socialist period (roughly 1921–1990), Mongolian cities became associated with industrialization and development, and the sparsely populated countryside, home to villagers and nomadic pastoralists, came to be considered as a space to be civilized and urbanized (Humphrey and Sneath 1999: 301), at least in public ideology. The implication was that "city versus countryside" was socialism versus a backward, feudal, and traditional way of life and that history was to be written as "the progressive nature of the socialist regime" (Kaplonski 1997: 57). In this way, the spatial distinction was simultaneously a temporal evolutionary distinction between presocialism and socialism.

It was essential to the identity of socialism – and to the realization of this identity – to depart from the past and the periphery, and moving to a new historical condition was to revolt against the past (cf. Žižek 1999). Things had to be destroyed, and an often specified number of enemies had to be killed (Humphrey 2002b: 29; Shimamura 2004: 208; Žižek 1999: 40); the summoning of imagined enemies, it seems, was more important than the existence of true enemies. In the words of one Mongolian: "They showed my father a paper saying he was an enemy of the people, and was to be arrested ... It wasn't necessary [to explain]. He was an enemy" (Kaplonski 1999: 97). It was imagined and realized that the past – i.e. the enemy – was *not* the present and the present was *not* the past, and hence, that the past was lacking in and lost to the present.

---

[8] One reviewer suggested that I use Derrida's notion of "spectre" (1994) rather than the dialectical expression "present absence", which points to the iconoclastic power of what "always remains" or the failure of iconoclasm "if any fragment escapes destruction" (Pietz 2002: 65; I thank Victor Buchli for this reference). I have, however, chosen to retain the latter expression, since a dialectical expression, I believe, much better conveys the importance of difference or split as potentiality – whether in (post-)socialist history, (post-) socialist historical narratives, magico-religious summoning of concealed powers (present and absent at the same time), or magico-religious images (where meaning is deferred). While the notion of spectre – as something which simultaneously is present and not present, inaugurates and reveals, and repeats and initiates (Derrida 1994: 10, 98) – might capture all that, it runs the danger, like so many other single hybrid terms, of moving attention away from their split and paradoxical nature. Even spectrality, it seems, can only be described through the use of oppositions (present/not present, inaugurate/reveal, repeat/initiate).

The purges of the 1930s were the most violent eruption of socialist modernity and its strategy of opposition, revolution, and historical rupture. At least 22,000 people died during the purges (Kaplonski 1999: 95), most of them Buddhist lamas; and 760 out of 771 Buddhist temples and monasteries were demolished (Baabar 1999: 370). As a strategy of radical critique, however, it had the unintended consequence of also bringing into being what it tried to destroy. "The labour of the negative", a phrase coined by Hegel and recently appropriated by Taussig (1999; see also Højbjerg 2002), is a notion that captures the dynamics of these unintended consequences; it is also a notion which, eventually, will lead us back to the range of ethnographic phenomena mentioned above concerning lack of knowledge as knowledge of lack. "The labour of the negative" points to the dialectic logic that socialism's attack on its imagined enemy backfired because not only did socialism's imagination of superstition serve to eradicate such superstition, but it did – while eradicating it – bring it into existence as superstition: that is, as something that was important and powerful enough to necessitate destruction. The point is that the force of destruction and the sheer amount of energy expended on superstition mystified "mystification". It fashioned an entity and gave it potential life.[9] Much "superstition" was lost, surely, but simultaneously an imagined space of absence was created. People were made to know that certain things existed of which they did not, and should not, know, and the negative came into being and gained power by virtue of being subject to destruction. We need to remind ourselves that many stories are circulating in Mongolia about how the socialist destruction of shamanic paraphernalia backfired and led to the violent and mystical death of the communists destroying it. An old woman in Tsagaan Nuur district in the northernmost part of Mongolia once told me of a man who drowned after burning a shamamic costume. Likewise, a revolutionary in a different part of Mongolia is said to have caused his own death and the death of all his descendants after burning a shamanic tree in 1930 (Yanjmaa 2000: 30).While nobody dared to touch the sacred stone cairn at the Dayan Deerh cave cult site in Northern Mongolia, one man, I was told, tried to shoot down a piece of silver from the wooden pole of a destroyed Buddhist temple nearby, and he soon died and so did his wife and children. Nowadays, previously suppressed – and, hence, angry – spirits are (re-)emerging among the Buryat Mongols in Eastern Mongolia to take their revenge for being neglected in socialist times (Buyandelgeriyn 2007), and some of them – the so-called *uheer* – "were made into outcasts of the socialist state" and their tormented souls are now returning to make trouble (Buyandelgeriyn 2007: 135; compare with the *shurkul* and *barkan*

---

[9]Interestingly, the labor of the negative is strongly reminiscent of the Mongolian notion of *hel am*, which concerns, among other things, the danger of 'a discourse of binary knowledge, where the effects can just as well be the opposite ... because opposites are integral to each other' (Højer 2004: 55[0]). *Hel am* concerns the fact that extreme and definite statements ('she is good/bad/beautiful', etc.) are dangerous because they act on people and are emotionally evocative. Stating things too clearly – as socialism did – evokes opposites/enemies and emotionality.

spirits of the Daur Mongols (Humphrey with Onon 1996)). The destruction, so to speak, recharged the battery of the shamanic paraphernalia, sacred trees, and "supernatural" powers destroyed. Now that socialism has been abandoned, people are left with this awareness of absence. What was considered to be a feudal past full of superstition in socialist times is today a potent space for magical possibilities and magical agency.

In a recent article, Buyandelgeriyn presents a substantial amount of ethnography which supports this claim, and she – like me – points to the productiveness of the lost Mongolian past when writing that "the more the Buryats [Mongols] believe in the loss of that tradition during socialism, the more shamanic rituals they generate" (2007: 128), but she stops short of attending to the constitutive indeterminate nature and generative capabilities of *perceived* absence within magical workings. Based on her understanding of emerging shamanic practices and spirit powers on the Buryat Mongols attempt to come to terms with historical loss, tragic past events, and existing post-socialist uncertainties, she relies mainly – like many others – on implicit "emotional-functional" explanations such as the Buryat Mongols need to find meaning, construct identity and history,[10] or alleviate suffering. Shamanic practices are means for dealing with "anxieties and uncertainties" (2007: 127), for making "misfortunes meaningful" (2007: 127, 128, 142), for offering explanations (2007: 130), for making "sufferings bearable" (2007: 142), and for controlling "the flow of misfortunes" (2007: 132); moreover, "economic anxiety has *pushed* the Buryats to seek help from shamans" (2007: 128, my emphasis). While Buyandelgeriyn's analysis does not necessarily contradict the present argument, I am – for now – less interested in "actually existing" historical loss (although this enters our equation) and the real traumas of past and present, or in what people psychologically, emotionally, and economically *need* to do, so to speak, than in what certain magical and modernist technologies do to people by working with – and creating – conspicuous and productive gaps where meaning and knowledge are constantly deferred. While everyone acknowledges that things – and revolutions – certainly did happen in the past (and also brought about traumatic events), the historical gaps take on particularly strong significance when merging with magical domains constituted in – and working with – a strong presence of absence and a constant deferral of meaning; a red sect lama whom we have mentioned below, for example, is much more inclined than others to evoke and engage with historical gaps and past mysteries. Following from this, absence cannot simply be seen as a product of socialist modernity, but is intrinsic to the magical technologies that are explored ethnographically in the following sections; like modernity, they can create imagined spaces of productive absence. The aim of the following ethnography is to show how magical technologies join the modern (post-)socialist space by making absence present, and how they are fuelled by absence and cultivate it.

---

[10] While also stressing the importance of historical rupture, the socio-psychological aspect is even more pronounced in an article by Shimamura (2004) whose focus is almost solely on the role played by shamanism in reconstructing the ethnic identity of the Aga-Buryat Mongols.

Manufacturing Absence in a Written Buddhist Charm

The manufacture of absence is well illustrated by a particular protective written charm created by one of my key informants, a so-called "red" Buddhist lama from Chandman'-Öndör district in the northern Hövsgöl province. Although the term "red" is unclear and diffuse when applied to particular Buddhist sects in Mongolia, it is often – and remarkably so in this case – used to refer to more "basic", ancient, and shamanic Mongolian religious traditions concerned with the requirements of everyday life at the periphery of centralized powers, as opposed to more institution-alized and dogmatic "yellow" Buddhist practices. The "red" lama brings to mind Barth's notion of the 'conjurer' (Barth 1990), secrecy being constitutive of the kind of knowledge he works with and of the way in which it is transmitted. Having been taught secretly in socialist times – or so he told me – by a high-ranking and powerful lama, he has a direct link to a potent past and, like many Mongolian shamans, he had a serious illness in his childhood. Doctors were unable to diagnose his illness or treat him, but one night a lama performed a *gürem* (ritual of exorcism to repel misfortune or sickness), and three days later he had dramatically improved. From then on he was interested in magic power (*id shid*) and eager to learn it. At first, he was taught the Tibetan alphabet by a "yellow" lama, and then a "red" lama reluctantly accepted him as his only pupil (*shav'*) at a time when it was illegal to practice any kind of religion. The latter started by introducing him to five religious books and some incense offerings (*san*), and finally – after five or six years – he was taught a number of secret mantras (*tarni*), the most secret of which was only "orally transmitted" (*amyn jüd be*). Along the way, he realized that he had been taught shamanic "things", and his teacher told him that he was to follow the red direction. He used a similar form of secrecy – of revealing things as concealed – to refer to his own abilities and religious education (which took place secretly in a remote area) and when – at other times – he told me about hidden treasures and mysterious happenings. This secrecy is also manifest in the written charm to which we will now turn.

This charm is written on a long piece of paper and can be divided into four sections. In the first section, the main text – a mantra – is written in black ink in Tibetan, a written language almost solely understood and read by lamas but never-theless recognizable as Tibetan scripture by most people in Mongolia. In the second, the names to be protected by the charm form a section between the initial and the final part of Tibetan text. They are written in blue ink in Cyrillic, the script most commonly used in Mongolia and therefore easily read and understood by almost any adult person in the country. In the third section, a whole range of destructive or enchaining tools and frightening weapons have been drawn below the main text on the front. The fourth section, on the reverse of the paper, contains a mantra written in Sanskrit, used for the consecration of the device.

The written charm was designed to be placed over the entrance to a Mongolian home, making the distinction between host and visitor crucial. From the description above, we would expect both host and visitor to perceive the device as a display of weaponry, inducing a sense of fear, protection, and physical power, associated with an enumeration of familiar names related to the household and surrounded by unintelligible – but recognizable – religious text. The point to be made here is that it is the unintelligible text that empowers the "familiar" device by providing a *level beyond complete understanding*, making it transcendent and powerfully "captivating" (Gell 1998: 68–72).[11] The incomprehensible – i.e. that which is beyond the comprehension of ordinary people – is evoked by the meta-sign of Tibetan scripture. In addition, the importance of the incomprehensible is emphasized by the red lama, who stresses the secrecy of the charm and warns the client against copying it. Also, he claims, the charm – and the mantra – will not be understood by Buddhist lamas from other sects. On the reverse of the paper, the Sanskrit mantra (*tarni*) for the consecration of the device is written in Tibetan letters. This mantra consists of incomprehensible syllables, which the lama knows by heart but which he cannot and certainly should not translate because their power derives from their mystical form as words without lexical meaning. As such, they are powerful rather than meaningful – they gain power from being beyond ordinary meaning and communicative understanding. They do not communicate power; they *are* power.

The charm's materialization of indecipherable "magical" knowledge, which is, however, decipherable as a paradoxical *knowledge of the unknown*,[12] is associated with well-known names (such as members of the household) written in a conspicuous blue color, and easily accessible symbols of aggression (axe, gun, etc.) and forced pacification (hobble and handcuffs). Its simultaneous embodiment of the known and the unknown makes the known and the unknown draw on the power of the other. The known world is mystified by embedding it in an agency without a known agent. Our imagination is provoked (what is behind the scripture?) and the form *elicits a reaction*, but not a specific action on our part. We have been acted upon, we have sensed agency, and agency has been elicited.[13] In other words, the sign works by virtue of referring to something beyond itself, or rather by containing this beyond within itself. It hides the content while conjuring it up; it creates by mystifying, it reveals by concealing. The charm is designed to provoke absence as such: that is, to *put absence to work* and to cause reactions. One might say it is less a matter of the particularity of "thinking through things" (Henare et al. 2007), than of something that simply makes us think (and do), much like the shamans' mirrors described by Humphrey, whose "design encourages a progression of thought" (2007: 175). Indeed, present absence *is* mirroring the unknown.

A sceptic might claim that the lama has simply used the written charm to mystify his client deliberately, but – apart from being unlikely – this claim is irrelevant for at least two reasons. First, the present argument concerns form in itself, and as such

---

[11] The principle is comparable to Gell's notion of "captivation" (Gell 1998: 68–72), although Gell introduces this term with regard to the effects of artistic virtuosity: Artistic agency ... is socially efficacious because it establishes an inequality between the agency responsible for the production of the work of art, and the spectators ... Captivation or fascination – the demoralization produced by the spectacle of unimaginable virtuosity – ensues from the spectator becoming trapped within the index because the index embodies agency, which is essentially indecipherable (1998: 71).

[12] This can be compared to Houseman's notion of "avowed secrecy" (1993: 213), where the excluded party is aware of the existence of a secret and of his/her exclusion from it.

[13] Cf. Strathern's notion of "elicitation" (1988: 296) and Gell's notion of "abduction" (1998).

deliberately avoids political, economic, and functional issues of strategic manipulation by individuals or collectives. The argument concerns what magical forms do to people (cf. Pedersen 2007), not the other way around. Secondly, it might be argued that the lama is just as mystified as the client (remember the Sanskrit mantra on the reverse of the paper), since the power and "meaning" of the mantra can never be made transparent (even to the lama himself), and that it is, paraphrasing Lévi-Strauss (1969 [1964]: 12), a question of mystification thinking through us. If form, for example the "pure" form of Tibetan or Sanskrit scripture in the charm, is opposed to content (or intention), yet only exists by virtue of content (as form has been created with a purpose by an agent and begs the question of what, or which intention, is behind it), then to create form is to create content or intention. Moreover, the more abstract the form becomes, as when form appears to be mystical, the more abstract, intangible, and pure the intentionality seems to become. It becomes, purely and simply, the elicitation of a reaction.

In what appears to be in line with the present argument, Bloch claims in a seminal article that religion and ritual are not about communicating in an ordinary locutionary sense, where a large number of potential choices are available to the communicators, but rather about creating a formalized situation where actors are caught and unable to resist – through ordinary argument – the demands made of them (Bloch 1989c: 24), because religion and ritual have "no 'truth' conditions" (1989c: 42). There is simply no argument to be made when language is formalized in ritual:

> It is because the formalization of language is a way whereby one speaker can coerce the response of another that it can be seen as a form of social control. It is really a type of communication where rebellion is impossible and only revolution could be feasible. It is a situation where power is all or nothing and of course in society total refusal is normally out of the question (1989c: 29).

Hence, ritual, religion, and formalization can be likened to a tunnel into which one plunges (1989c: 41), extinguishing any possibility of choice or creativity. We can follow Bloch to the extent that an irresistible demand is caused by what is acknowledged as form in the charm, but otherwise his argument appears to be an illuminating inversion of the present line of reasoning. Bloch argues that formalization turns reality into "a timeless placeless zone in which everybody is in his right place" and the elder "into an ancestor speaking eternal truth" (1989c: 44). The charm described above is certainly recognized as a religious form, but, apart from the fact that it is not placed in an expanded and fixed universe or cosmology with ancestors occupying the apex, the whole point about the charm is that it does not *contain* truth. The "minimal" formalization of objects that are recognized as religious form, but not locked to tightly knit cosmologies, and does not place one on a highway to eternal truth. Rather, such fragments of form direct one towards the indefinite, and as such make one open to any reaction. They are in a sense – and as opposed to Bloch – even more creative, as it were, than ordinary language because they allow any possibility (cf. Lévi-Strauss 1987 [1950]: 64). Bloch also concludes that religion is a special form of authority. If the present objects and powers, however, qualify as religion, they are – at least when it comes to the most "wild" fragments – what amounts to the least authoritative phenomena possible because they define actions minimally. They create a space where politics are minimized,[14] so to speak. If power, according to Bloch (1989c: 29), is all *or* nothing – either you plunge into the tunnel with no possibility of turning left or right, or you do not – then power in the present case is all *and* nothing. When you plunge into the tunnel, everything becomes possible, at least in principle. This should become clearer as we proceed.

Effects of Absence: Indeterminacy and Avoidance

Let us now turn away from religious objects and their inherent effects to a setting where people and their specific reactions to construed absences are more prominent. This is important because the absence designed in objects, such as the written charm above, does not have an effect in a cultural and historical vacuum. The above charm, for example, was made by a red sect lama living in the remote periphery of Mongolia, and it was made for a young Mongolian man living in the absolute center of Mongolia, the capital Ulaanbaatar. The latter needed the charm for the protection of family members. He would see the lama as embodying the periphery and a deep pre-socialist past in the form of a particular "red" Buddhist tradition practised on the threshold of an ancient Mongolian shamanic tradition. The lama would "do something" which the young man – in his own words – "did not know what it was". This included a ritual for consecrating (*aravnailah*) or enlivening the device, and the young man then took it to his home in the capital city. The lama had created a rare charm, an almost one-off creation; the only other instance of it – as observed by me and the young man – was placed over the door of the lama's own home. In the young man's own words, he wanted the charm because "he hadn't seen similar things in other places" and because the lama "did it on his own, made it himself" (singularity being the ontological premise for shamanic activity (Humphrey with Onon 1996)). A further reason, the young man added, was that "it did not seem to be completely Buddhist". The lama personified a continuity of the unknown, that is, a singularity; he embodied a lost past in the distant countryside and an esoteric semi-shamanic tradition, whose secrecy – one might argue – was even boosted during socialism, when it was forced to become clandestine and to avoid the use of tangible written material. The effects of the charm, then, are conditioned by such other powerful cultural forms as the socialist and post-socialist retrospective and prospective making of historical gaps and spatial distance.

Such conditioning through cultural forms is related to everyday concerns of people as well. In certain divination sessions described elsewhere (Højer forthcoming), an essential indeterminacy is brought about by the evocation of enigmatic and elusive religious objects and by powers that are brought to bear on clients' present misfortunes. Common to such powers is often their unwelcome and unexpected intrusion

---

[14] This is not meant to suggest that the charm – using symbols of aggression and being placed to protect a household – is not political or used politically, but that its *way of working* with layers – and, hence, being a form that simply elicits the anticipation of an intention – is minimally political.

into peoples' lives. Through divination sessions, then, people are suddenly brought into relations with powerful and precarious agencies, such as a hardly known Buddhist lama relative from the old days, a forgotten religious object once owned by someone in the family line, a spirit power in the landscape, or a spell caused by a dispute. These objects and agencies are often not known to exist beforehand by the clients in question, and throughout the divination session they are construed as – and remain – partly unfamiliar, indefinite, and evasive; they are revealed as concealed.

Now, the point is that such unknown powers are a distinctive kind of agency effecting "undirected movement". If present absence, as claimed with regard to the charm above, elicits reaction, then we should note that its specificity, rather paradoxically, is to elicit "any reaction" by forcing people into an exchange in relation with the unknown. Such reactive exchange scenarios might be of a very tense and erratic nature, which is not characteristic of more institutionalized religious practices, where agencies are related to in a more formalized and secure manner. When paying respect to Buddhist deities or pictures of deceased family members on a family altar, for example, Mongolians usually know what to do, and at *ovoo* (stone cairn) ceremonies, where spirit masters of the Mongolian landscape are celebrated, and educated lamas officiate at the formalized and highly predictable proceedings. While "mystification" does take place on such occasions, this mystification is contained and does not have the potential of the singular, exceptional, and fragmented form of a rare charm. At *ovoo* ceremonies, reacting to the known (unknown) is ritualized and hence relatively calm, and such occasions, besides being official, formal, and ceremonial, take place in a safe atmosphere. Exchange relations with the (known) unknown, however, are either "wild" and unpredictable or characterized by avoidance. This is conveyed in a story related to a young woman in Ulaanbaatar.

The story begins with the tragic suicide of the woman's younger brother when he was a young man in the mid-1980s during the closing stages of socialist rule in Mongolia. Staunch believers in the socialist system, her parents were neither "traditional people" nor practising Buddhists. They did, nevertheless, have an image of a Buddhist deity, inherited from her grandparents, at home, but it remained locked in their chest with other belongings and was never displayed publicly on an altar. The death of her younger brother was, of course, a great shock to the parents, and they decided, despite their atheist convictions, to visit a Buddhist lama. The lama told them that the deity in the chest had been lying upside down and next to a pair of shoes. This, they were told, had offended the deity, who had become angry and taken their son. The parents were now afraid of what the deity would do next, and they were unsure about "the wants of the deity", and how to treat it properly. They decided to hand it over to the main Gandan temple in Ulaanbaatar, where Buddhist lamas, they assumed, would know what to do and how to treat it. In turn they received a new deity from the same place. After the death of her son, the mother suffered mental problems and was hospitalized for a while. She was depressed for a long time and her hair turned grey almost overnight. One day, a few months later, the mother was cleaning the ground of the family's compound (*hashaa*) on the outskirts of Ulaanbaatar. She was sweeping up rubbish and burning weeds. Suddenly, she became furious and exclaimed that the gods had never helped her or her family. They had taken her son, she continued, and the gods would not help them in the future. She then took the new deity image from the altar and threw it on the fire. For many years afterwards, the family had no deities in their home. A few years ago, they acquired a new one, but now the parents have grown old and, as the woman relating the story explained, it is their last chance to "do some good" – i.e. gain religious merit – before they die.

The recently acquired deity does not relate to the first part of the story, and – as I have observed on many occasions and been told by numerous Mongolian informants – it is common in Mongolia for people to develop a renewed interest in institutionalized and "calm" religious practices concerned with reincarnation and gaining merit (*buyan*) as they grow old. The main point of interest in the story is the first part, from which a number of points can be drawn.

First, we have a clear case of an unknown power literally emerging after having been locked up for many years. The deity is inherited from a deep Buddhist past, which is radically separated from the contemporary atheist life of the family.[15] In the name of socialism the family has, so to speak, eclipsed the past; they have not destroyed the deity but have hidden it, and although the power of past religion has been dismissed, it has also been kept. What has happened, however, is that in creating a distance – in terms of both time and knowledge – to the power in question, it has changed from being a conventional actuality (a deity on the grandparent's altar) to becoming an erratic possibility (a locked-up power).[16] The parents are insecure. What does the deity want? What will it do next? The only way out is to give it away: that is, to sever their relation with it. The new deity, acquired from the Gandan monastery and thus emerging from present times, is initially thought to be more manageable, and it does not act in unpredictable ways.

Secondly, the story conjures up a fierce ambiguity and change of mind with regard to semi-alien powers and shows that *relations with the unknown are also unknown relations*: that is, relations that are uncertain, unpredictable, and capricious and can only be settled once and for all through avoidance. The parents are atheists, but Buddhism has remained a possibility; they have kept the deity and decided to visit a lama when their son died. They give away the god, not because they do not believe in it, but because it is not for them (and their insufficient knowledge) to handle it. They fear it and believe in it *because* they do not know it. Yet, their relation to religion

---

[15] Inside the Mongolian household chest are things that have been detached from people at moments of separation and transformation (Empson 2007: 123). Through such things, you keep only 'partial connections' (Empson 2007: 124-5) and 'difficult relations are maintained as open possibilities' (Empson 2007: 126). We might then – and in line with the notion 'present absence' – characterize the emerging religious powers as 'partial connections which allow people 'to cross boundaries' (Empson 2007: 126).And if the partial relations inside the household chest are concealed by – but necessary to – the visible agnatic relations displayed on the chest's surface, as argued by Empson, then we might also say that the hidden deity (i.e. supernature) is the concealed – but necessary – inside of socialism. We might even further speculate that socialism has served to 'shamanize' magico-religious practices, since it seems to be in the nature of the sacred artifacts/spirit powers of shamans, such as the *ongon* (spirit vessel), that they should be hidden from public view (see also Pedersen 2007: 150-1, 154, 157).

[16] In line with this, Empson writes that it is as if things kept at the bottom of the Mongolian household chest have a 'potential to move but must be contained' (2007: 123).

and religious powers is still unsettled, and when they receive a new deity, the mother decides to get rid of it, but in doing so she still proclaims a kind of belief in impulsively and furiously burning it, rather than just "clinically" throwing it out, and by claiming that the gods have never done anything good for them. Rather than declaring disbelief, she is – it seems – declaring what amounts to war. A constant change of mind, and a radical questioning of one's own relation to these powers, is intrinsic to such anxious relations with the unknown. But as long as one engages with the powers, they cannot be ignored. On the one hand, they are construed as revealed-as-concealed powers by lamas and diviners. On the other hand, people attend to them through a lens of self-declared ignorance (we have lost the knowledge) leading to both a lack of belief (how can you really believe in what is so unknown?) and an abundance of belief (the excessive fear of the radically unknown). These aspects converge to create a domain where much can be at stake but little is certain.

The tragic death of this woman's brother, and the mother's reaction to it, speak of a universe where the radically unknown is made to be imagined, because nothing known, familiar, and close to the family would cause such a thing to happen.[17] The unknown has, so to speak, a minimal ability to animate maximally because we do not know, quite obviously, what the unknown is. Hence, it animates maximally by releasing undirected action; reactions are unconstrained by what they react to because the "exchange partner" is unknown (even rejection of the agency as agency, i.e. deciding that it is "fake", is a possibility). The unpredictable (elicitation of) hyperactivity of the unknown is also suggested by Shimamura when he writes that among the Aga-Buryat Mongols, "ancestral spirits who were unknown to them were more actively seeking (demanding – *ug nekhekh*) their descendants" (2004: 206). The fact that they are unknown seems to make them more active, and often also more erratic and dangerous: "Shamans make a particular strong point by arguing that the erasure of an origin spirit's name from the genealogical record is one of the worst causes of misfortune, far worse than forgetting the spirits whose names do exist in the records" (Buyandelgeriyn 2007: 138). If the power of gods and spirits, then, is that they always have a residue of meaning that we seek but can never completely uncover (Swancutt 2006: 338), that is, a compelling unknown (cf. Pedersen's (2007) description of the "pulling" of the shamanic spirit vessels), then one might also argue – in line with the present argument – that the more unknown and residual the spirit powers, the stronger, the more compelling, and the more unpredictable they become. All such powers – of course – are concealed, but the more manifest the concealment, the purer the power becomes in eliciting uncontrolled reactions. In the written charm, the unintelligible form called forth a mystical content, accentuated by the lama, who emphasized the secrecy of the charm, and by the client, who was sure that he had now acquired a particularly powerful object. In a similar manner, the deities from the past conjure up

---

[17] It is also possible to interpret this story in psychological terms as a family trying to come to terms with a tragic suicide. While this is a possible explanation, it does not necessarily contradict the present one. The explanatory coming-to-terms (mistreatment of a deity), as well as the grief and anger, could quite obviously not be projected onto anything, but had to be perceived in a form that contained the possibility of agency.

layer upon layer of concealment: they are powers from another world, they are from a deep and unfamiliar past, and during socialism they were clandestine objects not for public view. The charm and the deity, as well as other past and unknown powers that are evoked, are vivid images animating people. At the heart of these agencies is disguise and absence. Obviously, this is not entirely a consequence of socialism, but socialism has created a topography of fragmented religious – and partly empty – forms, such as religious objects whose significance is unknown owing to the (believed) loss of knowledgeable people, places where monasteries and spirit powers were once located, and lost or stored possessions of deceased religious people: that is, places or "points" loaded with the energy of destruction and the vitality of a lost past.

Conclusion

The anticipation of the unknown is present in the effects of socialism and in magical modalities, and it is gaining renewed momentum through the fusion of magical absence and the radically "negative" effects of socialism. This mode of anticipation is already in itself an effect – not in the sense of creating an explanation or destroying another one as it fights over different cultural ideologies such as Buddhism or shamanism, but rather by virtue of giving itself away to other effects. People are drawn into relationships and worlds, not just in the manner of painting, clarifying and synthesizing new cultural landscapes of knowledge – although this quite obviously also happens – but in the sense of being drawn into landscapes constituted in, and gaining effect from, suspense or in the fact that they are not fully known.

In concluding this argument, I was made aware of a comparable argument made by Strathern (2004). She writes about the "procreativity of absence" in relation to Melanesian ethnography and suggests that

> the knowledge that they [vehicles for communication] are lost is not, so to speak, lost knowledge, it is knowledge about absence, about forgetting and about an unrecoverable background. That sense of loss stimulates the Baktaman initiators, it would seem, to making present images work ... The important thing is that the gaps are preserved ... It is as if they knew that by insisting on that absence they create their own creativity (2004: 97-8, emphasis omitted).

It is in this sense that I understand the magical workings of certain Mongolian powers as – in Strathern's words – "the 'one' form" doing "multiple work" (2004: 98). Yet, one is then faced with the problem of whether such absences simply concern a condition of being human, be this in Melanesia or Mongolia, or whether they can be actively produced or accentuated through the unintended effects of socialism, by means of religious artifacts, or through divination sessions. I would argue that both apply because this modality refers equally to the production of images and practices that enhances the sense of absence through their radical dialectical work, and to a way of attending to the world, where this absence is potentially perceived in all images. This enhancement can, as it has been argued, take place in more coherent, institutionalized, and formalized systems of religiosity like those analyzed by

Bloch and mentioned briefly above, or it can take place in fragments of minimal magico-religious form, as they have been dealt with here. In the former case, enhancing absence is, in effect, turning it to work for the present world as a kind of ideology (cf. Bloch 1989c). In the latter case, absence works on its own terms, so to speak, and produces multiplicity. This is not an absolute difference, though, as absence can only be evoked through a known form (Tibetan scripture, Buddhist deities) – often even related to a known presence (the personal names on the charm and its location in specific homes) – and because both contain the potential of the other. Multiplicity can be the starting-point of new ideologies, and existing ideologies can implode and be subverted or torn apart by the potential possibilities of absence as it exists in all magico-religious practices.

The difference is well illustrated by two approaches to the avoidance of spirit powers in the Mongolian context. Hürelbaatar (2002: 85) has observed that people in Inner Mongolia sometimes avoid making offerings to ghosts and new sites because, once initiated, these offerings become obligatory and cannot be broken. Such obligatory relations are tiresome, people say, and they often prefer not to establish them at all. In a similar vein, Buyandelgeriyn (2007: 131) has observed that once a spirit is accepted into a Mongolian family's pantheon, the relation cannot be broken and might turn into a psychological and economic burden. In these cases, we are dealing not with avoidance of initially dangerous powers, but with known powers that turn dangerous if already established formalized exchanges are abolished. In this case, you avoid the reciprocal obligation of formalized exchange, whereas in the cases mainly dealt with in this article, you avoid the uncertain relations implicated in exchanges with the unknown. In formalized relations with relatively known powers, the danger lies in breaking the relationship, but in the cases we are dealing with here, the danger lies in establishing it. A transformation from one to the other – from danger to obligation – is conveyed by Humphrey when she writes about the Buryat Mongols that: "When the offended spirit has been revealed, the shaman commonly orders the client to go out to the mountain (tree, etc.) residence of the spirit and perform the ritual called *alban*, which means duty, service or tribute" (2002a: 216).

What I have tried to reveal is a space that points not to the presence of institutionalized cultural knowledge – or not-entirely-present cultural imaginations or anticipations extending such knowledge to new domains (cf. Barth 2002: 2) – but to the presence of absence as such: that is, to what is important by virtue of not being here, by virtue of being a powerful centre of gravity where only nothing – or rather no thing – *is* yet. But the fact that only nothing is in this "gap" does not imply that this absence cannot be produced, or that it cannot be effective. Rather this space might be depicted as the non-cause for effects, or as an effect which is indefinite. The absence contains potential the effects of which cannot be contained; it just elicits (re)action.[18] And its unattainability – or its being relatively external to relations – is what gives it power. Thus, if cultural knowledge, so to speak, is elaborated inside our (cultural) minds, the presence of absence points to the power of the outside.

---

[18] In continuation of Gell (1998), we might define this (spirit) potential as the abduction of abduction.

References

Baabar (Bar-Erdene Batbayar). 1999. *Twentieth century Mongolia*, ed. C. Kaplonski; trans. D. Sühjargalmaa, S. Burenbayar, H. Hulan & N. Tuya. Cambridge: White Horse Press.

Bareja-Starzynska, A. & H. Havnevik. 2006. 'A preliminary study of Buddhism in present-day Mongolia'. In *Mongols: from country to city*, eds. O. Bruun & L. Narangoa, 212–36. Copenhagen: NIAS Press.

Barth, F. 1987. *Cosmologies in the making: a generative approach to cultural variation in inner New Guinea*. Cambridge: University Press.

——— 1990. 'The guru and the conjurer: transactions in knowledge and the shaping of culture in Southeast Asia and Melanesia'. *Man* (N.S.) 25(4), 640–53.

——— 2002. 'An anthropology of knowledge'. *Current Anthropology* 43(1), 1–18.

Bloch, M. 1989a. 'The past and the present in the present'. In *Ritual, history and power: selected papers inanthropology*, ed. M. Bloch, 1–18. London: Athlone Press.

——— 1989b. 'The disconnection between power and rank as a process: an outline of the development of kingdoms in Central Madagascar'. In *Ritual, history and power: selected papers in anthropology*, ed. M. Bloch, 46–88. London: Athlone Press.

——— 1989c. 'Symbols, song, dance and features of articulation: is religion an extreme form of traditional authority?' In *Ritual, history and power: selected papers in anthropology*, ed. M. Bloch, 19–45. London: Athlone Press.

Boyer, D. 2005. 'Visiting knowledge in anthropology: an introduction'. *Ethnos* 70(2), 141–8.

Buyandelgeriyn, M. 2007. 'Dealing with uncertainty: shamans, marginal capitalism, and the remaking of history in postsocialist Mongolia'. *American Ethnologist* 34(1), 127–47.

Crick, M.R. 1982. 'Anthropology of knowledge'. *Annual Review of Anthropology* 11, 287–313.

Delaplace,G. & R. Empson. 2007. 'The little human and the daughter-in-law: invisibles as seen through the eyes of different kinds of people'. *Inner Asia* 9(2), 197–214.

Derrida, J. 1994. *Spectres ofMarx: the state of the debt, the work of mourning and the new International* (trans. P. Kamuf). New York: Routledge.

Empson, R. 2007. 'Separating and containing people and things in Mongolia'. In *Thinking through things: theorizing aretfacts theoretically*, eds. A. Henare, M. Holbraad & S. Wastell, 113–40. London: Routledge.

Gell, A. 1998. *Art and agency: an anthropological theory*. Oxford: Clarendon Press.

Henare, A., M. Holbraad & S. Wastell, eds. 2007. *Thinking through things: theorizing artefacts ethnographically*. London: Routledge.

Hobsbawm, E. & T. Ranger, eds. 1983. *The invention of tradition*. Cambridge: University Press.

Højbjerg, C.K. 2002. 'Inner iconoclasm: forms of reflexivity in Loma rituals of sacrifice'. *Social Anthropology* 10(1), 57–75.

Højer, L. 2004. 'The anti-social contract: enmity and suspicion in Northern Mongolia'. *Cambridge Anthropology* 24(3), 41–63.

——— Forthcoming. 'Entertained by the unknown: divination in postsocialist rural Mongolia'. In *Unveiling the hidden: Contemporary Approaches to the study of Divination*, eds. A. Lisdorf & K. Munk. Berlin. Walter de Gruyter.

Holbraad,M. & R. Willerslev 2007. 'Transcendental perspectivism: anonymous viewpoints from Inner Asia'. *Inner Asia* 9(2), 329–45.

Houseman, M. 1993. 'The interactive basis of ritual effectiveness in a male initiation rite'. In *Cognitive aspects of religious symbolism*, ed. P. Boyer, 207–24. Cambridge: University Press.

Humphrey, C. 1992. 'The moral authority of the past in post-socialist Mongolia'. *Religion, State and Society* 20(3–4), 375–89.

——— 1994. 'Remembering an 'enemy' – the Bogd Khaan in twentieth-century Mongolia'. In *Memory, history, and opposition under state socialism*, ed. R.S.Watson, 21–44. Santa Fe, N.M.: School of American Research Press.

——— 2002a. 'Shamans in the city'. In *The unmaking of Soviet life*, ed. C. Humphrey, 202–21. Ithaca, N.Y.: Cornell University Press.

——— 2002b. 'Stalin and the Blue Elephant: paranoia and complicity in postcommunist metahistories'. *Diogenes* 49(194), 26–34.

——— 2007. 'Inside and outside the mirror: Mongolian shamans' mirrors as instruments of perspectivism'. *Inner Asia* 9(2), 173–95.

——— with U. Onon 1996. *Shamans and elders: experience, knowledge, and power among the Daur Mongols*. Oxford: University Press.

——— & D. Sneath 1999. *The end of nomadism? Society, state and the environment in Inner Asia*. Cambridge: White Horse Press.

Hürelbaatar, A. 2002. *'Tradition' as differently practised by the Buryat-Mongols of Russia and China*. Unpublished Ph.D. thesis, University of Cambridge.

Ingold, T. 2001. 'From the transmission of representations to the education of attention'. In *The debated mind: evolutionary psychology versus ethnography*, ed. H. Whitehouse, 113–53. Oxford: Berg.

Jing, J. 1996. *The temple of memories: history, power, and morality in a Chinese village*. Stanford: University Press.

Kaplonski, C. 1997. 'One hundred years of history: changing paradigms in Mongolian historiography. Inner Asia'. *Occasional papers of the Mongolia and Inner Asia Studies Unit* 2(1), 48–68.

——— 1998. 'Creating national identity in socialist Mongolia'. *Central Asian Survey* 17(1), 35–49.

——— 1999. 'Blame, guilt and avoidance: the struggle to control the past in post-socialist Mongolia'. *History and Memory* 11(2), 94–114.

Keesing, R.M. 1987. 'Anthropology as interpretive quest'. *Current Anthropology* 28(2), 161–76.

Lévi-Strauss, C. 1969 [1964]. *The raw and the cooked* (trans. J. Weightman & D. Weightman). New York: Harper & Row.

——— 1987 [1950]. *Introduction to the work of Marcel Mauss* (trans. F. Baker). London: Routledge & Kegan Paul.

Pedersen, M.A. 2001. 'Totemism, animism and North Asian indigenous ontologies'. *Journal of the Royal Anthropological Institute* (N.S.) 7(3), 411–27.

——— 2007. 'Talismans of thought: shamanist ontologies and extended cognition in Northern Mongolia'. In *Thinking through things: theorizing artefacts ethnographically*, eds. A. Henare, M. Holbraad & S. Wastell, 141–66. London: Routledge.

Pietz, W. 2002. The sin of Saul. In *Iconoclash: beyond the image war in science, religion, and art*, eds. B. Latour & P. Weibel, 63–65. Cambridge, Mass.: MIT Press.

Sahlins, M. 1999. 'Two or three things that I know about culture'. *Journal of the Royal Anthropological Institute* (N.S.) 5(3), 399–422.

Shimamura, I. 2004. 'The movement for reconstructing identity through shamanism: a case study of the Aga-Buryats in postsocialist Mongolia'. *Inner Asia* 6(2), 197–214.

Sperber, D. 1985. 'Anthropology and psychology: towards an epidemiology of representation'. *Man* (N.S.) 20(1), 73–89.

Strathern, M. 1988. *The gender of the gift*. Berkeley: University of California Press.

——— 2004. *Partial connections*. Walnut Creek, Calif.: AltaMira Press.

Swancutt, K. 2006. 'Representational vs conjectural divination: innovating out of nothing in Mongolia'. *Journal of the Royal Anthropological Institute* (N.S.) 12(2), 331–53.

Taussig, M. 1999. *Defacement: public secrecy and the labour of the negative*. Stanford: University Press.

Trevor-Roper, H. 1983. 'The invention of tradition: the highland traditions of Scotland'. In *The invention of tradition*, eds. E. Hobsbawm & T. Ranger, 15–42. Cambridge: University Press.

Watson, R. ed. 1994. *Memory, history, and opposition under state socialism*. Santa Fe, N.M.: School of American Research.

Yanjmaa, B. 2000. *Hövsgöl aimgiin Chandman'-Öndör sumyn tüühiin zarim asuudal (Some issues of the history of the Chandman'-Öndör district of the Hövsgöl province)*. Unpublished master's thesis (*diplomyn ajil*), National University of Mongolia, Ulaanbaatar.

Žižek, S. 1999. 'When the Party commits suicide'. *New Left Review* 238, 26–47.

Chapter 10
Seeking Providence Through Things: The Word of God Versus Black Cumin

Mikkel Bille

Introduction

Once again, I am riding with Ibrahim, a settled Bedouin in his mid-twenties, in his car a few kilometres from the village of Beidha towards Siq al-Barid in southern Jordan. This time I cannot stop wondering about the elaborate merchandise hanging from the car's rear-view mirror (Fig. 10.1). Pointing to the patterned cloth bag hanging in a white string and the handful of amulets with Qur'anic calligraphy, I ask him "*What is this for?*" Ibrahim answers: "*This one is the black cumin bag. It is put in the car as decoration. If you have a beautiful car some people might envy it. The black cumin will take the attraction to it instead of the car. The evil eye will not affect the car, it will affect the black cumin; they will break. As little as the seeds are; they break. The other is 'There is no God but God, and Muhammad is the Prophet of God'. This is Islam!*"

Puzzled by what appears a redundant use of different amulets against the evil eye, I point at the Qur'anic words and ask, "*but how are these different from the black cumin?*" He answers, "*These are God's and Muhammad's names. When anyone sees the car or a house, he will say 'God pray upon Muhammad' and he won't envy*". Not really feeling that his answers address my question I continue, "*If you already put the names of God and Muhammad, then why do you need the black cumin?*" Ibrahim explains, "*It is not a must to have the black cumin. You have to put God's names and 'God pray upon Muhammad'. The black cumin has been known for a very long time. The elders say that it is good against envy. But, 'There is no God but God' is better. When you put the black cumin, it will protect the whole car. God protects, but the black cumin is a tradition.*"

The conversation reminded me of a similar discussion on protective stones and amulets I had with Ahmad, another Bedouin in his late twenties from Beidha. Ahmad is well versed in Islam and he frowned at my questions. Unlike Ibrahim he

M. Bille (✉)
University of Copenhagen, Copenhagen, Denmark
e-mail: mbille@hum.ku.dk

M. Bille et al. (eds.), *An Anthropology of Absence: Materializations of Transcendence and Loss*, 167
DOI 10.1007/978-1-4419-5529-6_10, © Springer Science+Business Media, LLC 2010

Fig. 10.1 Prophylactic objects in rearview mirror. Photo by the author

said, *"Twenty years ago if you said this stone doesn't work, they would say, 'you are crazy! This stone protects me'. But now they discovered that the stone doesn't work. The stone is a stone; Nothing more".*

Clearly, in the past the stones and black cumin must in some way have seemed effective as protection against envy; indeed, to Ibrahim they still seemed to work. So I asked Ahmad how did the black cumin and stones work? Would people have to perform certain rituals with them? Ahmad's reply was intriguing: *"No, no, just put it and it protects you"*, and he started laughing, *"This is what people think, but not me! Don't hang it here or anywhere, because that means you don't believe in God. You have two Gods to worship if you put it here, because you think it helps you. No. Just depend on God and forget all the materials. That's the summary".*

Ahmad and Ibrahim are part of the Ammarin Bedouin tribe, which was resettled in 1985 in Beidha, North of the tourist site Petra. Settlement policies have facilitated increasing access to health clinics, mosques, schools, electricity and have changed the economy and livelihood of the Bedouin generally in the region, as well as resulting in changing tribal power structures. However, settlement has also left a sense of nostalgia among the Ammarin towards Bedouin traditions, as semi-mobile herders, dwelling in remote areas. Protective objects such as the cumin bag are part of these traditions, as Ibrahim explained. They constitute elements of a life form that is increasingly disappearing in the area, and which the young generation were rarely brought up with themselves, yet miss.

The conversations with Ibrahim and Ahmad highlight a contemporary conflict, which is also apparent on a more general level in Muslim's everyday life in the Middle East, between different understandings of specific material means of protection. In the southern areas of Jordan, this tension is a result of the promulgation of a particular kind of literal understanding of Islam during the last three decades. This particular version combats what is perceived as innovation to Islam (*bid'a*) often associated with Sufism and "folk Islam", such as saint intercession (*tawassul*), celebrating prophet Muhammad's birthday (*mawlid al-nabi*), or prophylactic items like the black cumin bag, etc. In essence, this understanding of Islam seeks "ridding the world of magic" (Gilsenan 2000) with the side effect of reformulating existing power structures – much like modernization policies. Furthermore, this version emphasizes a detachment from what its followers see as threatening materialism and instead preaches a need to focus on immaterial virtues, and the Word of God by replicating a "pure" Islam as it was believed practised and preached in prophet Muhammad's time.

The propagation of this version of a literal Islam is particularly evident in the case of the previously semi-nomadic Bedouin. Increasingly, the mosques have promoted a conformist teaching and through collective prayers publicly expose people's religious practices and dedication. Furthermore, schoolbook authors and policymakers have been heavily inspired by the Muslim Brotherhood,[1] thereby influencing the young generations (Anderson 2007). Technological developments have also enabled Islamic satellite television programmes transmitting from Saudi Arabia and the Gulf to reach distant areas communicating their particular Islamic understandings, thereby impact powerfully on people's religious perceptions and practices on a global scale.

The inception of this emergent version of Islam in the area lends very little to existing local traditions and religious understandings, but seeks, rather, to abolish these as un-Islamic inventions, as articulated by Ahmad in the above. Consequently, both the traditional objects for protection and different understandings of Islam in everyday life also become entangled more generally in the pronouncement of social hierarchies, religious knowledge and authority (see Lambek 1990).

Although people among the Ammarin are gaining increased access to material goods, asceticism and relying on the uncreated Words of God presented in the Qur'an are increasingly perceived as superior means of seeking providence and protection to that of non-Qur'anic amulets; "forget all the materials". This raises the pertinent question of how one can experience God when the absence of material form presumably is the ideal? Recently, Daniel Miller has aptly argued that "the passion for immateriality puts even greater pressure upon the precise symbolic and efficacious potential of whatever material form remains as the expression of the spiritual power" (2005: 22).

---

[1] Represented by the political party "Islamic Action Front" in Jordan.

In this chapter, I will investigate this *paradox of immateriality* as it unfolds in conceptualizations of presence, absence and efficacy among the Bedouin.

Furthermore, the protective objects are entangled in social negotiations of identities, where protective strategies are manifestations of vanishing traditions and forefathers' ways of dealing with the perils of life. Protective strategies confront both the sense of vulnerability and exposure, as well as performing publicly the morality and propriety of protecting people, places and things in accordance with the socially accepted ways of relating to cultural traditions.

What I am concerned with is not the absence of any objective material as such, but the negotiation of material efficacy, revolving around cultural and religious conceptualizations of specific kinds of absence that play potent roles in social life. This calls attention to an ambiguous and contiguous relationship between presence and absence that almost imbricates, yet avoids this through conceptualizing particular sensuous engagements with things. From the conversation quoted above, Ibrahim clearly showed us that materials are by no means forgotten, and the decomposition of the cumin beads proves their efficacy. Furthermore, even Ahmad would have artifacts with Qur'anic verses around his house and car. Paradoxically, then, the protective amulets containing the Word of God attest to an increase in material registers of protection (cf. Coleman 1996; Engelke 2007; Meskell 2004). If people should "forget all the materials" since they signify polytheism and religious ignorance, then how are we to understand the persistence of material objects in Ibrahim's rear-view mirror, and indeed with Ahmed? This paradox, I argue, suggests that we need to be careful not to conflate absence with "the immaterial", or as oppositions to presence and empirical matter, as all are subject to ambiguous classifications and experiences.

This chapter argues that there are particular logics underlying the continuous use of various protective objects, conceptualized through engagements with "irreducible materiality" and "immaterial things". Investigating this logic through notions of "multiple ontologies" (Henare et al. 2007; Viveiros de Castro 1998) may draw attention to ambiguous conceptualizations and experiences of presence and absence within specific cultural contexts. My overall suggestion is that the various strategies in use emphasize how adjacent registers of protective materials may co-exist locally in everyday life, exactly because of the lack of imbrications in sensuous efficacy in confronting harm – while other strategies that overlap in efficacy are discarded. The propriety of seeking efficacious protection is thus contingent upon the proper understanding of the materiality of efficacy and immateriality of God, and the announcement of which arouses unremitting social disquietude.

The Physicality of Protection

People protect themselves against many forms of risk, which often have more to do with ideas about dangers than their objective impact. A particular risk that people in Beidha and elsewhere in the Middle East fear is being harmed by the "evil eye".

The "evil eye" rests on the idea that a look of envy, even unintentionally, can cause harm and misfortune, such as childlessness, lack of success in transactions or illnesses (Abu-Rabia 2005). The evil eye is thought to have a very physical nature since it "touches" by looking – being a form of *haptic vision*. One of my informants explained: "*When you have a beautiful glass, and they just keep looking, you are afraid the glass may break*". This is further articulated by Bedouin proverbs of the evil eye being "more penetrating than a spear", or having the ability to "cut stone" (Al-Sekhaneh 2005: 158; Drieskens 2008: 70–79; Nippa 2005: 544–545, 568). We, as outsiders, may understand this physicality as metaphorical and the means of confronting it as magical. However, to Ibrahim the material decomposition of the black cumin proved that the look of the evil eye was a physical fact (cf. Mauss 2001 [1950]: 109).

Several prophylactic items and ritual practices have been used among the Ammarin to protect themselves against envy. The Black cumin bag (*hubbah as-sudda*) contains seven pieces of flint and three pieces of alum, aside from the black cumin.[2] The flint pieces are considered physically "hardest" and therefore better able to sustain and ward off the effect of the evil eye. The alum may be used for healing purposes against illnesses inflicted by the evil eye. The black cumin bag is placed somewhere visible in order to attract the evil eye. The proximate presence of protective objects enforces the malevolent person or force to see the amulet. As Ibrahim explained, the black cumin *absorbs* the envy causing the beads themselves to materially decompose. This complexity of various material registers within the same protective object – the hardness of the flint to deflect, the cumin to absorb, and the curative properties of the alum – creates a composite efficacy that has more to do with materially confronting the physicality of envy, than with the magical power of the "spirit" of or in the material (cf. Taussig 1993: 136; Pels 1998).

Other widespread protective amulets in this area of Jordan are the blue stone (*hajjar al-'ayn*) and the Guard (*herz*). Among the Ammarin, the blue stone is a two cm milky blue oblong stone, coated with a shiny varnish, hanging in a necklace around a woman's neck under the veil. The blue colour and shiny surface are thought to both attract and deflect the evil eye. Because the stone is hidden under the veil, it is not visible to a casual viewer, but it will nevertheless attract the malicious evil eye. The blue stone is often used in conjunction with other prophylactic materials, geometric or pictorial symbols, such as triangles, crescents, silver or cloves, to provide protection. The blue stones are also used in necklaces with other stones that are believed to cure illnesses, enhance prosperity or bring fortune. In that sense, these composite protective objects communicate with the invisible to attract positive powers while rejecting the negative (Nippa 2005: 553).

A third amulet regularly used is the "Guard". Whereas the black cumin bag is used in cars (and on camels), and the blue stone around women's necks, the Guard is used to protect the houses or tents (Fig. 10.2). It is made of beads from *Peganum harmala*. It is visibly placed in the reception rooms whereby potential envy is

---

[2] Occasionally tortoise shell is also used.

Fig. 10.2 Triangular guard in reception room. Photo by the author

absorbed by entering the centre of the guard, which renders the envy harmless. Like the other items, it is the proximity, ability to physically attract, absorb and interact with the envy of a potential perpetrator, which protect the space and person.

These various amulets, and others like them, are increasingly contested and are gradually vanishing as protective strategies in the villages in southern Jordan, due as mentioned to the impact of more literal teachings in mosques, schools and television. Their efficacy in all instances is perceived to work in similar *centripetal* ways in the sense that the physicality of envy is attracted to them, and either deflected or absorbed. Interestingly, these amulets' power hence work through the material, colour or form inherent to the object (Mershen 1987: 106).

Thus, these various material registers confront a physical phenomenon – the evil eye – capable of breaking things in an equally physical manifestation of material presence. The protective powers of these objects, I argue, are inherent in their "irreducible materiality" to use William Pietz's term (1985: 7); that is, deriving from the object's physicality itself, such as the decomposing cumin (Pels 1998: 101; Nakamura 2005: 22; Meskell 2004; see also Ingold 2007). The material properties of the amulets need to be "there" to be efficacious; their efficacy relies on their unambiguous physical presence to confront the evil with the physicality of the protective matter; the matter strikes back (Pels 1998: 91).

Belief in the evil eye is also a social mechanism of morality, which sanctions people not to desire the possessions of others, all the while explaining misfortune, bad luck and illnesses (Abu-Rabia 2005; Dundes 1981). Moreover, the social act of protection is also entangled in notions of Bedouin identity; particularly in a post-nomadic nostalgia of "how it was". The imposition of settled lifestyle during the last two decades has to a large extent rendered herding and tent life impossible. The tent, coffee pot and camel are primal objects in this nostalgia. Yet, protective amulets also materialize "Bedouin" conceptions of the world and means of coming to terms with vulnerability and danger. The amulets are ambivalently positioned, simultaneously acting as material anchors of Bedouin traditions and nostalgic reminders of a life less dependent upon material consumption, while also acting as proofs of ignorance to "proper" ways of protection against envy; i.e. Divine, rather than magical or physical protection.

This ambiguity situates protection as a material phenomenon on a socially potent scene with continuous tension between emerging religious and vanishing cultural identities as (semi-) nomadic Bedouin. The social stakes are high in allegations of ignorance, and disrespecting cultural roots causes social exclusion, and there are great amounts of cultural capital invested in gossip of "incorrect" behaviour. As my informant Hussein, and others like him, clearly pointed out in relation to the amulets: "*Humans always have to ask God to protect them from the Devil, and mention God (by praying and reading). In the past the people were ignorant. All of them ignorant*". Clearly then, neither the amulets nor the Words of God, as I will now turn to, are detached from social or material relations, but are heavily invested in negotiations of knowledge, hierarchies and authority.

The Ambiguous Immateriality of the Word of God

The reliance on physicality to confront envy – on the one hand the intangibility of envy, and on the other hand the occurrence of physical changes – has become a problematic issue. As Ahmad would argue, the protective measures to ward off the evil eye resemble acts of polytheism (*shirk*). Instead, the protective materials should be replaced by "forgetting the materials". That is, by an intentional absence of objects relying on an irreducible materiality. The absence of certain kinds of materials enforces attention to the superiority of seeking providence in immaterial sources; a providence that involves preparation and anticipation of Divine support for future eventualities, even if these are not immediately apparent to the believer. The efficacy of such "absence" instead relies on the contiguity of God through *Baraka* (blessing) or *dhikr* (remembrance of God). The two most known ways of achieving this is through saint veneration and the Word of God as presented in the Qur'an.

The Petra region has many tombs and shrines from Biblical and Islamic times. Most renowned to the general audience is the shrine of Moses' brother Aaron at Jebel Haroun, to where people from the area would perform biannual pilgrimages. Many other local saints are buried in the region, and the people are referred to as *awlia* (singl. *weli*) meaning "friends of God" or saints. As "spiritual representatives" the saints are considered closer to God and, at least until recently, are thought to be able to influence God. They are not "lesser gods" as much as they are (or were) seen as *intercessors* between human and God. The *weli* describes a charismatic and knowledgeable person, who transmits *Baraka* bestowed on him/her by God through various kinds of contact (Meri 2002: 59–73, 101–108; Renard 2008; Marx 1977). In the Beidha area they are associated with the ascetic character of the *faqiir* (cf. Jaussen & Savignac 1914). This again highlights the perception of the superiority of "forgetting materials" to achieve divine providence and blessing, but as we shall see, it relies on the paradox of immateriality.

While *Baraka* is "one of those resonant words it is better to talk about than to define" (Geertz 1968: 33), it is generally considered to be (1) prosperity and favour bestowed by God, (2) a wish, invocation or greeting asking for such a favour to be granted to someone else, or (3) an expression of praise to God (Stewart 2001: 236). It is a "benevolent power which radiates from the holy place to everyone who comes in contact with it" (Canaan 1927: 99). Thus, I would argue, despite its immaterial and intangible nature, it is a highly material phenomenon, as it emanates from people, places and things. In that sense *Baraka* is a *centrifugal*; an emanating force, securing providence for people, places and things in the vicinity of its material medium. This mode of seeking providence through intercession relies on a sense of *being-in-touch* emotionally; an intimate, immediate and passionate closeness with God through the *weli*.

For the Ammarin in Beidha, the tomb of the *weli* Salem Awath, was until recently a central place to obtain healing, blessing and future prosperity. Many families in Beidha claim descent from him, and he is highly respected by other tribes. People would perform prayers, burn incense and offer animals to seek providence through him, and they would tie white or green rags on his grave (Fig. 10.3), as a sort of "contact magic" to remind the *weli* of a personal wish or prevent misfortune (Canaan 1927, 1930; Kriss & Kriss-Heinrich 1960a; Mauss 2001 [1950]; Meskell 2004; Taussig 1993).

Fig. 10.3 Saint tomb in Wadi Arabah. Photo by the author

During the last 10 years, however, people have increasingly dissociated themselves from this sort of intercession because the tradition has come to be seen as un-Islamic.[3] This is based on the theological argument that the participants ask the saint for *Baraka*, rather than God directly, whereby they commit heresy by worshipping not the immateriality of one God, but the saint both as secondary divine medium and material form.

Replacing the worship of saints, the Word of God as written in the Qur'an has gained further pre-eminence as protective strategy within recent decades.[4] Muslims understand the Qur'an as God's own uncreated and literal words. They existed previously in Paradise and were passed on to the Prophet Muhammad by the archangel Gabriel. Hence, they are the foundation of religious thought in any Muslim community, and are the message and guidance from God to humanity in all aspects of people's lives. The relationship between the words, text and material of the Qur'an and the practitioners' senses hold a particular role: "to hear its verses chanted, to see the words written large on mosque walls, to touch the pages of its inscribed text creates a sense of sacred presence in Muslim hands and hearts" (McAuliffe 2001: i). Because of this profound relationship between the Qur'an and the experience of God, the very words of the text employ a markedly different materiality than those of any other book. As Clifford Geertz (1983: 110) describes this relationship, "the point is that he who chants Qur'anic verses [...] chants not words about God, but of Him, and indeed, as those words are His essence, chants God Himself. The Quran [...] is not a treatise, a statement of facts and norms, it is an event, an act".

"Qur'an" literally means "recitation", but the Qur'an as a material book is termed *mushaf* (from the word *sahifa*, singular for "page"), suggesting that through different classifications of the same object – from an empiricist position – the immateriality of the one and physicality of the other are emphasized. In that way, despite historically written down after the life of the prophet, "the character of the Quran as a book in the Western sense is far less pronounced than its identity as a recited 'word' [...] the quintessential Muslim 'book' denies its writtenness" (Messick 1989: 27–28).

The Qur'an is believed to contain the most powerful *Baraka*. Hence, aside from guiding humanity, material artifacts with Qur'anic verses also protect the believer against misfortunes and malevolent forces. But more powerful than the Qur'an as a material book, is its commitment to memory that shapes an evocative nearness to God (El-Tom 1985: 416); that is, its internalized nature creates a sense of immediacy and *being-in-touch* (in Runia's (2006) sense). In this way, acts of

---

[3] This interpretation, drawing particularly on *salafi* and *wahabi* readings of the Qur'an and Sunna, is contested in other places in the Middle East for example by arguing from a *hadith* describing how a blind man was allowed intercession by prophet Muhammad. The denunciation of intercession is adopted by most Ammarin despite claiming to adhere to the *shafi* school of Islam that holds a less strict position on the matter.

[4] It must be emphasized that there is no direct opposition between a "Bedouin" and an "Islamic" identity, rather these are intrinsically linked among the Ammarin. Furthermore, the Word of God has held a position as protective strategy throughout history, but it is important to emphasize the current increase and dominance of this material register among the Bedouin.

recitation and remembrance (*dhikr*) of God shape a contiguous relationship that offers safeguarding. Interestingly, the words themselves in materialized or verbal form impose the remembrance on people, as a pervasive "affecting presence" (Armstrong 1971), whereby the Qur'an is "both the occasion or catalyst for *dhikr* as well as what should be recalled, the object of *dhikr*" (Madigan 2001: 372).

Inherent in the Qur'an is therefore both a tension and a connection between the physical (*mushaf*) and the immaterial (*Qur'an*: recitation). The proper understanding of this relationship is continuously creating social tensions, implying potential allegations of misconduct and misunderstandings of the Divine. The Qur'an offers a sense of "closeness" to God through remembrance of his words on the one hand. On the other hand, there is the theological obligation not to worship the Qur'an as a *material* book in itself, despite its powerful *Baraka*. Protection through the Word of God therefore becomes a socially potent question of the proper understanding of presence and absence of material efficacy. Therefore, the issue addressed here also extends beyond questions of objects' effects, to a question of the ability for the objects to cause those effects in a suitable way – both in terms of social life and protective efficacy (cf. Gell 1992, 1998).

The Word of God, particularly evident in the soundscape of the village through the call to prayer penetrating spaces and bodies, and in everyday speech acts, is used to invoke divine power, blessing and protection. The continuous recitation of divine names and phrases from the Qur'an acts as repetitive remembrance that generates a sense of *being-in-touch*, which becomes a vehicle against sorcery or harm. Likewise, when entering a house or a car, starting dinner, killing a goat, accidentally breaking a thing, etc., people would immediately utter variations of the *basmala* ("In the name of God the Compassionate, the Merciful"). When seeing a thing that potentially could be an object of admiration, such as a telephone, car, jewellery, etc., the words "*maa shaa' allah*" ("what God wills") are uttered as a self-reflexive mechanism. Protection through the *Baraka* invoked by the soundscape of the Word of God is not as much about understanding every word, but about sensing the divine presence, which acts as a moral and ethical regulating mechanism of behaviour (Graham 1987: 96, 104; see also Hirschkind 2006).

More than just part of the soundscape, the Words of God are also increasingly entering the market for religious commodities (Starrett 1995; D'Alisera 2001) and domestic architectural form (Dodd & Khairullah 1981; Campo 1987; Metcalf 1996). In Beidha, they are printed over doors, on posters on cars or amulets like the Chinese merchandise in Ibrahim's car, or in one case in letters of a man's height spelling "Allah" in purple tiles in a kitchen (Fig. 10.4). Most reception rooms have at least one golden frame with either one or all of the 99 names of God, the *basmala*, or verses from the Qur'an, particularly verse 1, 113, 114 or the powerful "Throne Verse" (2: 255). Another way of shaping closeness is through letting the fingers slide between each of the 33 beads on a rosary string (*sibha*) three times as bodily mnemonics of God's 99 names. All of these objects, verbal and bodily gestures impose themselves on people for them to remember God. They invoke passion, enlightenment and morality, and are ascribed internalized ontological efficacies by individuals. I had previously asked Ahmad about his perception of the shift in protective practices and the sensuous engagement with the Qur'an:

Fig. 10.4 Allah in tiles. Photo by the author

'If you asked me this question in the past, at least 40 years ago, or before, I would answer "I use the amulet to protect me" because I am uneducated, but now even if I use the amulet, I use the Qur'an to protect me, it is God's words I use to protect me. In the past they believed that the amulet would protect them, but now they use the Qur'an and Qur'an verses in the house so that God will protect them if they have his words in the house. We do not exactly believe that the Qur'an as a book, or as a material in our house, protects us. […] We use the words from the Qur'an to connect with God; our senses, our soul, directly with God'.

This internalization of the Words as offering a direct link is also apparent in healing practices. During the healing ritual of "Drinking the Qur'an" among the Ammarin, the healer would take a glass of water and utter Qur'anic verses over the water, and prescribe the patient to drink it as a residuum of *Baraka* (see also O'Connor 2004: 174). Thereby, the *Baraka* of the words are materialized and internalized through water. In another more material version a piece of paper with a Qur'an verse written on it would be dissolved in the water and then consumed (El-Tom 1985). In other places the same idea is presented in a variation where water is poured over the edges of the Qur'an into a bowl (Donaldson 1937: 266).

Yet, in Beidha some uses of Qur'anic verses are controversial, particularly the Qur'anic talisman. The talisman is a personal charm with the Words of God written on paper or cloth by a special Qur'anic healer, e.g. a *Dervish* (Al-Krenawi & Graham 1997; Kriss & Kriss-Heinrich 1960b). The effectiveness of the talisman relies upon both the reifying power of Qur'anic words and the physical transmission of Qur'anic blessing (O'Connor 2004: 164). Most people in Beidha now denounce such objects as illicit magic, sorcery and polytheism. The problem is that by wearing the talisman, people take the Word of God with them to impure places such as the toilet, or the healer may take verses out of context or write them wrongly. Furthermore, people would rely on the material properties of proximity, rather than through the immaterial ideal of *being-in-touch,* as expressed by Ahmad saying *"Without God in your mind no material will help you!"* In other words, the problem is not that the words are objects on the body, as "repositories of power" (Tambiah 1984: 335), but that they are reduced to instrumental matter, rather than internalized and engaging in a sensorium of *being-in-touch.*

The material manifestations of the Word of God also have another function aside from actively reminding and healing: Their mere physical presence seems to be beyond that of reading and meaning and to relate instead to the words themselves being part of a protective strategy. This should also be seen in the context of official numbers, stating that 26% of the inhabitants in Beidha are illiterates,[5] with practical illiteracy being much higher. The point is, I would suggest, that in terms of protection, rather than being meaningful, the Words of God are powerful. However, this leads to a very careful regulation of understanding and use of the religious objects, since a "good Muslim" must resist sacralizing objects and thereby risking *shirk* (polytheism). Quite obviously though, defining this sacralization is a matter of ambiguity. Using calligraphic Qur'anic ornamentation in an illiterate's home may be seen as Islamic, since it instantiates the divine in hearts and minds. Using Qur'anic verses on paper set in a necklace may conversely be seen as illicit magic. The point here is not to pass theological judgement, but rather to show local variation in the conceptualization and engagement with the Word, and that such variation is contingent upon ambiguous approaches to the materiality of seeking providence.

The talisman along with saint veneration are denounced by many as *jahiliyyah*: belonging to the Age of Ignorance, either as pre-Islamic or contemporary conduct, which goes against Islamic culture, morality and way of thinking and behaving. It is from this perspective of the social potency of announcing practices *jahiliyyah* in a post-nomadic setting among the Bedouin, that the physics of the black cumin and other non-Qur'anic amulets to absorb and deflect, and the presence of a protective blessing in heart and mind through the Word of God that the initial conversation with Ibrahim and Ahmad must be understood.

Reformulating Absence

With the increasing influence of literal Islam, the act of protection has been reconfigured to rely more on achieving intimate divine presence and blessing than on proximate matter. The Word of God becomes part of the ethics of anti-materialism,

---

[5] According to the Jordanian Department of Statistics.

which, paradoxically, is not reflected in an attendant lack of materials. Quite the contrary, objects with the Word of God are rapidly circulating with different receptions among Muslim communities (D'Alisera 2001; Starrett 1995).

By applying the Word of God to things, people can claim to stay true to worshipping God's immaterial qualities and thereby avoid allegations of materialism. The local Islamic preacher would have blue stones and cloves hanging in his car in a decoration with Qur'anic words without problems, and yet he would fiercely denounce the use of the blue stone alone or the Qur'anic talisman for that matter. The application of the Words of God re-classifies a thing into something ontologically entirely different. The propriety invested in dealing with the Word of God is contingent upon conceptualizing how the material and immaterial aspects are adjacent, never overlapping or separate, but linked together through comprehending its ambiguous materiality: more than immaterial and less than material. To make sense of the conceptualizations of it in Beidha, I will argue that as the literal Word of God, the Qur'an is an "immaterial thing", although the Ammarin do not refer to it in these terms. To make this conceptual leap, I must emphasize that the physicality of the book – as *mushaf* – is at times acknowledged, but what matters about the Qur'an is its *Baraka*, recitation and *dhikr*; externalization and internalization. Its physicality is downplayed (or avoided), and so of little or no relevance as protective strategy, even if the Words of God throughout history have been elaborately materialized – for example in calligraphy. Yet, in the immediate everyday engagement, discourse and perception of the Word of God, they are less than material; an "immaterial thing".

The notion of "relative materiality" developed by Michael Rowlands (2005) suggests in this case that technologies of seeking providence highlight how some things are "more" (and irreducibly so) or "less" material, and these may be complementary protective strategies depending on the perception of the propriety of using materials against envy. Certainly, the words themselves are enmeshed in a process of objectification, but as Maurer (2005) argues, they are neither considered material nor ideational, but "both and neither". The application of the Word of God, I argue, transforms an otherwise mundane object into an "immaterial thing" and in terms of its relative materiality emphasizes an immaterial source of protection. The notion of "immaterial thing" is thus not just a conceptual riddle of oxymoronic classifications, as the "both and neither" statement may insinuate. Instead, it relates to the sensuous engagement with the ontology and adjacency of things and their affecting presence "asserting their own being" (Armstrong 1971: 25). The riddles are *real*: "Drinking the Qur'an", the use of the word "Qur'an" as "recitation" to describe a book, or Ibrahim who instead of saying "decoration with written Qur'anic words", describes his car decoration as *"There is no God but God"*. These are examples of the cultural practice and reality of such oxymoronic classifications.

With this strategy of protection, emphasis is on the direct, unmediated link to God (see also "live and direct" in Engelke 2007), and thus highlights the problematic nature of seeking *Baraka* through saint veneration in developing the understanding of Islam. God becomes present through remembrance or recitation evoked by even a few of God's words or names. Thus, the immateriality of a protective strategy is sustained by conceptually dematerializing the object that communicates the protection. What is important for most informants is that the manifestations of the Word of God constantly influence the believer to *remind* him/herself of God, whereby God offers protection; not the "thing", but the words.

The materialization of divine words and repetitive formulas convey an understanding and sensorium of *being-in-touch* with a protecting God. In local ontology, the Qur'an *is* the Word of God, and does not just represent it. The Qur'an is an immaterial thing, and thus to some degree absent at least from what ontologically may be classified as clear-cut "matter". I thus wish to argue that in this context when asking questions about presence, what is emphasized is the deliberate absence of what is conceived of as "material" or bound in a register of "presence" that relies on irreducible matter, and instead highlighting the intimacy of *being-in-touch* with a supreme God through the intangibility of *Baraka*, *dhikr* and recitation.

Amulets, such as the black cumin, on the other hand, are conceived of as "satellites". They are external from the body, having their own (efficacious) life. They receive the evil eye precisely because of their spatial proximity and physics of absorption and deflection. Hence, the non-Qur'anic amulets are "more" materially present in local ontology and deny any reduction of their matter (except as proof of their efficacy).

The protective registers of the black cumin and the Word of God hence rely on very different protective qualities and engagements between people and envy, which forces us (once again) to question dichotomies such as material and immaterial. As Lynn Meskell argues, "for *things to work* they must be beyond the object-as-taxonomy approach that we are comfortable with in Western societies. There must be a pervasive presence, constant influence and agency travelling between spheres" (2004: 27). It is the co-existence of *centrifugal* and *centripetal* efficacy as well as the difference in modality of "presence" that allows for the continued – although contested – use of both registers. The tombs of the saints, however, are a more contested matter, exactly because of the imbrications with the Word of God in terms of relying on emanating *Baraka* through intermediary material form.

The engagement with the past and the landscape through saint veneration and sacred places has rapidly changed. Ibrahim would, for example, not go on the pilgrimage to the tomb of a local saint, since this relied on the intercession of blessing and *being-in-touch* with a saint to provide providence. Thus, closeness to God through intercession and saintly providence is now nearly obsolete, as blessing is increasingly achieved directly through the Word of God. Some saint tombs are even actively destroyed.

The persistence of material strategies, such as the black cumin or infrequent surreptitious acts of saint worship, should not simply be seen as social resistance and retaining traditions in light of contested settlement policies by ignoring religious arguments. Nor should the public dissociation from these practices simply be seen as acts of sycophancy towards the authority of those presumably knowledgeable in Islam, to gain better social standing. The basic concern about what one protects oneself against has not changed considerably during the last 20 years of settlement in terms of envy and spirits. But the concrete means of seeking providence have emerged as a delicate, tangible and socially potent matter that raises continuous disquietude in everyday life as people experience misfortunes. The shift in regimes of protective knowledge creates tension in terms of senses of roots and Bedouin identity, in that Bedouin knowledge and social hierarchies from the past are questioned, exactly because the traditional protective objects rely on the proximity of irreducible materiality to confront the evil eye.

"Nostalgia inevitably reappears as a defence mechanism in a time of accelerated rhythms of life and historical upheavals" Svetlana Boym (2001: xiv) tells us. In this case, nostalgia revolves around the way the increasing absence of a nomadic life form imposes itself in formulations of memories and identities. Settlement has brought education and increasing religious awareness to the Ammarin, but also a rapid social transition where concrete houses, agriculture and tourism have for most parts replaced tents, caves and herding goats and sheep. Here, tent life, goat herding, coffee rituals and other aspects of engagement with material culture associated with the Bedouin identity become material reminders of a Bedouin life style that is largely abandoned, but which continues in oral traditions and to some degree in protective practices. When asking about what it means to be a Bedouin, one is confronted with informants pointing to the desert landscape and the increasing absence of tents and herds that present themselves as illustrative of the rapid change of the roots of Bedouin identities. This has created a distinct sense of loss and utopian anchor among the young Ammarin, raised in villages, who shape narratives of the loss of "Bedouin culture". This notion of Bedouin becomes essentialized as nomadic pastoralism at some undefined time between the arrival of the rifle and the car, through "hyper-nostalgic reminders of a glorious Bedouin past of which their ancestors perhaps never partook" (Wooten 1996: 72). As Susan Stewart poetically puts it, "Nostalgia is the desire for desire" (1993: 23). This mourning of the past establishes links with history in the present through what *remains* as anchors for nostalgia, which act to negotiate the past, as well as re-imagining the future (Eng & Kazanjian 2003).

Conclusion

Classifying, transforming and using ideas of whatever constitutes "matter" as a protective strategy is not only ambiguous in this context, it is also a way of showing and reaffirming alternative identities and religious awareness. Perhaps even more importantly, by partly denying the physical properties of the Word of God (at least in terms of any binary opposition between materiality and immateriality) people are reaffirming their reluctance to rely on materials for protection by transforming a thing into something conceptually "less material" by applying Qur'anic scripture. The anti-material ideals of the divine presence through material absence are thus achieved by a cultural reformulation of what constitutes matter and efficacy.

For the Ammarin, the question of the materiality of protection is thus one of understanding various modalities of presence and absence. The socially entangled nature of the diverging strategies of protection has led to current attempts to dissociate oneself from materialism, in order to avoid allegations of backwardness and heresy on account of the perceived superiority of immateriality.

To Ibrahim, the black cumin was complementary to the Words of God as they fulfilled different modalities of presence. The use of the black cumin was based on the knowledge of what his Bedouin forefathers had been using for generations, and a way of life and cultural identity that Ibrahim and others like him feel increasingly alienated from today. The objects are markers of cultural identities. More than this, through the very properties of the materials he is convinced of the efficacy of the amulets by the physics of absorption, and deflective properties of the flint against the physicality of the evil eye.

On the other hand, a different solidarity and belonging as a modern enlightened Muslim is presented by the efficacy of experiencing the presence of God through "immaterial things". The Qur'anic frames and merchandise are also markers of identity, but rather than marking Bedouin roots, they mark solidarity with a moral and religious identity focusing more on being a Muslim. Ibrahim wanted both, and to him the two ways of materializing protective efficacy were not mutually exclusive. Ahmad, on the other hand, would have none of this and wanted instead explicitly to "forget all the materials". From a material perspective, obviously, he did not fully comply with this, but in local ontology he did by making use of Qur'anic objects classified as "immaterial things". Not exactly a thing, but neither immaterial, rather both, conjoining material and immaterial, a presence through the absence of a *certain kind of material efficacy*.

Rather than describing a result of social change, the protective objects are mechanisms of change. The objects both describe and act as a social display of the means of coming to terms with vulnerability, physicality of envy, and experiencing the Divine, as well as negotiating a post-nomadic identity. Thus, in terms of the providence of *Baraka* through reciting, remembering and surrounding oneself with things, the Word of God, as immaterial things, suffices. Hence, investigating everyday conceptualizations of absence reveal how absence as a cultural phenomenon has both ontological and epistemological implications of being the ideal of anti-materialism, as well as confirming the sense of nostalgia related to a rapidly changing Bedouin culture.

References

Abu-Rabia, A., 2005. The evil eye and cultural beliefs among the Bedouin tribes of the Negev, Middle East. *Folklore,* 116(3), 241–254.

Al-Krenawi, A. & J. R. Graham, 1997. Spirit possession and exorcism in the treatment of a Bedouin psychiatric patient. *Clinical Social Work Journal,* 25(2), 211–222.

Al-Sekhaneh, W., 2005. *The Bedouin of Northern Jordan. Kinship, Cosmology and Ritual Exchange,* Berlin: Wissenschaftlicher Verlag Berlin.

Anderson, B., 2007. Jordan. Prescription for obedience and conformity, in *Teaching Islam. Textbooks and Religion in the Middle East,* eds. E. A. Doumato & G. Starrett, London: Lynne Rienner Publishers, 71–88.

Armstrong, R. P., 1971. *The Affecting Presence. An Essay in Humanistic Anthropology,* Chicago: University of Illinois Press.

Boym, S., 2001. *The Future of Nostalgia,* New York: Basic Books.

Campo, J. E., 1987. Shrines and Talismans: Domestic Islam in the pilgrimage paintings of Egypt. *Journal of the American Academy of Religion,* 55(2), 285–305.

Canaan, T., 1927. *Mohammedan Saints and Sanctuaries in Palestine,* London: Luzac & co.

Canaan, T., 1930. *Studies in the Topography and Folklore of Petra,* Jerusalem: Beyt-Ul-Makdes.

Coleman, S., 1996. Words as things. Language, aesthetics and the objectification of protestant evangelicalism. *Journal of Material Culture,* 1(1), 107–128.

D'Alisera, J., 2001. I ε Islam. Popular religious commodities, sites of inscription, and transnational Sierra Leonean identity. *Journal of Material Culture,* 6(1), 91–110.

Dodd, E. & S. Khairullah, 1981. *The Image of the Word. A Study of Quranic verses in Islamic Architecture,* Beirut: American University of Beirut.

Donaldson, B. A., 1937. The Koran as magic. *Moslem World,* 27, 254–266.

Drieskens, B., 2008. *Living with Djinns. Understanding and Dealing with the Invisible in Cairo,* London: Saqi Books.

Dundes, A., 1981. *The Evil Eye: A Folklore Casebook,* New York and London: Garland Publishing.

El-Tom, A. O., 1985. Drinking the Koran. The meaning of koranic verses in Bertu erasure. *Africa: Journal of the International African Institute,* 55(4), 414–431.

Eng, D. L. & D. Kazanjian, 2003. Introduction, in *Loss: The Politics of Mourning,* eds. D. L. Eng & D. Kazanjian, Berkeley: University of California Press, 1–25.

Engelke, M., 2007. *A Problem with Presence. Beyond Scripture in an African Church,* Berkeley: University of California Press.

Geertz, C., 1968. *Islam Observed,* New Haven: Yale University Press.

Geertz, C., 1983. *Local Knowledge,* New York: Basic Books.

Gell, A., 1992. The technology of enchantment and the enchantment of technology, in *Anthropology, Art and Aesthetics,* eds. J. Coote & A. Shelton, Oxford: Clarendon Press, 40–63.

Gell, A., 1998. *Art and Agency: A New Anthropological Theory,* Oxford: Oxford University Press.

Gilsenan, M., 2000. Signs of truth: Enchantment, modernity and the dreams of peasant women. *Journal of the Royal Anthropological Institute,* 6, 597–615.

Graham, W., 1987. *Beyond the Written Word,* Cambridge: Cambridge University Press.

Henare, A., M. Holbraad & S. Wastell (eds.), (2007). *Thinking Through Things. Theorising Artefacts Ethnographically,* London, New York: Routledge.

Hirschkind, C., 2006. *The Ethical Soundscape. Cassette Sermons and Islamic Counterpublics,* New York: Columbia University Press.

Ingold, T., 2007. Materials against materiality. *Archaeological Dialogues,* 14(1), 1–16.

Jaussen, A. & R. P. Savignac, 1914. *Coutumes Des Fuqarâ, Mission Archéologique En Arabie,* Paris: Librairie Paul Geuthner.

Kriss, R. & H. Kriss-Heinrich, 1960a. *Volksglaube im Bereich des Islam. Band I,* Wiesbaden: Otto Harrassowitz.

Kriss, R. & H. Kriss-Heinrich, 1960b. *Volksglaube im Bereich des Islam. Band II,* Wiesbaden: Otto Harrassowitz.

Lambek, M., 1990. Certain knowledge, contestable authority: Power and practice on the Islamic periphery. *American Ethnologist,* 17(1), 23–40.

Madigan, D., 2001. Book, in *Encyclopaedia of the Quran,* ed. J. D. McAuliffe, Leiden, Boston: Brill, 242–251.

Marx, E., 1977. Communal and individual pilgrimage: the region of saints' tombs in south Sinai, in *Regional Cults,* ed. R. P. Werbner, London; New York: Academic Press, 29–51.

Maurer, B., 2005. Does money matter? Abstraction and substitution in alternative financial forms, in *Materiality,* ed. D. Miller, Durham and London: Duke University Press, 140–164.

Mauss, M., 2001 [1950]. *A General Theory of Magic,* London: Routledge.

McAuliffe, J. D., 2001. Preface, in *Encyclopaedia of the Quran,* ed. J. D. McAuliffe, Leiden, Boston: Brill, i–xiii.

Meri, J. W., 2002. *The Cult of Saints among Muslims and Jews in Medieval Syria,* Oxford: Oxford University Press.

Mershen, B., 1987. Amulette als Komponenten des Volksschmucks im Jordanland, in *Pracht un Geheimnis. Kleidung und Schmuck as Palästina und Jordanien,* eds. G. Völger, K. Helck & K. Hackstein, Köln: Druck- und Verlaghaus Wienand, 106–109.

Meskell, L., 2004. *Object Worlds in Ancient Egypt: Material Biographies Past and Present,* Oxford: Berg.

Messick, B., 1989. Just writing: Paradox and political economy in Yemeni legal documents. *Cultural Anthropology,* 4(1), 26–50.

Metcalf, B. D. (ed.) (1996). *Making Muslim Space in North America and Europe,* Berkely: University of California Press.

Miller, D., 2005. Introduction, in *Materiality,* ed. D. Miller, Durham and London: Duke University Press, 1–50.

Nakamura, C., 2005. Mastering matters: Magical sense and apotropaic figurine worlds in Neo-Assyria, in *Archaeologies of Materiality,* ed. L. Meskell, Malden: Blackwell, 18–45.

Nippa, A., 2005. Art and generosity: Thoughts on the aesthetic perceptions of the *'arab,* in *Nomads of the Middle East and North Africa. Facing the 21st century,* ed. D. Chatty, Boston: Brill Publishers, 539–572.

O'Connor, K. M., 2004. Popular and Talismanic Uses of the Quran, in *Encyclopaedia of the Quran,* ed. J. D. McAuliffe, Leiden, Boston: Brill, 163–182.

Pels, P., 1998. The spirit of matter. On fetish, rarity, fact, and fancy, in *Border Fetish. Material Objects in Unstable Spaces,* ed. P. Spyer, London: Routledge, 91–121.

Pietz, W., 1985. The problem of the Fetish I. *RES: Journal of Anthropology and Aesthetics,* 9, 5–17.

Renard, J., 2008. *Friends of God. Islamic Images of Piety, Commitment and Servanthood,* California: University of California.

Rowlands, M., 2005. A materialist approach to materiality, in *Materiality,* ed. D. Miller, Durham: Duke, 72–87.

Runia, E., 2006. Presence. *History and Theory,* 45(1), 1–29.

Starrett, G., 1995. The political economy of religious commodities in Cairo. *American Anthropologist,* 97(1), 51–68.

Stewart, D. J., (2001). Blessing, in *Encyclopaedia of the Quran,* ed. J. D. McAuliffe Leiden, Boston: Brill, 236–237.

Stewart, S., 1993. *On Longing: Narratives of the Miniature, the Gigantic, the Souvenir, the Collection,* Durham: Duke University Press.

Tambiah, S. J., 1984. *The Buddhist Saints of the Forest and the Cult of Amulets,* Cambridge: Cambridge University Press.

Taussig, M., 1993. *Mimesis and Alterity: A Particular History of the Senses,* New York: Routledge.

Viveiros de Castro, E., 1998. Cosmological deixis and Amerindian perspectivism. *Journal of the Royal Anthropological Institute, n.s.,* 4(3), 469–488.

Wooten, C., 1996. *From Herds of Goats to Herds of Tourists: Negotiating Bedouin Identity Under Petra's 'Romantic Gaze'.* Unpublished M.A.: The American University in Cairo.

Chapter 11
Presencing the Im-Material

Victor Buchli

Introduction

I would like to consider here the rather paradoxical nature of the immaterial: that in order to conceive the immaterial, one must always try to understand it in material terms. I want to suggest that this is not so much a paradox but an artifact of our particular terms of analysis and in fact an ideological effect of the productive dualisms that structure social life (Miller 2005). We need this apparent paradox in order to gird the dualisms that make our social categories possible. What exactly is the relationship between the material and immaterial? I propose to cast this question in different terms; in relation to the notion of propinquity as an alternative way of seeing this relationship, and also as a way of understanding in a different manner what Michael Rowlands has observed regarding the multiplicities of materiality and relative degrees of materiality and immateriality at play in social and historical life (Rowlands 2005). I want to argue that our understandings of the relationship of the material and the immaterial and the issue of multiple materialities might be more profitably understood when considered in terms of propinquity. I will examine this issue in relation to different understandings of the prototype, one derived from the notion of the prototype and its technologies in early Christian life, focusing on Christ as the divine prototype, and the other, a more recent technology of the prototype, namely rapid prototyping, and in particular rapid manufacturing. I want to see how examining both technologies of the prototype, their conceptualizations and implementations might help us gain a better understanding of multiple materialities and of how the relationship between prevailing notions of the material and the immaterial and its apparently paradoxical nature might be more profitably engaged.

V. Buchli (✉)
Dept. of Anthropology, University College London, Gower Street, London, WC1E 6BT, UK
e-mail: v.buchli@ucl.ac.uk

M. Bille et al. (eds.), *An Anthropology of Absence: Materializations of Transcendence and Loss*, 185
DOI 10.1007/978-1-4419-5529-6_11, © Springer Science+Business Media, LLC 2010

The Absent Present, Propinquity and Things

First, I want to engage with this issue in terms of early Christian technologies for the presencing of the divine, in particular the Christ prototype. I want to suggest that different material registers serve to presence in distinct sensorial ways that can be co-present and incommensurable to one another, each register turning away from one another and not productive of a Durkheimian unified "moral" and "material" density (Durkheim 2001) as we traditionally understand this within the social sciences. Why should a particular register work and not another? This is so, I would argue, because of a "commitment" as understood by the philosopher of science, Joseph Rouse, to a given material register's efficacy and the community and forms of knowledge that are produced within that "commitment" (Rouse 2002). The contentious examples from the Christian tradition are about the terms by which this commitment and community are sustained and negotiated. I will use examples from Christian iconoclastic and ascetic traditions to illustrate how examining these issues in terms of propinquity might work in facilitating novel assemblages of social life such as the early Christian ecumene.

I would like to look at the issue of presence and in particular the absent present and contrast it with the idea of "propinquity", of degrees of nearness in different registers, rather than presence. I understand presence here in colloquial Euro-American terms of corporeal, visual, and physical co-presence, what we might normally refer to as empirical reality. Propinquity rather facilitates presence in terms of relation, analogy, nearness in time, or nearness of place – conventional empirical reality, understood in terms of visual and physical co-presence, can be thought of as just one form of propinquity among many others.

The Absent Present

The question of the absent present seems every bit as paradoxical as the idea of immateriality – the two are related concerns. To say that something is here but not present is merely to assert a particular sensorial engagement over another. Typically, I would argue, this means a visualist one of physical proximity – all of us being co-present, physically near and visually available to us in terms of a corporeal proximity to one another in the same room, village, place, building, encampment, etc., as we might understand it in colloquial empiricist terms. This is what Durkheim would refer to as the "moral" and "material" density that constitutes social life (Durkheim 2001).

It is also worth noting that it is ethnographically evident, however, that what is visually co-present, what we might otherwise call empirical reality in the colloquial Euro-American tradition, is often thought of as decidedly unreal, or at least as highly unstable. To many people, what is in fact real, stable, and enduring, is beyond what is physically co-present: the realm of the ancestors, totemic connections, constitutive cosmologies, the presence of God, etc. The body and the material world emerge and decay – they are unstable – what is stable, however, are the cosmological principles, which structure the world. To say something is present and yet absent is to understand this absence in terms of physical and visual co-presence. Ancestors, the dead, cosmology, and God are most emphatically present, but not apprehended in terms of visual and physical co-presence that the term "absent presence" signifies. As a result, various complex technologies have been devised which are commonly glossed as "ritual activity" to presence these entities in a given material register, which in another context, say the colloquial empirical, might be thought of as "absent."

Gavin Lucas and I referred to this process of presencing absence as the peculiar cultural project of materialization that archaeology produces, rendering presence within the material register of corporeal, visual and physical co-presence (Buchli and Lucas 2001). Another word for this is that peculiar diagnostic "thing", which we call "material culture." This presencing in terms of physical co-presence then makes the artifact produced within archaeology available for wider social projects within this vitally productive dualism, such as having a "cultural heritage" comprising "artifacts" and "monuments" that make one "visible" within the nation state and thereby facilitate a viable form of socially sustainable life.

Presence, of course, can be rendered in different material registers beyond the visual and physically co-present. Presence can be spectral in terms of cosmology, it can be atmospheric, it can be sound, it can be light, temperature, etc. It can work in a number of different understandings of the senses and the hierarchies of knowledge we associate with different senses at different historical times and social contexts, as Claassen and Howes have shown in their work on the anthropology of the senses (Claassen 1993, Claassen and Howes 2006, Howes 2005). These different registers and how they can be seen to testify to different kinds of immaterialities are what I would like to discuss here in reference to two historical settings of the prototype. I am interested in the prototype, because of its immateriality, being not quite materialized, stabilized physically or expressed in durable form, existing merely as a mould or abstract referent. Furthermore, the prototype is useful here, because, by definition, it typically attempts to transcend the visual and physical terms of co-presence, as we understand from Alfred Gell (1998).

The Prototype and Propinquity

The two forms of the prototype I am interested in here are implicated in two forms of transcendent universalism: the prototype of the early Christian era and the technologies emerging from rapid prototyping in the early twenty-first century. Early Christian prototypes are very instructive here in terms of how they worked within their material registers and their resulting social effects. Early Christian prototypes served to presence the incomprehensible divinity of the universal God over scales of time, place, and local tradition that transcend immediate visual and physical co-presence, through his earthly material manifestation: Christ. I will discuss this in terms of a number of material registers and their effects, relating to time, assemblage, embodiment, mimesis, touch, and seeing. Then, I will discuss the innovative registers that emerged during the Protestant reformation furthermore in relation to hearing and typography.

Likewise, the examples of early twenty-first century rapid prototyping or 3-D printing in the present day suggest analogous processes. For example, the current collaboration between the Hage Gallery in London with the German company Eon, a 3-D manufacturing developer, attempts a transcendent universalism within the conditions of neo-liberal globalization with their first iteration of a rapid manufactured pavilion. As the Hage Gallery's March 2008 press release rather straightforwardly suggests: "..., the CAD data (drawings) can be sent via email. This data can be used to manufacture the pavilion on an E-Manufacturing machine anywhere in the world, therefore, incurring no shipping cost, taxes, or duties." Whole realms of space, geography, time, the nation state, tax regimes, and labour markets and with them union agreements are overcome with the click of a mouse. Both technologies, antique and modern represent an unbounded universalizing materiality of extraordinary scope and power that is intimately linked with the political economies of their time. Both technologies also exploit what we call, with a certain ambivalence, the immaterial, in order to realize their respective powers and control over the material world, and both create settings with productive dualisms that radically reconfigure our relations, physically, politically, economically, and sensorially with the world at hand.

As mentioned, presence/absence dichotomies make a certain assumption of a material register and sensorial hierarchy: namely, that it is visual, corporeal and physically present. Our understanding of empirical reality is usually in such terms. We might see this as rather just one aspect of propinquity – as a means by which at-handedness and nearness are achieved in addition to analogy, relation and nearness of time and place. What we normally consider the immaterial can be seen as more of an ideological effect of a socially productive dualism as I will explore below. By considering the absent present in terms of propinquity and its various means of presencing the immaterial rather than in the colloquial terms of physical and visual co-presence, we can begin to overcome what appears to be a stymieing paradox.

A certain philosophical consensus regards the question of the immaterial as essentially a nonsense, but a very important one – a paradox that goes to the heart of the question's socially productive power. If we consider the philosopher Irving Thalberg on this issue, then what we call the immaterial does not really support the apparently radical dualism contained within the word pairing of material and immaterial (Thalberg 1983). Philosophers such as Irving Thalberg (1983) and Richard Rorty (1970), in struggling with the paradoxical question of the "existence" of the "immaterial," both argue that the question is merely one of degree and how that degree is described and in what context. As Thalberg notes, other refutations of material states are materially conceived: "Instead of saying that a nonalcoholic refreshment contains no alcohol, we can list its ingredients – the minerals, flavourings, or sweeteners it contains. However, when theorists attempt to explain the sense in which mental happenings are nonbodily, positive information is scanty" (Thalberg 1983: 108). The immaterial and the dualism it presupposes are logically unsustainable from a philosophical point of view. Thalberg frustratedly throws up his hands: "We have yet to learn what dualists are asserting" (1983:113). Rorty (1970) specifically understands this in terms of understanding the purely "mental" or "immaterial" as being a socially contingent understanding of the "incorrigible" (that is being irrefutable or not open to verification). There are no other means of refuting the statements of a purely mental nature and means of understanding it in some other "nonmental" way, in terms of a logical opposition in "physical" terms. Rorty argues that eventually if all incorrigible statements of states of being could eventually be described technically in terms of the measurements of something like an imaginary "cerbroscope," then an identity between such incorrigible statements and something empirically described could be made, and the assertion of something as "mental" and "immaterial" would then be impossible. Rorty is careful to note however, that ultimately this is a social question of "matters of taste": "reference to mental states might become as outdated as reference to demons, and it would become natural to say that, although people had once believed there were mental states, we had not discovered there were no such things, [...and] we might simply cease to talk about them at all (except for antiquarian purposes)." (Rorty 1970: 422). This becomes a matter of taste then, no more an ontological issue, and by default the philosopher throws the issue into the realm of the social and socially contingent needs. "For as long as people continue to report, incorrigibly, on such things as thoughts and sensations, it will seem silly to say that mental entities do not exist – no matter what science may do. The eliminative materialist cannot rest his case solely on the practices of scientists, but must say something about the ontology of the man on the street" (Rorty 1970: 422–23). Rorty throws the problem squarely back to the social scientist, and, I would argue, in particular upon the shoulders of the anthropologist to help explain and understand the "mental" and other instances of the "immaterial" and other "matters of taste."

Icons, Idols and Books: Haptic Vision and Visual Co-Presence

In this section, I would like to consider a number of distinct Christian technologies of presencing the immaterial, which suggest different ways in which propinquity works to achieve presence across a number of different material registers. In particular, I would like to address the notion of propinquity and the issue of the absent present in relation to the long historical Christian problem of icons and idols. Idols for instance are a good and extreme example of a register, where propinquity is achieved through visual and physical co-presence. The object in itself assembles various elements to create presence. That is why if the idol is destroyed, then the Divinity that inheres is destroyed as well. Icons work otherwise; icons distribute presence because they refer to a prototype. The prototype is absent in the register of visual and physical co-presence; it is not *there*. That is why one can destroy an icon without affecting the prototype. When one destroys an icon of Christ or the icon of the Byzantine Emperor, neither the Emperor nor Christ will be affected. Rather, the physical artifact is merely a conduit, where propinquity, nearness, is achieved haptically through an icon.

To illustrate how, consider the Byzantine art historian Barber's observation of the homily delivered by the Patriarch Photios in 867 at the unveiling of the apsidal mosaic of the Enthroned Theotokos in the Hagia Sophia, Constantinople (Istanbul) (Fig. 11.1).

Here, the haptic visuality of the icon functions as the means by which the circuit of viewer, icon, and divine prototype interacts to presence the divine:

> "No less than these, but rather greater, is the power of sight. For surely whenever the thing seen is touched and caressed by the outpouring and emanation of the optical rays, the form of the thing seen is sent on to the mind, letting it be translated from there to the memory for the accumulation of a knowledge that is without any error" (Patriarch Photios, 867 cited in Barber 2002: 136).

This, of course, is a demonstration of classical antique theories of vision. But in order for these theories of vision to work, a different material register needs to be

Fig. 11.1 "The Enthroned Theotokos" Hagia Sophia, Istanbul 2009. Photo by the author

in effect, not the register of visual and physical co-presence. Presence within this register is able to achieve a spatial and temporal dimension that the material register of visual and physical co-presence cannot – being too local and too circumscribed.

Classical notions of haptic vision understand vision as a superior form of touch: where particles of light emanating from what is seen actually physically touch the viewer. Similarly, another metaphor deriving from the Aristotelian tradition was that of the seal – whereby the image of what is viewed is impressed, like a seal onto the viewer – an imprint of vision on the soul: "as a seal-ring acts in stamping" (Frank 2000: 125). Both metaphors exploit an understanding of viewing as a form of physical touching with all the implications of "contagion" in the conventional sense of bacterial contagion that touch brings with it. Alternatively, the vision of the viewer could be seen to actually reach out and touch the object (ibid: 123–124). What is common to these diverse antique notions is the issue of touch either from the eye (as rays outwards) or towards the eye (as particles touching, or imprinting). There is equally great power and danger in the haptic quality of seeing following Frank's observation that "Most dangerous was visions' power to connect the viewer so intimately to its object that the adhesion could damage the soul beyond repair" (ibid: 131). As Frank notes citing the Bishop Nemesius of Emesa, sight and touch both encompassed the key properties of "contact, participation, and initiative" (ibid: 132). This merges into what she refers to as a "tactile piety" centred on sight that represented a convergence of senses that to modern sensibilities are typically segregated resulting in an entirely different bodily and epistemic frame. Vision allowed one direct tactile contact with the divine in these encounters, "it was a form of physical contact between the viewer and the object" (ibid: 133).

As mentioned earlier, idols by distinction are characterized by a visual and physical understanding of co-presence. That is, the idol is in fact the deity, and the deity can of course be harmed if the idol is harmed or destroyed (see Pietz 1985, 1987, 1988). As archaeologists and anthropologists within the Euro-American tradition, many feel the same way when an artifact is destroyed. This is an outrageous act of vandalism, which constitutes a true and authentic loss and harm to our communities such as the destruction of communal cultural heritage. This is possible because in both settings there is a similar understanding of the material register and sensorium in terms of presence rather than other forms of propinquity that is achieved in terms of visual and physical co-presence. When one destroys an idol, the deity is affected, when one destroys a cultural monument, culture is irrevocably lost.

Of course, as we know in the debates over icons and idols in the Christian Byzantine and later Reformation traditions, the two registers can exist side by side. One person's idol is another's icon. Sometimes, not acknowledging one another in the same time and place – or as in the case of the iconoclastic controversies of the eighth century and the Protestant Reformation they are in mortal conflict with one another.

Vision and Materiality

The understanding of vision in relation to specific material registers is particularly instructive in early Christian contexts. In particular, the early Christian tradition focused on three material elements, which Byzantine scholars would refer to as "bread, bone and image" or the Eucharist, relic, and icon. Here, it is important to distinguish two forms of seeing: "seeing at" versus "seeing past" (Frank 2000) or "being towards" (Barber 2002).

The image of the ascetic in the early Christian period is particularly useful in understanding this register and the terms of propinquity at play. The development of an ascetic physiognomy allowed pilgrims to "see past" towards the light emanating from within the ascetic. It was the body's mortification and decay through ascetic practices that allowed the light of divinity to shine through and touch the pilgrim and bring him or her closer to the divine (Frank 2000: 161). Decay and radiant divinity were inversely proportional to one another. Such an eye in these circumstances possessed penetrative powers. They could see past external surfaces and appearances and discover the secrets within emerging more and more vibrantly with the decaying ascetic body (ibid: 168) much as in later understandings of the icon, the wood and paint of the icon allowed one to see past the image and apprehend the prototype. As such, within this material register, the surface of things are not signs with meaning behind them, that is a material signifier behind which lies immaterial meaning – but actually productive of meaning itself and the novel relations entailed thereof (see also Henare et al. 2007, Pinney 2002).

These decaying ascetics assumed monumentality but one that is much different from our conventional contemporary understandings of monumentality. One such living monument was St. Simeon the Stylite. He is reputed to have lived continuously on the top of a column for 37 years in the Syrian Desert in the first part of the fifth century A.D. As Gillespie (2000) notes regarding ancient Mayan practices, stillness functioned here similarly to evoke a form of monumentality that was further heightened by boasts of inanimacy by desert ascetics to facilitate a fusion between living flesh and object into an enduring human/material monument or icon of ascetic work presencing the divine. Lives such as St. Simeon the Stylite were perceived as "living artefacts of a distant culture" (Frank 2000: 75) invoking earlier Biblical lives and times. This often involved learning to be able to "see past" the human circumstances of these ascetic individuals by the pilgrims who visited them or the listeners and readers of the vivid accounts of their lives, and to see the "angelic" shine emerging through and to recombine these details into a vision of ascetic life that combined the Biblical past with the as-seen and as-experienced practices of the holy desert ascetic (ibid: 77).

This unifying and tactile form of seeing works in later Byzantine contexts to unify and refigure what would otherwise be in modern terms conventionally distinct bodies of material culture: "bread, bone and image" which provide and facilitate contact with the divine. The haptic gaze in relation to "bread, bone and image" presence the absent sacred thereby becoming an extraordinarily powerful local technique for presencing absence. Within these early Christian understandings during the first millennium A.D. in the Mediterranean region, there is the sense and acknowledgement that "bread, bone and image" are in themselves inconsequential (see also Barber 2002 regarding eighth/ninth century iconoclasts). Efficacy lay not in the objects themselves but in the haptic power of the eye of the beholder. But this eye is not passive, rather it is an eye that is able to "touch" and make physical contact with the divine (see also Eck 1998 on *Darsan* and haptic vision).

As regards "bone," early Christian fathers such as St. Jerome acknowledged that a relic is nothing more than "a bit of powder wrapped in a costly cloth" (Frank 2000: 176). It was however the haptic eye of the beholder that constituted the relics as a prophet "as if they beheld a living prophet in their midst" (Jerome in Frank 2000: 176). Haptic vision constituted the reality of a prophet's presence, visually reassembling form out of diverse elements. Similarly, the icon/image according to Barber is "...a means of extending the relic's touch through a tangible reiteration," (Barber 2002: 23). An icon is both a depiction and a relic, being both original and a copy – a copy in the sense that it is a copy of the original prototypical image, and a relic in the "haptic" sense by which it has had physical "contact" with the prototype and thereby is an extended and distributed aspect of the original.

This notion of "seeing through" as opposed to "seeing at," suggests a tactile and active, disaggregating engagement with the material/visual world. This is an engagement that is interpenetrative, where it is difficult to discern where one thing ends and another begins. These are not stable surfaces of engagement, but ones that are highly porous "through which gifts can be given," and hybrid entanglements made. This world is "seen past" not so much to get under the surface of things but to get through them and engage in the circuit of divinity that early ascetic Christian understandings of materiality attempted to facilitate. Thus, the relic/image serves within a particular register of propinquity, facilitated by haptic vision, to assemble and presence the divine by relational similarity either through a piece of the body or an artifact close to the body in addition to mimetic formal resemblance to the prototype as in the conventional forms of icon painting.

However, the status of the Eucharist and "bread" negotiates this problem in another vein. The Byzantine iconoclastic controversies of the eighth and ninth centuries were not so much a debate over the idolatrous nature of icons and the sin of idolatry. Rather, it was a question of technique, how better to presence (or rather establish contact with) the divine and anchor social relations in the present on earth. It was not a question of how truthful an icon could be, but how best the material world could accommodate infinity (Barber 2002: 59). In short, what terms of propinquity and their attendant sensorial registers could presence the divine most effectively. Icons and representations of divinity in themselves were not so much reprehensible. What was questioned was whether or not they were effective at doing what they were supposed to do. Iconophiles emphasized how the haptic relation both visually and physically presence the divine. This idea however, was challenged by iconoclasts who had argued that the efficacy of the material medium of the icon, or the relic, was limited. It was not up to the task of presencing the divine, being of non-divine, material, and mundane origin (wood, paint, etc.). Rather, the Iconoclastic Council of 754 was able to argue for the Eucharist as being the most effective presencing of the divine because of Christ's declaration at the Last Supper in relation to the bread and wine, that "this is my body" and "this is my blood" (Barber 2002: 79). The painted image was never able to make that direct connection in terms of relational propinquity with the divinity of Christ. The Gospel record of this utterance on the part of Christ himself, however, pointed to a more direct opportunity to presence the divine through the mimetic actions of the Eucharist. Since Christ consecrated bread and wine as a representation of his flesh and blood, the Emperor Constantine V was able to define the Eucharist as an icon and more effective means of presencing the divine: "The bread which we take is also an icon of his body, having fashioned his flesh, so that it becomes a figure of his body" (ibid: 80). If Christ himself had chosen these material forms as appropriate representations, then they are superior to all other material forms such as wood and paint, which were not consecrated by Christ originally (see Ginzburg 2002, Engelke 2005, Vilaça 2005). Here, we have a situation where propinquity is achieved relationally by mimesis and analogy with the Eucharist.

Iconophiles such a Nikephoros argued, however, for the efficacy of figurative icons also in terms of propinquity and mimetic analogy: "The icon has a relation to the archetype, and is the effect of a cause. Therefore, because of this, it necessarily is and might be called a relative. A relative is said to be such as it is from its being of some other thing, and in the relation they are reciprocal. Likeness is an intermediate relation and mediates between the extremes, I mean the likeness and the one of whom it is a likeness, uniting and connecting by form, even though they differ by nature" (Nikephoros in Barber 2002: 116). Thus, haptic visuality is able to tie together incompatible materials, crude materials such as wood, with the divine (the figure of Christ) through the mimetic work of the figural icon and more importantly the constitutive eye of the observer. Furthermore, Nikephoros argues in relation to the workings of the icon that by "Making the absent present by manifesting the similarity and memory of the shape [the icon] maintains [with its archetype] an uninterrupted relation throughout its existence" (Nikephoros cited in Barber 2002: 119), thereby achieving propinquity and presence through novel means.

Typography, Text, Words and Things

With the Protestant Reformation, new understandings of vision emerged with optical inventions such as the camera obscura and typographical print, which created a setting where the technologies in which presence was understood and then refigured within a new configuration of the sensorium. This understanding of the sensorium is more familiarly modern and the setting in which our Euro-American ocular-centric sensorium emerges.

However, with these changes in the sensorium, new questions regarding the problem of presence and the material registers in which this is to be understood emerge. Idolatry in the Christian sense remains an issue. Like in the earlier Byzantine context, the controversy, despite the heated rhetoric of iconoclasts, was more about the appropriate technology by which the divine could be presenced and how the universal Christian ecumene could be assembled. For instance, Michalski notes how "For Luther, Christ is not immanently connected with any given external *(res externa)* and only in the sacrament of the Eucharist can he be 'bound'" (Michalski 1993: 177), thereby echoing earlier Byzantine aniconic sentiments.

In the wake of Gutenberg's printing press, there is a shift in sensorium with an emphasis on hearing as opposed to vision or touch. Michalski notes that visual cognition at this time is seen as something superficial and harmful, citing the earlier Lollard leader Wycliffe writing before the Reformation, "that which nourishes sight poisons the soul" (ibid: 185). Protestants privileged hearing over seeing as the more powerful and veracious sense (ibid: 185). Hence, the opposition of pulpit vs. picture; word vs. image.

This realignment of the immanence of the material was reiterated in the iconoclastic statements of John Knox during the English Reformation. This was a question of degree in terms of how the Christian ecumene could be presenced. There was not an innate hostility among thinkers towards images, merely a sense that they could be misused. The issue was what other means were available that were less susceptible to misuse. Echoing earlier heretical and Byzantine sensibilities regarding the immanence of the material, Michalski observed how John Knox, while on the galleys in Catholic captivity, was given an image of the Mother of God. He responded by saying: "Mother? Mother of God?, this is no Mother of God: this is a painted board – a piece of wood, I tell you, with paint on it! She is fitter for swimming, than for being worshipped" added Knox and flung the thing into the river (Michalski 1993:187). This radical confusion and instability of material affordances exemplified the inadequacies of such image-based technologies for presencing the divine in favour of the word sustained by print, the vernacular, and the sermons of the pulpit. Karlstadt and Haetzer both referred to Isaiah 44:16–18 as a rejection of the material work of art, deprecating the materiality of idols: "He [the sculptor] cut down cedars, takes a holm or an oak...With a part of their wood he warms himself, or makes a fire for baking bread; but with another part he makes a god which he adores... Half of it he burns in the fire, and on its embers he roasts his meat and eats it...from what remains he makes a god, his idol" (Michalski 1993: 187–8). This illustration from Isaiah demonstrates this perceived instability of wood as a medium with multiple and promiscuous affordances as being entirely inappropriate to presence the divine.

The Reformation preoccupation with the abuses of idolatry was fuelled by the possibility of a more direct, and one might say efficient presencing of the divine through the word and the impact that the printing press made towards universalizing the word through print. Cummings (2002) notes that the solution to idolatrous abuse was to move from the unstable materiality of images to text. Every parish was to order its bibles from printers (Cummings 2002: 185), and people were actively encouraged to read the Bible. As Cummings states: "The objection to images, as to pilgrimages, and relics, is based on a rigid adherence to the rule of the book: the people are warned 'not to repose their trust and affiance in any other works devised by men's fancies besides Scripture'" (ibid: 186). The relative immateriality of the word was profoundly implicated in this new semiotic realignment: "books for images' was the rallying cry of this radical new attitude" (ibid: 186). However, as Ong (1967) notes, this immaterial quality was materially produced. This was a denial of the embodied, social, and communal quality of the word in oral-aural culture in favour of a produced immaterial word as opposed to "marks on a visual-izable surface" that deny the exteriority of the world in relation to the typographical word of God (Ong 1967: 280). As Cummings notes "bibliolatry was paid for by iconoclasm" (Cummings 2002: 187), and more revealingly bibles were to be funded by a tax on candles placed before images.

But books too could also be seen as a vehicle of idolatry. If the book is fetishised made idol-like, then it inhibits the establishment of the Christian ecumene fixing the divine and the presence of Christ idol-like within the book itself (see also Engelke 2005). Here, power is in one place and not dispersed within and through-out the Christian community by being fixed in time, space, and place, and being co-terminus, that is located idol-like within the book "thing," which is visually and physically co-present. These debates are really over the question of an adequate technology and effective material register and the terms of propinquity with which to achieve the Christian ecumene of the Reformation. This was an anxiety over the segregation of two material registers and their relative instability and promiscuity in relation to one another. What was at risk was a misrecognition of what a given material register could do, manifest the Christian ecumene or its polar opposite idolatry. The iconoclastic acts, removal of images and their destruction was to insist on the distinction between these two registers when they were in fact rather unsta-ble, producing through these actions the relevant divisions between the material and immaterial that girded the productive dualisms being contested in Reformation social life.

Recent Understandings of the Prototype: Rapid Manufacturing

We touched upon the idea of immateriality of the early Christian era and the Christian prototype at the beginning of our Common Era and now move to the pres-ent, and touch briefly upon the most recent understanding of the prototype: the technologies of rapid prototyping and rapid manufacturing which emerged from it. As St. Jerome (Frank 2000: 176) said, a relic is nothing more than "a bit of powder wrapped in a costly cloth." Rapid Manufacturing is also a matter of powders envel-oped in elaborate and costly technologies that radically reconfigure many of the productive dualisms shaping social life, namely those between organic and inor-ganic matter, object and subject, sign and signifier, the material and the immaterial. The Hage pavilion mentioned earlier is a good example of some of the issues at stake here. Early Christian technologies of the prototype were the means by which a radical rupture with traditional pagan society and a new universalism in the figure of the Christian ecumene were created. Time, space, and social relations were radically reworked within these technical and conceptual means available to the early Christian church. As with the first technology of the prototype of the Western tradition in the beginning of the first millennium, and with this most recent technology of the prototype at the beginning of the third millennium, we are also confronted with the disruptive capacities of these worthless "powders" such as the powders at the heart of Rapid Manufacturing which force us yet again to reconsider the relation between the material and the immaterial and the absent and present.

"These worthless powders" and their affordances lie at the heart of the efficacy of Rapid Manufacturing in the present day, where Rapid Manufacturing has been heralded by some as the Second Industrial Revolution of the twenty-first century (Hague et al. 2005). Emerging from the fast developing area of rapid prototyping, this new technology produces three dimensional objects of any imaginable shape that were once impossible to create by any other method, thereby offering what engineers refer to as total "geometric freedom" (Hague et al. 2005) (Fig. 11.2).

Simply put, an object is conceived three dimensionally on a computer (in CAD [computer aided drafting software]), and the digital information (translated into a .stl file [standard triangulation language]) is then used to build up the object additively, unlike conventionally subtractive methods, through highly fluid media such

Fig. 11.2 Lamp Shade printed by Materialise.MGX, "The Damned", designed by Luc Merx, Milan Furniture Fair 2007. Photo by the author

as powdered polymers, or metals (among others) with a micro layering technique (such as laser sintering and stereo lithography) into an actual three dimensional artifact. These three dimensional printers can range from free standing personal factories (*Perfactory®*) about the size of small copy machine to units large enough to print out a three dimensional life size figure of a man. The CAD image can be created anywhere in the world and transmitted digitally anywhere else, to be built up, virtually instantaneously depending on the media used. No solid materials are being manipulated – only a binary digital code, powdered elements, and liquids. Its uses are wildly diverse, producing anything from medical prostheses, to automobiles, lampshades, spare parts on space missions, and fruit bowls.

Described as a "disruptive technology" by many observers and developers of the technology that upsets traditional design and manufacturing practice (Hague et al. 2005), Rapid Manufacturing poses a series of problems for conventional Euro-American understandings of materiality at the beginning of the twenty-first century. At stake are assumptions critical to Western thought such as the ontological separation of living and dead matter, of thought and thing, nature and culture, subject and object and of creativity and authenticity, which Rapid Manufacturing further disrupts almost completely. Because it can print out objects three dimensionally, it is able to avoid the conventional restrictions of matter and manufacturing constraints (Hague et al. 2005). It can construct solid objects that can be composed of hybrid materials, ceramic to polymer to metal for instance all fused at the micro level. Its largest application commercially is for dental implants, hearing aid cases, and medical prostheses. Human bones, teeth, etc. can be scanned and printed out three dimensionally in various materials to create prostheses based on the precise dimensions of an individual. Currently, there is production and research in progress that enable the three dimensional printing of human tissue using living cells which is currently available commercially as the *Envisiontec 3-D Bioplotter,* which can print human tissue for implantation.

Rapid Manufacturing thus challenges a number of our prevailing assumptions of artifacts and their social dimension as well as our understandings of presence and propinquity. Artifacts once thought of as the passive reflections of our intentions have recently been understood in terms of their recalcitrance and their ability to resist our projects by virtue of their materiality – what Keane refers to as "bundling" (Keane 2005). This recalcitrance is now also taken as an indication of a certain independent agency manifested as an irreducible datum that shapes our social and material worlds. The technologies of Rapid Manufacturing call these conventional understandings of material recalcitrance within anthropology and the social sciences into question. For within this emergent technology, objects begin to exhibit, it would seem, apparently no recalcitrance at all – in fact what we create can be almost as exact as we want it to be relative to the restrictions imposed by traditional manufacturing. Traditional material resistances encountered in conventional manufacturing are negligible, if non-existent. As a "Second Industrial Revolution," Rapid Manufacturing calls into question the great social edifices of the First Industrial Revolution, with its contingent social hierarchies and inequalities so trenchantly criticized by Marx and generations of historians and social scientists since. Rapid Manufacturing suggests that the classical social structures associated with production are further challenged: creator and producer, worker and capitalist are one, distanced physically from one another only by the proximity of their machines. In this light, questions of propinquity in relation to issues of labour and migration, global flows of investment and capital are all profoundly implicated when an artefact can be purchased online, instantly customized and then printed out anywhere in the world as promised in the press release for the Hage Pavilion mentioned earlier. The "vicious bifurcation" (Whitehead 2000) that has constituted our understandings of the empirical world and girded the productive dualisms constituting social life, and the "objects" and "subjects" forged therein are almost conflated and entirely obliterated in the creative and manufacturing processes underlying rapid manufacturing, when the digital representation and physical thing are difficult to meaningfully differentiate in time and space much like the Christian icon and its prototype. Propinquity in terms of physical and visual co-presence is confounded as the artifact can be seen to exist in a distributed spatial and temporal context that is outside colloquial understandings of empirical presence.

This leads to another issue: the new terms by which people and things are refigured and assembled. Rapid Manufacturing emerging within the social changes wrought by globalization and digitization forces us to rethink our received understandings of social relations within traditional notions of production and exchange and traditional productive dualisms. For instance, the classical problem of the alienated worker and ruptured social bonds is potentially even further exacerbated by the extreme individuation suggested by the desktop personal factory (*Perfactory®*). The industrial town and its institutions of labour and social life, vast landscapes and distributive networks that might produce a given "widget" is supplanted by the highly individualized personal factory in one's office. Normal flows of globalization are disrupted as objects can be created at point of need at any time rather than produced somewhere else with traditional tooling and materials at another location/country and transported (by air, sea, or land) to the point of use.

As our conventional understandings of "life", the "real", "virtual" and "authentic" become unstable and are further challenged when considering "printed" human tissue, so too are notions of time associated with the manufactured object, which is based on a past prototype, and accumulated experience upon which innovations are based, contingencies planned for and produced. Traditional anthropological notions in the social sciences of "consumption" "appropriation," "authenticity," and "alienation" are entirely refigured when the increasing trend towards "mass customization" in manufacturing and their attendant social and political hierarchies are conflated with Rapid Manufacturing. This is the dilemma that manufacturers must confront when considering when a branded commodity is customized to such a degree that it might stop being that brand. Additionally, time takes on a new and unexplored social dimension. As can be expected within such a radical reconfiguration, our temporal focus shifts – past linear modes of envisioning future scenarios based on cumulative patterns of previous experience are replaced by an open ended futurity. Unanticipated needs are met at unanticipated times. All contingencies are apparently mastered. As with the emergence of the Christian prototype, which created a radically new frame within which to presence the divine universally within a radically distinct temporal and geographic frame, so too does Rapid Manufacturing produce a radically new frame within which to consider the nature of the artifact and temporality. If the only stable entity is the ostensibly immaterial code and if its iterations in three-dimensional print are technically endless and limitless, what is the status of the artifact in terms of its location in time and space? How might it be collected and what might collecting actually mean, if the only stable entity is the code – as an .stl file or as an iteration of given printing in physical form, in terms of physical and visual co-presence? And what kinds of social commitments and collectivities can then be seen to ensue? What then might be the status of conventional notions of the empirical? Questions regarding the simulacrum and aura from Benjamin to the question of the "distributed artefact" of Alfred Gell take on a renewed significance within this disruptive technology, much as the original Christian prototype did at the beginning of our Common Era with a new understanding of propinquity and "nearness."

This material register advanced by new technologies such as Rapid Manufacturing in many ways would seem to express in the most perfect terms the materiality of neo-liberalism with its ability to produce extreme forms of individuation. But as many observers (Povinelli 2001, Ong 1967, Sassen 2007, Rose 1998) have noted, such technologies of self are profoundly locally inflected. Similarly, the rise of Rapid Manufacturing as fluid and universalizing as it might appear emerges within specific settings and assumes new and unexpected dimensions precisely because of its specific material register and its local inflections. This has been most certainly the case historically as we have seen, and this is certainly only to be expected in this new register of the apparently immaterial.

There is of course a certain unexpected material recalcitrance in this new form of apparent "immateriality": the jagged quality of the surface. So useful in some medical applications for its mimicry of the naturally rough surfaces of bone, they are the direct result of the shape of the information: the triangulation of stl.files and its slicing up horizontally along the vertical z-axis. However, as things are layered, the vertical z-axis suggests a material dimension and recalcitrance shaping the object in a specific way unique to the technology – creating a novel form of recalcitrance different from our conventional understandings. The main areas of future development for this technology is not in manufacturing, those issues have more or less been resolved, but in the development of software programming (Hague et al. 2005), which shapes the data and then shapes its material iteration in specific ways as in the jagged edges produced along the vertical z-axis. This material recalcitrance emerges from the specificities of material components whether powder or liquid and the means by which digitized information is created and thereby shapes matter. Thought and thing are no longer in a dichotomous relation to one another, but actually mutually constitutive of each other. Our traditional opposition and insistence on the immateriality of thought and information is challenged when sign and signifier, "immaterial" thought and "material" thing, are in fact difficult to distinguish and disentangle. This "disruptive" technology disrupts much more widely than in simple manufacturing – as we know from the First Industrial

Revolution, its social impact had much greater significance than simply making more things cheaply and efficiently. An example from the aerospace industry shows how the extreme localization of production, where design and manufacture can take place in the same space and room, radically undercuts the role of unionized labour in terms of transportation, manufacturing, and quality control, profoundly upsetting conventional labour relations (see Hague et al. 2005). These impacts are only now being felt but are sure to be further articulated and complicated with time as increasing industrial interests from high design, to aircraft production, auto manufacture, medical and dental prostheses etc. continue to exploit and advance this technology while ideas of authenticity, liability, authorship, and globalized distribution are challenged by its uptake (see Hague et al. 2005).

In addition, existing market conditions and manufacturing traditions structure the ways in which the technology is taken up, emerges and is then socialized within industry and by consumers. Marketers must figure out how to insert themselves these settings. Within Rapid Manufacturing, a different material register emerges with its own novel forms of recalcitrance, unanticipated by engineers and designers but a direct consequence of the materials used, the shape of the information, and the printing machines, which execute these designs as well as the current limits of economies of scale. An initial emphasis on polymer powders and a relative material fragility akin to bone and glass has already suggested a specific trajectory of emergence into the wider public sphere as in high design (Fig. 11.2). It is within these settings that Rapid Manufacturing positions itself to emerge in high design light fixtures referring to the price points of similarly delicate and translucent artisanal glass such as Murano or as in the texture of medical prostheses resulting from the vertical axis of modelling in CAD that produces very small jagged edges analogous to that of natural human bone. Limits set by vigilant labour unions, economic scales of production, and intellectual copyright along with its points of entry into market structures will assemble this potentially universalizing technology and forge it within the emerging requirements of local interests and reconfigure them in novel ways.

Conclusion: Propinquity and Presence

By way of conclusion, the two examples of the prototype presented here suggest how our understanding of presence in relation to the material might be more profitably pursued in terms of propinquity. Our conventional notions of presence that privilege visual and physical co-presence in the Euro-American tradition is confounded by the workings of the prototype in both the early Christian and late modern contexts discussed here. Our preoccupations with presence and absence privilege a particular form of propinquity, one based on visual and physical co-presence. However, when we consider these two contrasting technologies of the prototype, then we might be able to consider different material registers and constitutive sensoria. Presence can be facilitated in radically different material registers achieving propinquity, such as the technologies of the icon discussed in the Early Christian period, where pagan concepts of time and place are refigured by the universalizing and radically restructuring technologies of the Christian prototype to create new forms of community in terms of the universal Christian ecumene and with its new understandings of time and place. In contrast, new forms of propinquity are emerging with new technologies in the present day, such as Rapid Manufacturing, which challenge conventional notions of visual and material co-presence, and serve to further confound dominant Euro-American categories of time, space, and materiality through an emerging and radically "disruptive technology." The productive dualisms that insist on the radical segregation of the material from the immaterial and the "incorrigible" norms the immaterial sustains are here confounded as well with new emergent "commitments" and social entanglements that are just beginning to emerge and become the focus of study. Analytical categories such as "material culture," the status of what constitutes the empirical and the ontological categories that these objectifications sustain are being reworked. As one can see with the material and discursive *in*distinction of "immaterial," binary code and "material" discrete "thing" as represented by Rapid Manufacturing and the extraordinary productive capacities of these "worthless powders" within this material-discursive frame (pace Barad 1998), an understanding of the material and the immaterial emerges that our conventional understandings of presence and absence are not quite adequate to understand except as a particular and socially contingent and productive aspect of propinquity among many others.

References

Barad, K. 1998. Getting Real: Technoscientific Practices and the Materialization of Reality. *Differences* 10(2), 87–128.

Barber, C. 2002. *Figure and Likeness: On the Limits of Representation in Byzantine Iconoclasm.* Princeton: Princeton University Press.

Buchli, V and G. Lucas, eds.. 2001. *Archaeologies of the Contemporary Past.* London: Routledge.

Claassen, C. 1993. *Worlds of sense: exploring the senses in history and across cultures.* London: Routledge.

Claassen, C. and D. Howes. 2006. The museum as sensescape: Western sensibilities and indigenous artifacts. In *Sensible Objects: Colonialism, Museums and Material Culture*, eds. E. Edwards, C. Gosden, and R. Phillips, 199–222, Oxford: Berg.

Cummings, B. 2002. Iconoclasm and bibliophobia in the English Reformations, 1521–1558. In *Images, Idolatry, and Iconoclasm in Late Medieval England*, eds. Dimmick, J.; Simpson, J.; Zeeman, N., 185–206. Oxford: Oxford University Press.

Durkheim, E. 2001. *The Elementary Forms of Religious Life.* Oxford: Oxford University Press

Eck, D.L. 1998. *Darśan: Seeing the Divine Image in India.* New York: Columbia University Press.

Engelke, M. 2005. Sticky Subjects and Sticky Objects. In *Materiality*, ed. D. Miller, 118–139. Durham: Duke University Press.

Frank, G. 2000. *The Memory of the Eyes: Pilgrims to Living Saints in Christian Late Antiquity.* Berkeley: University of California Press.

Gillespie, S. 2000. Maya Nested Houses: The Ritual Construction of Place. In *Beyond Kinship: Social and Material Production in House Societies*, eds. Joyce, R. and S. Gillespie, 135–160. Philadelphia: University of Pennsylvania Press.

Gell, A. 1998. *Art and Agency: An Anthropological Theory.* Oxford: Clarendon Press.

Ginzburg, C. 2002. *Wooden Eyes: Nine Reflections on Distance.* London: Verso.

Hague, R.J.M., Hopkinson, N. and Dickens, P.M., eds. 2005. *Rapid Manufacturing and Industrial Revolution for the Digital Age.* Chichester: John Wiley and Sons Ltd.

Henare, A, M. Holbraad, and S. Wastell, eds. (2007) *Thinking Through Things: Theorising Artefacts Ethnographically,* London: Routledge.

Howes, D., ed. 2005. *Empire of the Senses: The Sensual Culture Reader.* Oxford: Berg.

Keane, W. 2005. Signs are not the garb of meaning: on the social analysis of material things. In *Materiality*, ed. D. Miller, 182–205. Durham N.C.: Duke University Press.

Michalski, S. 1993. *The Reformation and the Visual Arts: the Protestant Image Question in Western and Eastern Europe.* London: Routledge.

Miller, D. 2005. Materiality: an introduction. In *Materiality*, ed. D. Miller, 1–50. Durham N.C.: Duke University Press.

Ong, W. 1967. *The presence of the word: some prologemena for cultural and religious history.* New Haven: Yale University Press.

Pietz, W. 1985. 'The Problem of the Fetish, part I'. *Res* 9, 5–17.

Pietz, W. 1987. The Problem of the Fetish, part 2: The Origin of the Fetish. *Res* 13, 23–45.

Pietz, W. 1988. The Problem of the Fetish, part 3: Bosman's Guinea and the Enlightenment Theory of Fetishism. *Res* 16, 105–123.

Pinney, C. 2002. Visual Culture. In *The Material Culture Reader*, ed. V. Buchli, 81–86. Oxford: Berg Publishers.

Povinelli, E. 2001. Radical Worlds: The Anthropology of Incommensurability and Inconceivability. *Annual Review of Anthropology* 30, 319–34.

Rorty, R. 1970. Incorrigibility as the Mark of the Mental. *Journal of Philosophy* LXVII, pp 399–424.

Rose, N. 1998. *Inventing our Selves: Psychology, Power and Personhood.* Cambridge: Cambridge University Press.

Rouse, J. 2002. *How scientific practices matter: reclaiming philosophical naturalism.* Chicago: University of Chicago Press.

Rowlands, M. 2005. A materialist approach to materiality. In *Materiality*, ed. D. Miller, 72–87. Durham, N.C.: Duke University Press.

Sassen, S. 2007. *Territory, Authority, Rights: from medieval to global assemblages.* Princeton: Princeton University Press.

Thalberg I. 1983. Immateriality, *Mind* XCII(365), 105–113.

Vilaça, A. 2005. Chronically Unstable Bodies: Reflections on Amazonian Corporalities. *Journal of the Royal Anthropological Institute* 11(3), 445–464.

Whitehead, A.N. 2000. *The Concept of Nature.* Cambridge: Cambridge University Press.

Part VI
Commentary

Chapter 12
An Anthropology of Absence: Commentary

Lynn Meskell

Archaeologists are accustomed to responding to absence, to reading the spaces and bygone traces of materials and practices, as well as assembling the social worlds of people now departed. The often haunting fragmentary remains that are bequeathed to us, the palimpsest and the void itself – plus the material and immaterial methodologies employed to interpret and revivify the past – are often more telling and carry greater psychical weight, than dealing with the myriad intact artifacts that have endured.

More redolent are the spaces and scars that signify, not only the object that once was, but the very process of object absence, disappearance or decay. The political pairing of the twin towers in Lower Manhattan and the Bamiyan Buddhas in Afghanistan (Colwell-Chanthaphonh 2003; Meskell 2002), their respective erased monumentality and the imperative for surrogate materialization, are now well-worn examples. In fact, these things do more "work" in their current void state, than they perhaps ever performed during their use-lives. Absence is extremely productive. As the editors make clear in their Introduction, rather than constructing an oppositional relationship between presence and absence, we might more fruitfully consider an ongoing intercalation between the thing-in-itself, the ways we conjure its materiality, and the practices by which it is known, recalled and remembered. In fact, materiality itself always encompasses immaterial qualities, and it would be wrong to conflate materiality with physicality alone. As Bille (Chap. 10) reminds us, moreover, we need to be careful not to conflate absence with the immaterial either, or as oppositions to presence and empirical matter, since all are subject to ambiguous classifications and experiences. Instead, the editors draw our attention to the complex intersections, repudiations, and tensions between what is considered present and absent in everyday lifeworlds. This is both evocative and well grounded, and potentially charts a new way forward in our consideration of materiality.

Disappearance and erasure represent differing, though permeable, domains. Why do some things go unnoticed, without nostalgia and longing, while others are value-laden with symbolic and emotional attachments? Not all things are equal;

L. Meskell (✉)
Department of Anthropology, Stanford University, Stanford, CA, USA
e-mail: lmeskell@stanford.edu

M. Bille et al. (eds.), *An Anthropology of Absence: Materializations of Transcendence and Loss*, 207
DOI 10.1007/978-1-4419-5529-6_12, © Springer Science+Business Media, LLC 2010

some things are easily discarded or jettisoned, others relinquished, mourned, commemorated, and so on. Recall Hegel's (1977) wonderful exegesis on materiality and thingness through his description of the most mundane of commodities, salt. Captured in the present time, the thing we know as salt embodies the simple togetherness of a plurality, and these many material and immaterial attributes also have determinate qualities. Thingness allows both the immediate presence and manifold potentialities – colour, taste, shape, weight, texture – all interpenetrating, each is everywhere and at the same time, without being separated. They are connected by the "indifferent also" for Hegel, the "medium or thinghood that holds them altogether in this way" (Hegel 1977: 69). Bundling together qualities, features and associations provides a similar framing for Keane (2003), a way of suturing the visible and invisible into the indivisible. But why do some things *matter* more than others? Perhaps it is because their mattering is more multivalent, more multilayered and thus impossible to clearly disentangle.

At the time of writing, during my field season at the Neolithic site of Çatalhöyük in Turkey, we are surrounded by house walls with scars and voids from the ancient retrieval of wooden posts. Many floors were cleaned and bins were emptied out at the end of a building's life, and yet the human bodies flexed beneath the plastered platforms in the north portion of houses remained in place over the generations. Some 9,000 years ago, the inhabitants of Catalhöyük removed the skulls and horns of wild beasts and embedded the remains of dangerous animals, such as bear paws, in plaster (Hodder 2006: 199). Before the buildings ended their use-lives and were filled in and successively built over, these specific nature/culture objects were scoured from the walls leaving cuts and voids, then possibly circulated to other houses, reused, or buried elsewhere. In the case of the bear paws, the plastered remains of one paw were uncovered some years ago in an infilling layer in Building 24 at the excavation site. Other kinds of highly charged removals are reflected in the ancient burial records, such as the precise postmortem severing and removal of human heads, and sometimes limbs, in a small number of occurrences. Head removal and later retrieval was reserved for a few individuals, suggesting a significance or tension around the process of separating and reassembling heads and bodies. Headlessness was a pervasive motif across various media at Çatalhöyük: headless figurines, paintings of headless humans, plastered skulls, embedded animal heads and horns, and headless human burials (Meskell 2008). Of course, those things left behind that were buried in houses (both features and objects), infilled and then built upon, could also be seen as "working" things or an embodied absence, albeit hidden from the everyday. This reminds me of Buchli's point that what is real and enduring can often be that beyond the physically copresent; what the discipline of archaeology reveals is a "presencing of absence" (Buchli and Lucas 2001).

The archaeology of Çatalhöyük is salient here since it reveals ingrained daily practices and recurrent contextual patterns around removal, retrieval and resignification with a remarkable resilience, enduring over some 1,400 years. The evocation of everyday practices of materializing absence is one of the chief aims of this book: rather than concentrating on the dramatic, easily dismissed examples, the chapters underline the quotidian micro-practices that unfold and complicate everyday life. Many of the obvious pitfalls have been avoided by the authors. For example, all discard or disappearance could have been considered highly charged, in the same way that all objects were recently considered to be imbued with "agency"; absence could simply have been cast as the new optic to examine death and loss; absence and immateriality could have been read as isomorphic, like presence and physicality; just as other utilitarian or dichotomous modes of interpretation could have been employed. This would have made for a predictable volume. Instead, we are encouraged to reconsider the efforts of organ donor organizations to reposition the sublated organ as the donor's heroic sacrifice that concomitantly extends his/her life; or that the disappeared victims of civil wars might perform a more valuable political service if their missing status is extenuated; or the compelling productivities that are rendered when political erasure coupled with the perceived loss of traditional spiritual knowledge enables Mongolians to recast their magico-religious practices.

This commentary necessarily focuses on just a few themes and cannot encompass every contribution or the full scope of any author's extensive fieldwork. Because of my own interests too, I have identified a handful of nodal issues including the mobilization of absence as en effective political strategy; the "work" that removal and absence performs – the *matter* of absence to quote Buch (Chap. 5), and the paradoxical need for materialization or commemoration in the face of stated intangibility; the materialization of loss and simultaneous encapsulation of pasts and futures; reworking of a not-quite-past event in heritage futures; and the use of disappearance or erasure as a tactic of control and cleansing.

Let me start by drawing on some of the slippery and seductive spiritual materialities laid out by Bille and Buchli (Chaps. 10 and 11). Both Islamic and Christian traditions problematize human relations with the object world, particularly the reification, veneration, and deification of specific things, even those that may dwell in the religious realm in the first instance. It is a fine example of what Miller (2005: 22) has identified as a "passion for immateriality" that inevitably exerts greater pressure on the production of material forms. While there is a need to have didactic tools and mnemonics for the immaterial deities, entities, and teachings, these object lessons always have the danger of becoming devotional things in themselves. This means that physicality and propinquity in Buchli's words, as well as constancy and efficacy, inevitably entrap us in a passionate but ambivalent engagement with thingness. These studies show how truly promiscuous things are. In Bille's fieldwork, this slippage is reflected in the tightly negotiated tension between two interlinked traditions, Bedouin and Muslim, and their respective philosophies of material presence. Desire for apotropaic objects such as stones, black cumin, amulets, and curative minerals that ameliorate vulnerability and risk within the Ammarin Bedouin community is countered by the negative association of objects and objectification in the copresent Islamic tradition. It is the irreducible materiality of apotropaic objects that creates a composite efficacy, harking back to Hegel, or a synthesis of properties that work in centripetal ways such as the classic fetish (Meskell 2004; Pels 1998; Spyer 1998). The problem in Islamic doctrine is the exact relationship between the words, text and material of the Qur'an, as Bille outlines. Despite doctrine requiring the absence of devotional or commodified objects, there is a burgeoning world of goods: religious posters, amulets, jewelry, or the name of "Allah" scripted in purple tiles. Objects serve as mediators or proxies, mnemonics, despite all the intentions.

The coexistence of divergent religious strictures around presencing the transcendent is also laid bare in Buchli's treatment of the paradoxical immaterial in his discussion of the idol and icon (see also Belting 1994; Davis 1997). This historic problematic also touches on the unstable category of the fetish, since the idol meshes visual and physical copresence via its materiality, while the icon rather references an absent prototype. Erasure of the idol means destruction of the deity and cleverly Buchli employs the "archaeological artifact" as a contemporary echo of this association in our own era. Destruction of a cultural monument is tantamount to cultural annihilation, whereas other forms of nearness or propinquity could potentially reframe loss in tangible terms, but not encompassing all of culture's intangible presence. In Bille's examples, apotropaic objects afford productive material engagements, in Buchli's those same instabilities underscore the artifice and duplicity of religious objects: "this is no mother of god: this is a painted board"; or consider the sculptor who carves a god, an idol, from wood then uses the rest to make a fire. Despite the desire to eschew the worship of things in Christian and Islamic spheres, the paradoxical need for embodiment and commemoration of the immaterial still summons a material presencing.

So too in the world of partible selves, donor economies and corporeal medical technologies – absence requires a physical marking and is simultaneously called upon to perform a moral, future-oriented task. For organ donor organizations, like those Jensen (Chap. 4) studies, absence is staged and storied to create positive personal links with grieving relatives and sediment the organizational directive to secure future donations. The language of loss is rather transmuted into a productive and heroic, life-giving force: it is explicitly framed as a "gift" with all the Maussian (Mauss 1990) associations of circulation, reciprocity, sublation, extension of self, and so on. The continued circulation and presence of the donors (read deceased) through their organs makes legible and heroic, both their sacrifice and ultimately, their death. Their dispersed fame (Munn 1986) such as "helping 84 people in 24 different states," tangibly conjures the departed person and secures their future according to Jensen, achieving "absence with a future" no less. But more than this materialization of absence, the creation of new objects stemming from this partible process are called for: medals, quilts, T-shirts, coffee mugs, and so on. Even when loss is denied, we seem to require concretization, memorialization, and an outpouring of things as markers, proxies, and reminders. Commemorative representations are also studied in Parrott's (Chap. 8) contribution. Through fieldwork in households in London, Parrott has studied the material practices of remembering dead relatives, and she shows that the commemorative displays are dynamic assemblages that go beyond the material positing of a simple one-to-one relation between the living and the dead; the objects by way of which the deceased are commemorated are sites of contestation, expressive of equal contestation when the deceased were alive.

Anchoring the absent and amalgamating pasts and futures simultaneously, is evinced in Hastrup's (Chap. 6) fieldwork in post-tsunami South India. Working in the disaster-affected village of Tharangambadi, she documents how the 2004 tsunami remains an ever-present, enduring threat in the present and in an anticipated future. As if mirroring that temporal sequence of past to future, villagers have been unwilling to discard the damaged artifacts of loss, brandishing them as signatures of the disaster, keeping and integrating them with those goods that survived and others purchased after the event. Anything can become an index of the event whether ruined, intact or postdating the tsunami: each narrates and materializes the intangible moment. Conversely, what is out of place, according to Hastrup, is the black marble column engraved with the names of those from the village who perished. During her fieldwork, she never witnessed anyone from Tharangambadi visiting or discussing the memorial. Indeed, it has been long argued that monuments actually betray memory, since memory is internal and subjective and thus incompatible with public display and musealization (Huyssen 1995: 258). Such markers remain distanced and separate from grief, yet at the same time supposedly objectify the emotion: an object taken out of history, by history, as Hastrup reminds us. Monuments might be seen to do the work of remembering for us, and thus be psychical substitutes that hive off the loss and mourning. Clearly, in this instance, the inscribed column is a failed monument, while the damaged goods of everyday life offer new avenues for creative nostalgia and future refashionings. The question of anticipation is also a theme in Sørensen's (Chap. 7) study of contemporary Danish cemetery culture. By ascribing to an archaeology of the contemporary, Sørensen demonstrates that blanks left on gravestones serve, by way of their very blankness, as potent ways of creating an immediate bond between the present and living on the one hand, and the absent and deceased on the other. By seeing the voids on the gravestones as materializations of an anticipated reunion between the persons separated by the death of one, Sørensen makes the point that it is not necessarily or merely the deceased who is absent, but equally the surviving bereaved, thereby once again complicating the too neat distinction between the present and the absent.

Lars Højer's (Chap. 9) contribution also describes the creative new potentialities that erupt in the face of erasure in post-socialist Mongolia. He touches on an important new strand of thinking, absence of knowledge, what some scholars have called agnatology (Proctor 2009). Absence of knowledge has a productive or generative aspect, although contemporary Mongolians imagine that the past was a time when the category of loss itself was absent; back then "people knew all those things" about magic and ritual. Højer inverts this nostalgia, however, arguing that in the wake of loss productive space opens for new magical technologies to emerge. After the 1930s purges one major consequence was the emergence of the very practices it sought to destroy, in the spirit of Hegel's "labour of the negative." That is, the great expenditure on the eradication of superstition only led to other forms of mystification that has allowed potent magical possibilities in the present. From this study, at the national scale and also at the level of individual shamanic practices and objects, we are reminded of the work absence enables, the space it frees up, and the very matter of absence itself, rather than imagining it as simply oppositional to materiality. In a similar vein, Renshaw's (Chap. 3) study of Republican dead bodies from the Spanish Civil war recast as 'seeds' shows the creative potentials of loss, empowering a new political and future-oriented social movement that refuses to forget and makes the victims more potent some seventy years later. Here too, loss and absence serve the present and those living in the present for their current political (in Renshaw's case) or socio-religious (for Højer) projects.

Taken together, this exciting group of scholars confronts us with the familiar dualities of presence and absence, material and immaterial, past and present, and complicates our categories. Absence and loss do not have to be tied to mourning and nostalgia. Rather, they can proffer a future-driven strategy to reimagine oneself, one's community and its practices. New technologies also enable innovative narratives to be crafted, where even death is not the end of bodily existence and physical presence can endure in salutary ways. Looking back to the past is equally concerned with futurity and placing oneself in the present, whether it is within the realm of photographs, gravestones or tsunami damaged saris. I also see great potentials here to reconfigure our current disciplinary obsessions with "intangibility", which has become so prevalent and problematic in anthropology and heritage studies, not to mention organizations like UNESCO. Here too, valorizing immaterial or performed culture has led to an extensive system of documenting, monitoring, managing, and legislating that only serves to fix and materialize culture. What is impressive about this volume is the seamless integration of ethnographic research, archaeological accounts, and material culture studies. While the contributors take presence and absence as their core concern, they offer a broad swathe of methodologies to access and reveal those issues. Together, these authors map out new ways to think about materiality and immateriality, not exactly as end products or nodal points, but as a spectrum of engagements and entrapments, captured nicely in the idea of presencing. They remind us that our practices, negotiations and even repudiations, constantly impel us to both extend back in time and reach out toward possible futures.

References

Belting, H. 1994. *Likeness and Presence: A History of the Image before the Era of Art*. Chicago: University of Chicago Press.

Buchli, V., and G. Lucas. Editors. 2001. *Archaeologies of the Contemporary Past*. London: Routledge.

Colwell-Chanthaphonh, C. 2003. Dismembering/disremembering the Buddhas: renderings on the internet during the Afghan purge of the past. *Journal of Social Archaeology* 3:75–98.

Davis, R. H. 1997. *Lives of Indian Images*. Princeton: Princeton University Press.

Hegel, G. W. F. 1977. *Phenomenology of Spirit*. Oxford: Oxford University Press.

Hodder, I. 2006. *The Leopard's Tale: Revealing the Mysteries of Çatalhöyük*. London: Thames and Hudson.

Huyssen, A. 1995. *Twilight Memories: Marking Time in a Culture of Amnesia*. NY: Routledge

Keane, W. 2003. Semiotics and the social analysis of material things. *Language and Communication* 23:409–425.

Mauss, M. 1990. *The Gift: The Form and Reason for Exchange in Archaic Societies*. New York: W. W. Norton.

Meskell, L. M. 2002. Negative heritage and past mastering in archaeology. *Anthropological Quarterly* 75:557–574.

Meskell, L. M. 2004. *Object Worlds in Ancient Egypt: Material Biographies Past and Present*. London: Berg.

Meskell, L. M. 2008. The nature of the beast: curating animals and ancestors at Çatalhöyük. *World Archaeology* 40:373–389.

Miller, D. 2005. "Introduction," in *Materiality*. Edited by D. Miller, pp. 1–50. Durham: Duke University Press.

Munn, N. D. 1986. *The Fame of Gawa: A Symbolic Study of Value Transformation in a Massim (Papua New Guinea) Society*. Durham: Duke University Press.

Pels, P. 1998. "The spirit of matter: on fetish, rarity, fact, and fancy," in *Border Fetishisms: Material Objects in Unstable Places*. Edited by P. Spyer, pp. 91–121. New York: Routledge.

Proctor, R. 2009. "Agnatology: a missing term to describe the cultural production of ignorance (and its study)," in *Agnatology: The Making and Unmaking of Ignorance*. Edited by R. Proctor and L. Scheibinger, pp. 1–33. Stanford: Stanford University Press.

Spyer, P. Editor. 1998. *Border Fetishisms: Material Objects in Unstable Places*. New York: Routledge.

Index

Lightning Source UK Ltd.
Milton Keynes UK
UKOW06n2019260417

299983UK00012B/95/P